MY LIFE IN THE DARK

A MARRIAGE BUILT ON LIES

Memoir

KATHLEEN M. KLINE

First published by Dragonfly Editing And Publishing 2024

Copyright © 2024 by Kathleen M. Kline

All rights reserved. No part of this publication may be reproduced, stored or transmitted in any form or by any means, electronic, mechanical, photocopying, recording, scanning, or otherwise without written permission from the publisher. It is illegal to copy this book, post it to a website, or distribute it by any other means without permission.

First edition

ISBN: 979-8-9869256-3-9

This book was professionally typeset on Reedsy. Find out more at reedsy.com

*This book is dedicated to those I tried to protect —
as well as all of you who have, are, and need to do the same.*

*You are worth it.
They are worth it.
It is worth it.*

*This is a memoir.
It is written from the perspective, memory, and experiences
of the author.*

*Please note:
Some names have been changed
to protect some of the identities of those involved.*

Acknowledgement

Many encouraged me over the years – before these sets of experiences were ever going to be a book. Before many of these events ever took place. June, who is a woman who shared her story with me decades ago and told me she knew I would not stay married to my husband — and this was before the realizations that you will read within these pages. She did not show any frustration when it took me five years to move on what she saw.

Thank you June for your loving support and continued friendship. You have always been one of my blessings.

There are wonderful men and women out there who helped me which, in turn, helped my children. While for some of you, your names may not be known or may have been forgotten – *you and your actions have not been forgotten and NEVER will.*

To my family, thank you for your help, both direct blood members and my in-laws. *Thank you for your understanding when I was quiet and for the love and understanding you showed over the years as well as now.*

I appreciate the members of the Stallion Springs Writers Group and the Aspiring Memoir Writers, an international group, who listened, read, and gave feedback which helped me reach the clarity I hope I've achieved.

Thank you, Carolyn V. Hamilton for the suggestion of the color red on my cover.

Thank you, Francine Westgate, for your work with me on my cover.

Thank you Daniela for your encouraging support over the years of this project.

Thank you David for your support even as you learned what those you loved endured.

I

Psalm: 34:18

The Lord is near to the brokenhearted and saves the crushed in spirit.

Chapter 1

Cody's line about 'leaving to protect our family' did not sit right with me. His excuses — 'The military was following' him, wanted him to 'work for them again,' and he *had* to leave so he 'wouldn't be placing the family in danger' were making me question many things. My husband's resurfacing paranoia worried me. I was convinced his time in the Army had left him with more PTSD than either of us had realized.

I need to better understand his behavior. Uncle Zuck ... I need to call Uncle Zuck. I can't call from the ranch phone. Maybe I can stop at the payphone, on the way back from school. Cody won't care if I take the kids in and drop them off at school tomorrow. I nodded to myself. *That's what I'll do.*

I brought my ex-government agent of an uncle up to speed with Cody's recent actions and comments. Even my uncle had serious reservations about Cody's state of mind.

"We need to find his military records, so you can get him some mental help," my uncle's words came slow, steady.

Once home, I started to look through the house for the documents, but I was forced to stop as I found Cody rummaging through boxes. I busied myself with a dust rag while I waited for him to go out and work with the horses. When he pulled the pinto mare out of her stall I resumed my search. But I found nothing in the house.

I can't go out to look through the boxes in storage, he'd see me. Hum. Maybe I should call Sheryl and request her help, under the guise of getting Cody set up with medical insurance through the Veteran's Administration. Yeah. That could work. And I'd still be keeping with Cody's marital rule ... what happens in the marriage stays just between us.

"Okay," my computer-savvy sister, Sheryl, said, "no problem. It's gonna take me a few days ... but I'll get back to you as soon as I have some information."

"Thanks sis. I don't want to raise Cody's suspicions as I try to get him this help that Uncle Zuck agrees Cody needs and with him being here all day and night, well ... I just really appreciate you using your research skills to help me out here. I wouldn't even know where to begin to look."

As the weekend rolled around Cody packed our six-horse trailer with most of his belongings and three horses, even the chestnut mare he had given me just a couple of years ago for my birthday. He was still saying he was leaving to protect the family.

"When I call you," he said as he lowered the latch securing the trailer door, "a year from now, I want you to load up the kids and bring them to me wherever I am."

I scowled and rolled my eyes in the darkness.

Oh yeah, sure... that's what I am going to do! NOT! My blood began to boil. *Does he think I'm like a puppy dog and I will follow him like he's some irreplaceable master? He's delusional. Where does he get off thinking he can go off for a year and I'll just scamper to his feet? Why does he think I'm that gullible? That stupid?*

I frowned.

"I'd better get going or I won't ever leave," he said in a staged low voice as he turned and wrapped his arms around me – the stiff embrace telegraphed his insincerity.

Confusion, anger, and loss swirled within me as he hugged me goodbye.

We stood at the back of the trailer, only a couple hundred feet from the house. I was sure he whispered in hopes of not waking our 5-, 8-, and 10-year-old. After all, this way he didn't have to answer their multitude of questions about why he was leaving us.

I was glad for the dark of the late September night as tears started to fall.

CHAPTER 1

Unable to move I watched him get in the truck and drive off the ranch. I stood there, in the brisk moonless night, watching ... watching ... just watching the red taillights get smaller and smaller as he crested the hill and was gone.

Days later the silence of ranch life was interrupted by the phone.

"I can't find any record that Cody served in the U.S. Army or any branch of the military," my sister reported. "What branch of the service did he say his brother was in?"

"We've got to find it. He really needs it," I encouraged with a little more urgency than I wanted.

"Why, what's up?"

Oh shit, I said that out loud. "Um…" I hesitated and then filled her in. "He had said Bill was in the Army too," I finally answered her original question.

"Okay, that's what I remembered too. Let me work on this. Sorry it's taking a while, but we are real busy here at work and…."

"No worries sis, he's not here an' I certainly don't know where he is, so there's less of a rush ... at least for now."

"Right. But this is important," she added.

My sister's search for my brother-in-law, Bill – William Walton, who we had been told died in Vietnam, brought little hope.

"I'm a tad confused," Sheryl admitted, a few days later over the phone. "I found two William Waltons in the U.S. Military Fatal Casualties database."

"They have a data base for that ... that you can search through?"

Although it was 2001, my time on the ranch seemed to keep me in the dark when it came to technology.

"Yes."

"I didn't know…. Guess that's why I called you."

I smiled as if she could see my face.

"I did find one William Walton who is a junior and black, the other was white and could be the dead brother, but I'm just not sure this is Cody's brother. Didn't you say their family was from Texas?"

"Yes."

"Well, it says this Walton is from Washington."

"Okay," I said filled with defeat. "Thanks sis. I'm at a loss where to look now."

"Have you spoken to anyone on his side of the family?"

"No. I didn't want to worry them. He's always said, 'Keep things that go on in this family to ourselves.' But I ... I guess it's time to ask his family for information, huh?"

"Do you want to call them, or would you like me to do that for you?"

"If you want," I said, glad for the assistance, "you could call either of his oldest brothers – Jim or Phil...." I felt some sense of hope. "The second oldest brother's wife, Kathy," I remembered aloud, "called a couple of years ago, and said she was doing a genealogy project.... Maybe you could call for the same reason. Plus, the information could be helpful to your genealogy research."

"Great idea. I could do that. Why don't I call the oldest brother?"

"Okay," I mumbled, grabbed my phone book, and gave her the number.

"Let me do some more research. I'll get back to you."

Come Monday, I managed to get the kids up and meet the bus at 7:45. The 9/11 attack still dominated the news. The endless horror, uncertainty, and wide-felt grief minimized my own worries. Then the phone rang.

I picked it up before the third bell.

"Hi." It was my oldest sister. "I want you to sit down an' put down your coffee."

I sat down on the off-white couch which had been donated to us after the Christmas day fire took my family's home. But the coffee cup remained in my hand. My suction cup-like palm and my dry fingers held it. My never-ending supply of coffee was the only thing I knew for sure of late.

"Okay. What?" I said into the receiver.

"Did you put your coffee down?"

I shook my head and set the half-full cup down on the coffee table.

"Okay, it's down now," a touch of sarcasm laced my words.

"I talked to Jim, and I was able to ask a bunch of questions." Her veiled attempt at cheer was short lived.

"When did you talk to him?"

CHAPTER 1

"Yesterday morning."

Thoughts of Jim, my oldest brother-in-law, and his wife Moy flooded my mind. The time we'd met, in Spokane. How much I liked them. How kind they seemed to be.... The images were coming too quick.

"So ... what did ... you find out?" my words came slow at first. "When was Cody in the military?"

The acid increased in my stomach.

"I found out that his real name is Michael... Patrick... Walton, he was not born in Texas, he was born in Alberta, Canada, he was born February 19, 1953, not 1952, and you're not his second wife... you're his third," Sheryl was on a roll.

I guess she thought it best to get all of this new information out in the open.

"He was married the first time when he was eighteen years old..." she continued, not giving me a chance to interrupt with questions. "... to a lady in Canada and they have four children together."

Her words were like knives sending an ache to my chest or was it just my stomach that seemed to heave up into my throat? My pulse raced. The floor seemed to be swallowing up the couch with me on it, me unable to escape.

"Are you there?" a gentle sweet voice hit my ear,

"Was he even in Nam?" I asked, hopeful that I could hold on to something I had been led to believe as the truth over the last twelve and a half years.

"No."

"What do you mean he wasn't in Vietnam? Who lies about that? What about the scars, where did they come from? He has four other children. How can that be? He's always said, 'Kids and family were so important' to him. I've never even heard him mention any children! I remember I asked him before we ever got married if he had any kids. He said, 'No.'"

After my rant, long moments of silence passed. The quietness fought to dominate the ringing in my ears, the spasms in my gut, and the sharp pang in my chest. Shallow breaths were all I could muster.

"I'm sorry," sorrow filled my sister's voice, or was it pity? "Did I do the right thing by calling Jim and asking him all those questions?"

I tried to gather my wits. It was a struggle.

Take a deep breath. Again. It will be okay. I coached myself.

"Yeah .... Yeah, you did good. And to think I was worried about contacting any of my in-laws because I thought he was a Vet. who was going bonkers, and I didn't want to cause them any undue worries, especially this soon after their mom passin' away," my voice trailed off to a whisper.

"Well, he wasn't in Nam. According to Jim, Cody wasn't even in the military. The only one of the siblings that was in the armed forces was the oldest brother," Sheryl said, adding with a light chuckle, "but that does not mean Cody hasn't lost his marbles."

Her attempt at humor fell on deaf ears.

"My entire life with him has been a lie," the words stuck in my craw. "A fraud. Oh my God!" My voice cracked, I began to gag, and the tears stung my eyes.

The realization of a full decade-plus of deceit swelled up within me. I sat there, still unable to move. My strength was draining down my arms and out my fingertips. I couldn't even raise a hand to wipe the tears away. "What do I tell our children?" I said as my body went numb.

"Tell them the truth. Someone has to and it would be best if it came from you."

My oldest sister gave me the only answer possible. I knew this deep down inside, somewhere. Or at least I would have yesterday.

"Yeah, you're right."

"Jim's waiting for a call from you. He said he's more than willing to answer any questions you have."

"How 'bout why didn't anyone tell me before?" I retorted.

An awkward pause hung in the air, only to be stopped by my sister.

"I don't know. But you should call him."

"Yeah, yeah I will." I shook my head. *What am I going to say to him?* "What did **you** say to him? How come he told **you**?"

"Well, I introduced myself and said I was doing a surprise Christmas present for you and the kids, a genealogy project, a family tree. Jim was

CHAPTER 1

very friendly and helpful."

"Do they have any idea that their brother has begun acting strange again?"

"No. But Jim sounded like he has been expecting the call for some time."

Wow! So, he's been expecting this call for... what ... twelve years?

I tried to wrap my mind around why he kept this all to himself. "Thank you for doing this for me," my voice was weak and mouse-like.

"You're welcome ... I think." The dead space between us grew to an uncomfortable level for both of us. "At least you know ... some truths ... now," my sister's gentle voice soothed me. Almost.

"But now I don't know anything. Do I?" It was a rhetorical question I did not expect her to answer.

"When are you going to call Jim?"

"I'll call him right now. Talk to you later." I looked down through tears at the white handset and mustered up enough strength to depress the soft gray key that read "Talk". I knew I needed to phone my eldest brother-in-law, Jim. But that was going to have to wait until I had a fresh cup of caffeine.

Chapter 2

Minutes later I gathered enough strength to get up. After I refilled my cup, I walked to the makeshift office, just off the kitchen. I opened the cabinet door, looking for a thread of confirmation.

Where is it? I lifted document after document. *I remember him saying the wrong middle name to the cop. But what name did he give?*

"There it is!"

I held the folded incident report with unsteady hands. I hesitated, with the knowledge that the confirmation of one simple fact, his real middle name, could be on that document.

And then what Sheryl said would be true.

I released an unsteady breath. I cautiously unfolded the paper to find that Cody *had* slipped up. Memories of that evening played like a movie, a "B" Movie.

"I was drivin' down the mountain road and the brakes went out on the truck I was drivin'," Cody explained to the officer that sat with us at our dining room table. "I was comin' around that curve, and I couldn't get it stopped. I was forced to jump out as it went over the side of the mountain. I jumped out and I think I hit a tree," he added pointing to the cut above his eye.

"Okay. So how did you get here, home?" the officer asked.

"Well, this nice lady, Ter ..." Cody stopped, and glanced over at me. I

CHAPTER 2

nodded.

"Yes, she said her name was Terri," I said as I glanced from Cody to the officer. "She said she saw the white truck go over the side."

"She and her friend were nice enough to drive me home," Cody added.

"So, you were in the truck by yourself?" the officer asked.

"Yes."

"Okay, I need to go back and get some information," he pulled out his pad of incident reports. "Let me get the correct spelling of your last name Cody."

"W-a-l-t-o-n."

"And your middle name?"

"Patrick."

I glanced to the other end of the table where our apprentice, Julie, sat. A matched confusion filled her eyes.

"That bump on your noggin must be worse than it looks, your middle name isn't Patrick, it's Michael!" I said in disbelief, worried I might need to take Cody to the ER.

"Yeah, it's Michael," our apprentice echoed.

"Okay. Do you have your driver's license?"

"Yes," Cody said, handing it to the officer.

"And you're the registered owner of the vehicle?"

"No, it's Julie's truck," Cody said.

The officer lifted his eyebrows as he looked across the table. "This was your truck?"

"Yes, sir," Julie answered calmly.

"Do you have insurance?"

"Yes," she said as she pulled her insurance card out of her wallet.

The officer took down the information he needed and continued with his questions.

"What were you doing up on that road?"

"I had been goin' up to see a client about his horse," Cody offered up.

It was then that Cody continued to answer questions. He repeated his account of events that led to him being brought home by strangers.

"You wouldn't happen to have the name and number of the lady who gave you the ride home, would you?" the officer queried.

"I do." I pushed my notepad over to the officer. "I got it before she left." The officer flashed a small smile.

Now, almost a year and a half later, I saw it. There was no doubt. It wasn't Cody bumping his head that caused him to say the *wrong* middle name. It was the bump on his head that made him screw up and tell the truth.

Chapter 3

As the international call went through, I paced.

"Hello," it was my sister-in-law Moy. Her sweet voice brought a moment of comfort to me.

"Hi Moy, it's Kathleen."

"Oh yes, let me get Jim for you," she said without hesitation. I continued to pace as she handed the phone off.

"Kathleen, I am glad you called," Jim greeted me with his usual cheer like it was an everyday call. "I had a wonderful chat with your sister, is it ... Sheryl, yesterday."

"Yes ... yes, she told me." I extended my strides through the kitchen and living room, retraced my steps, lap after lap.

Our fifteen-minute chat revealed little, if any, new information. Unless you count the fact that it was painfully clear I was learning way too many new facts about the man I had shared the last thirteen years with.

Ask him. Ask him. Get it over with. Ask him, I coached myself.

"I do have a question, Jim...." It felt like a badger was in my belly. I took a deep breath and then asked, "Why ... didn't you ... ever ... say ... anything?"

"I did ... as soon as someone asked."

I grew silent. At least on the phone.

As soon as someone asked! My knees buckled. I stopped pacing and sat on the nearest piece of furniture. *As soon as someone asked! What the hell! It's been over twelve years... asked? How was I to know to ask? How was I to know I* had *to ask for the truth?*

"Maribel really wants to speak to you," Jim's words halted my internal struggle. "Are you going to call her?"

My brow furrowed as frustration covered my face.

Well, you've given me her phone number, and this is the fourth time you mentioned this.... "Yes ... I guess I will," I said with much hesitation. *I don't know if I can call her... it's his first wife.*

"She's expecting your call," Jim pushed.

Expecting my call! What the ...? Why is he pushing so hard for me to call his brother's first wife? Why'd she want to speak with me? What kind of things does she have to tell me? Oh my God, what if they're still married?

Before hanging up, I promised to call my husband's first wife. But minutes crept by before I dialed the phone number of the stranger.

"Hello, is Maribel there?" I tried to sound confident. But I know I failed.

" Yes, this is she."

"It's Kathleen ... Cody's ... or ... is it Mike's ... wife," I shook my head in disbelief as I heard my own words.

"Yes, from Colorado," Maribel responded.

"Wait, you know where I live?"

"Yes, and I know you have three kids."

I heard the distinct sound of ice cubes hit the sides of a glass.

Disheartened I asked, "Why is it you know so much about me ... and I know nothing about you?"

"Because the oldest two brothers come by, often, to check on the kids and me. They always have. Phil even showed us pictures once. I guess he was down there and met up with you."

"Yes, yes, a few years back. He brought their mum down with him in his big rig and there were a few others. Jim ... Guy ...." The pit of my stomach rose into my throat.

They all knew. They all knew Cody was living a lie. They all knew. His mother knew. Oh my God, we were living a lie!

The silence created by my dismay was not interrupted until I heard Maribel pour something over the ice.

CHAPTER 3

"Do you mind if I ask some questions?" I delicately inquired.

"No. Go right ahead."

"Are… are … are you two … still married?" dread made the words hard to deliver.

"No. No, we aren't," her words rushed out, "we've been divorced for many years now."

"Oh thank God, at least I know he's not a polygamist," I retorted. *Well, I hope.* "And you have … four … children?" the quiver in my voice took me by surprise, but I did nothing to steady it.

"Yes. The oldest is…"

Better write this down, this is too much to remember. A rush of adrenaline coursed through my veins as I grabbed my day planner and opened it to a random date. I jotted down names and ages, as she spoke. *And grandchildren? What? I wonder if he knows there are five grandbabies?*

I peered up at the clock. It was 12:10. I had lost all track of time.

Oh my god, the youngest! I need to catch her bus. They drop off at 12:15!

"I've got to go. I've got to get my youngest from the bus. Thank you so much for taking my call. It was so sweet of you," I tried not to sound too rushed, but the longer the call went on, the more the queasiness grew in my stomach.

"If you need anything, don't hesitate to call."

Yeah… that's what everyone says.

It was now 12:25.

Oh my god, I missed the bus, I just know it. What would they do with Bella? Where would they take her? Take her? Oh god. Another failure. Good job Kathleen!

I grabbed the local phone book, flipped to the Yellow Pages, and stopped at "S" for schools. I dialed the number while my stomach acid etched the lining of my gut.

"Hello," I tried to steady my voice as I gave my name, "My youngest is in the morning kindergarten class…"

"Yes, Barbra said you weren't at the bus stop, and she didn't feel comfortable leaving her off there, so she brought her back to the school."

"Can I come get her," my panic subsided, but I still sounded like I was begging... for permission and for forgiveness. "I am sorry, I got caught on a long-distance phone call and..."

"Yes. Yes, you can. She'll be here with me in the office until you get here. Don't worry. It's going to be okay. Take your time."

"I'll come get her now. I promise. I'll leave right away."

I grabbed my keys and headed to town. Although I accelerated up the long dirt driveway as fast as I could, I didn't need to attract any unwanted badged attention once out on the highway. I monitored my speedometer as I passed the prison half-way between our ranch and town.

Breathe. Slow down. They've got her. She's not lost. She's okay. I instructed myself as I drove. *The baby is okay. Oh my god. It's all true... breathe! Worry about this shit later. Later. Take care of the babies. Figure this shit out later.*

I barely got the Jeep in park before I jumped out and rushed into the office.

"There you are Lovie. I am sorry I missed the bus," I said as I wrapped my arms around my little blonde kindergartner.

Chapter 4

"While we're in town, why don't we go to the grocery store," I said as I strapped Bella into the Jeep.

I struggled to change my focus and improve my mood. It was not until hours later, as I sat down to dinner with our three kids, that I broke. As I pushed the rice and kielbasa around on my plate, I could no longer hold back the tears.

"Momma, what's wrong?" my son, Ethan, asked.

Moments passed before I found my voice.

"Well, it seems your father," I swallowed hard, still unsure how much information to impart to my 10-, 8- and 5-year-old. "Your father has not been honest with us. It seems his *real* name isn't Cody and ... and he ... has four other kids ... in Canada."

Anger flashed on our 8-year-old daughter's face.

"Whatcha mean?" she blurted out.

"Well, Lovie," I said as I wiped the tears away from my own eyes. "It seems his real name isn't Cody Walton. It's Michael Walton. And I found out today that you have two older half-brothers and two older half-sisters."

Tears welled in our son's eyes as I answered the few questions the youngsters had.

"Let's eat up. We still have horses to feed and school to go to tomorrow and ... I'm sorry," I said as I made eye contact with each of my beauties. We finished dinner in silence, except for the random sniffles around the table.

That night my 8-year-old, Emma, helped me feed and water the horses. My Rottweiler, "Coojoe", stayed close at my heels, he refused to let me out of his sight. As I threw hay to Cody's 21-year-old stallion, Spangled stuck his head out over the bottom half of the Dutch door. His muzzle caressed my cheek. I stopped, reached my arm up around his head, rested my hand on his mane, and laid my face against his.

"Sorry old man. I don't think he's ever comin' back."

Spangled blew air out his nostrils as he took a step back as if he had come to understand English. There was sadness in his eyes.

After evening chores were done, the kids and I snuggled in tight as we watched a TV show about a cowboy-styled ranger before we all headed for bed. I tucked the kids in bed and climbed into my own down the hall. As I curled up in the fetal position and cried, the dog curled up on the floor, just beside the bed. Coojoe was determined to be as close to me as he could. He knew something had to be up. After all, he hadn't spent a night in the house since the week we brought him home.

The sun rose, yet brought little comfort as we tended to our routines. No additional questions were offered up from the kids. We all just did chores and ate breakfast before I took them up to the bus.

"Hey, give me a hug." My maternal reward was granted before each of my beauties climbed the steps of the bus. "Have a good day you three. Love you," I said, filled with joy as I watched my children.

The bus drove off. I headed down the driveway and up to the barn. I busied myself with the six horses, the one in the barn and the five out in the pasture – they all needed to be fed. More than an hour later it was time for more coffee and a call from my sister.

Chapter 5

I glanced up at the clock as Coojoe and I walked through the house.
Nine forty-five here means /:45 there. Sheryl'll be at work soon. Better grab some coffee.
Like clockwork, at 9:50 the phone rang.
"Hey there," I said as I patted my Rotty on the head.
"Hey. How are you doing?"
"Okay, I guess," a sigh accented my words expressing more exhaustion than I expected.
"How'd it go ... did you tell the kids?"
"Yeah. Yeah, I did." I sat on the couch. Coojoe settled in beside my feet. "They took it pretty hard. Poor E-man was angry. Said, 'All I ever wanted was brothers and he denied me that!'"
"Yeah." I heard my sister's long nails hit the keyboard. "Whatcha gonna do?"
"Well, I am gonna go find some divorce papers and get them filled out."
"You sure?"
"Yeah. I can't believe he made me into a liar! All of these years! Effin' lying. Me tellin' his lies! He's made me into a liar..." my voice trailed off to an angry whisper.
"Sis, how can you be a liar when you didn't know what you told people wasn't the truth? How were any of us to know that what he was tellin' us all wasn't the truth?"
I shook my head. My agitation grew with each heartbeat. Coojoe looked

up, then nuzzled my hand.

"I'm okay boy," I said as I stroked the fur on his head.

"You've got the dog inside with you?"

"Yeah, he's helping keep an eye on the kids ... and me," I said focused on his peanut brittle-colored eyes. "He hasn't left my side."

As I smiled, he relaxed and lowered his head.

I brought my sister up to date on my talk with the oldest brother-in-law and my husband's first wife. Midway through, the second line beeped in my ear. I checked at the caller I.D. It read "Blocked".

"I gotta go. It might be him. Bye for now." I pressed the "Talk" button, and I answered the call-waiting. "Hello."

"Hey there." It was him. "How you and the kids doin'?" he asked in a chipper tone, like him being gone was a normal thing.

"Not so good Michael Patrick Walton," I said as I struggled to restrain the rage that flared within me.

"What did you say?" anger filled his voice.

"Not so good Michael ... Patrick ... Walton."

"Oh."

Silence filled the line.

Did he hang up?

I pulled the phone back from my ear and saw the caller I.D. still read "Blocked".

"So ... you know?"

"Yeah. Yeah, I know." The top of my head got warm as my blood pressure rose. "So why? Why did you think it was necessary to lie to me?"

"I don't know."

A slow game was played out – my attempt to see what he would own up to and him unsure of how much I actually knew. All awhile him still not coming clean on anything.

"And not from Texas huh?" I broke the silence.

"No...."

"Canada...?"

"Yah."

CHAPTER 5

"Well, that explains why you didn't want me to go or should I say wouldn't *let* me go up to say goodbye to your mum, my mother-in-law, with you last year." He confirmed nothing so I continued, "Now what Lizzy, said makes sense. She said you picked up and left quickly after you found her askin' your siblin's why they called you Mike, instead of Cody. That really had her confused," I shared with him, for the first time, what one of our apprentices had said the summer before. "And four other kids. Four other kids! What the hell?"

I reached for my coffee cup in hopes I could calm my mind, heart, and soul. After a sip, I grabbed up my day-planner and turned to the page with his children's names on it. I read their names aloud.

"Yah, I haven't seen them in a long time," was all he offered up.

Is that all you have to say? Four kids! Twelve and a half years and that's all you have to say? Dumbfounded, I sat quietly for a few minutes.

"Why didn't you ever say anything about them?" The silence lingered. I pressed him. "We used to live like 300 miles away from them. That's less than a half a day's drive! We drive farther than that to go to a horse show!" He still gave nothing. As my anger rapidly grew, I pressed on. "Tell me!"

I realized my rage was not getting me the answers that I wanted or needed. I took a deep breath, calmed myself, and asked again in a calmer, softer voice, "... tell me, what did you think I would've done if I'd known about the four kids? What? WHAT?" I demanded.

"I ..." he started, but the dead air remained between us.

"You think I would've left you? Not married you?"

"Yah," the sad tone in his voice did little to me. It was a feigned sadness that I had heard too many times.

"Well, you're wrong, dead WRONG! When we lived outside Spokane, we lived 300 miles away from them!" My head shook in disbelief. "I would have had you build a room on the darn house, and we would have shared custody with Maribel." Just when I didn't think the silence could get any quieter, it did. The quiet moments stretched. "I might have only had one kid of my own, but we could have shared custody and you would have been in those beautiful babies' lives."

"I didn't know...."

"You didn't ask!" my disgust for him erupted.

"Who told you about her?"

"It doesn't matter." It was time for me to get more information, information from him, not give it. "She's a real nice lady though."

"Huh?"

"Oh yeah, I had a nice little chat with your first wife, about the kids an' all." I could barely hear him breathing over the line. "Why? Why'd you think you had to lie about everything? Why?"

"I don't know," he said again.

Bull shit. You lied! You chose to conceal so much. You ... you didn't trust me enough to tell me the truth.

I heard a horse blow air out its' nostrils, so I walked to the door. Out the glass storm door Coojoe and I could see the kids' chestnut mare at the base of the stairs. She was here for her good morning pets.

"So, where are you?" I asked him.

"Oh, down south from the ranch," he offered up.

"Where'd you go down south?"

"Oh, just down here a ways from the ranch."

Still not tellin'. Don't want me to know, huh? What's the big secret? Who does he know south of here?

The dog now leaned his head against my leg. I sighed as Mike just kept me on the line, in dead silence.

"Molly's just outside the front door. I need to get out to her. I gotta go."

With that, I ended that meaningless and exhausting volley of untruths.

Chapter 6

As I opened the storm door Molly did not back away. She merely tucked her chin in and transferred most of her weight to her back legs. Coojoe walked down the stairs between us and headed out into the yard.

"Mornin' pretty girl," I said as I closed the door behind me. "Whatcha up to this mornin'?"

Molly rebalanced herself as I sat on the stairs. Her muzzle in my lap. Simultaneously we took deep breaths, we drank in the scents of each other.

"I'm glad you're here too girl."

I stroked her jowl. She relaxed even more now that one of her humans was with her. I lost track of time as we enjoyed the warmth of the sun.

"I gotta get going and get some chores done girl," I said, reluctant to get up. When I stood Molly did not move. "I'll be out later girl."

I tousled her forelock and went inside.

I found myself back at the cabinet where I had located the traffic citation. I rummaged through the papers we had brought back from the church rental. The one we had stayed in, months earlier, after the house had burned to the ground.

There it is, that zip-lock bag with a stack of papers in it.

I grabbed them, stopped by the coffee pot for a refill, then sat on the couch. My heart sunk as I read the header: "Dissolution of Marriage".

Oh my god! It felt like my stomach lurched up into my throat. *So... was this his plan ... leaving all along?* **He's the one** *that had me find that office supply* store.

I remember being confused when he made the request, but after the house fire I was not fully focused on my marriage. I was more focused on surviving, helping the kids survive.

He's the one that went in to purchase the packet of papers ... after the house burnt down. What did he say... 'It might be better for the insurance... if we are divorced.' What the...?

"Better for the insurance my ass! It was just better for you! You asshole! I bet you've had this planned for a long time!" I said through gritted teeth, as if he would hear me. "To hell with you!" I nearly spat the words out as I pulled the stack of papers out of the bag, just before I grabbed a pen.

The ink started to flow. I filled in the spot for respondent first: Cody Michael Walton a/k/a Michael Patrick Walton.... Over the next two hours I hesitated only long enough to grab a pencil.

Best to do this in pencil in case I need to change anything. I encouraged myself. *After all, this is the first set of divorce papers I've ever filled out.*

Next, it was time to find someone to check these documents over.

Where will I find a lawyer who's willing to **just** *check these over?*

I grabbed the phone book and turned to "A" – in the yellow pages. I decided to call attorney Davis. It wasn't a tough choice. He was the only one listed in my town. I was forced to leave a message after the beep. A day later, the attorney and I made an appointment for next Tuesday, 11 a.m.

"I can wait four more days," I patted Coojoe on the head. "I can wait four more days."

The weekend came and went without any calls from Mike. I did make a call to my uncle to catch him up on the turn of events.

"Hi Uncle Zuck. It looks like we can stop looking for Cody's military records."

"Why is that? Did you find them?"

"No. It seems he's been tellin' lies. He's never even been in the military. Matter of fact, there's twelve lies on our marriage certificate."

"Oh, Kathleen I'm sorry." There was a genuineness to his words. "I thought something was up. We just don't go after one of our own. Matter

CHAPTER 6

of fact we've always been told not to. Our superior officers ordered us not to."

"Yeah, well. Now it's all out in the open."

"Okay, if you need anything else, you let me know."

"Thanks Unc'."

With that call completed, I called my folks and updated them.

As the days of the week moved on, I immersed myself in the normality of ranch life. I fed and watered and even got to take my time to make sure the stalls were clean. The ordinary comforted me. It gave rise to a clearness of mind that helped me review the dissolution paperwork, one more time.

My solace was interrupted by the phone. I walked over and picked up the handset.

Four-o-three area code... hum. I wonder who's calling from Canada.

"Hello," even I heard the uncertainty in my greeting.

"Hi. It's Maribel."

Maribel? The first wife? Why?

A queasiness erupted.

"Yah, I wanted to check on you and see how you're doing?" The concern in her tone was palatable.

But am I just imagining that?

"Wow. Um... I'm... okay," I scratched my head. *It's been a week since we met and ... and she's calling to check on me? Why is his ex-wife checking on me? Why would she do this? I'm no one to her. Why is she calling?* "I'm okay ... I guess."

I took the phone to the couch and sat.

She continued with her questions. I answered them, with trepidation, but I answered them. The inquiries seemed to be more of a comparison of marriage notes than any interrogation. But still, why?

"Did he drink a lot while you were together?" she asked.

"No," I hesitated and thought about the few times I'd seen him consume alcohol. "Nope, as a matter of fact, I think I've only seen him drink twice over the twelve years. Once at the wedding and once about the time of our anniversary, that first year of marriage when we were invited to a neighbor's for supper. Did he drink when yah'll were married?"

"Yah. It was the only time he was nice to me," she said.

I swallowed hard as I heard her words.

"So ... he was abusive to you too?"

"Yah. The kids used to hide under the table as he took turns at me ... with his fists," the sadness in her voice was undeniable.

"He hit me too ... but only a couple of times."

I did my best to block the memories that began flooding back.

"You were lucky," she said with a shaky voice as I heard ice cubes clink against a glass in the background.

"Lucky ... I guess."

I sighed in disbelief. *Lucky! How the hell was I lucky. The bastard laid his hands on both of us! Oh my god!*

The moments of silence that followed brought an unexpected comfort.

"So, he just recently left you, huh?" she asked.

"Yes, he left me here on the ranch in Colorado."

"Well, it sounds like you lucked out there too. When he left me ... he left me in a tent with four kids. One was even in diapers."

"While one was in diapers?" disbelief filled my voice. "How could he do that? How could anyone do that to you?"

My mind was filled with the image of a tent and four kids running around.

"Yah, he doesn't give a shit about anyone else," she added with disgust. I could hear her taking a drink of something and the ice cubes clanked again.

"It shows."

"Yah. He used to love to set things on fire."

Her words stung my ears, but could I have heard her correctly? *'He liked to set things on fire?' Is that what she just said?* I doubted what I'd heard. *She didn't just say, 'He liked to set things on fire?'* Fear surged through me. *Did she?*

She continued, "Yah. One time we were sittin' at the dinner table, and he kept lookin' out the window ... at the truck, like he was waiting for something." She sighed. "And after a while the hay in the back of the truck caught fire. He just sat there and continued eating. I remember sayin', 'we

CHAPTER 6

need to call...' and he cut me off, raisin' his voice to me and all... 'no, wait, wait a bit,' he said. And he refused to call the fire department until the truck was on fire."

What the eff...? I shook my head, flabbergasted.

"Wasn't he worried it would start the house on fire?"

"No. We'd already had a house burn down. Guess that didn't worry him anymore."

My jaw dropped open.

What did ... did she just say? "Oh my God! Your house burnt down, too?" I did not try to hide my dismay. "So did ours, just last year, on Christmas day!" I said as my voice dropped to a near whisper. *This is too much. Too much. He's put more than just our kids' lives in danger! Ours wasn't the first time! More than once! Oh my god!*

I swallowed hard, but something seemed to still stick in my craw. My stomach lurched. I became nauseous.

As we continued to talk, I jotted down notes, mental notes. *I can't wait until eleven. I hope I have these papers done correctly, 'cuz the sooner I file 'em the better!*

"I've got to go meet up with an attorney who agreed to check over papers I am wanting to file this week."

I couldn't decide if I was more unsettled by this weird and kind phone call or by my impending appointment.

I peered up at the clock, 10:30. My hands trembled. I grabbed my paperwork and headed out to the Jeep.

"Hi Molly," I greeted the mare. "Coojoe, no," I patted him affectionately as I opened the car door. "You stay here and watch the ranch," I added as I shut the door.

The lawyer's office was only five miles from the ranch, so I ended up early for my appointment. I sat, nervously, in the car.

I wonder how close I got to getting these papers right? How much will I need to change?

After a few minutes, I got out of the car, took a deep breath, and went inside where 'hellos' were exchanged.

Filled with a desire to not waste this man's time I handed him my papers as I sat on the edge of the chair before him. Mr. Davis reviewed the documents, line by line, page by page. Twenty minutes later he spoke.

"You said you filled these out by yourself?"

"Yes. Yes, sir I did."

I interlaced my fingers and tried to limit my fidgeting.

"Hum... well, you've done a pretty good job," he said encouragingly. "Why'd you fill it out in pencil?"

"Well, I figured you'd find a lot of things I needed to fix." A short uncomfortable chuckle escaped my throat.

"Okay." He nodded. "Why aren't you asking for alimony?"

"Well, I spoke with his ex-wife, and she said he's never paid her any and I only found out he had four older kids two weeks ago." I shrugged my shoulders. "I figure he's not gonna pay me anyways."

"Okay. Then you might want to ask for the entire ranch in the settlement instead of just fifty percent." He looked up at me and grinned. "But you did very well."

A timid smile sprouted on my face as he handed me my papers back. We stood. I pulled out a ten-dollar bill and extended my hand forward.

"I told you I only charge five dollars to help women who are needing help," Mr. Davis said with a smile.

"I..." *Well, I can't ask him for change.* I glanced down at the worn carpet. "I don't have any change." I looked up at him. "Will you take this, please?" I said with hesitant upturned lips.

He smiled.

"Okay. Now don't forget to write over all that in pen before you file it," he said as he escorted me to the door.

I turned back toward him. Brought my focus up, and I found his kind eyes encouraged me.

"Thank you. Thank you for being so generous and kind and looking over my papers," my sincerity dripped off each word.

"Oh, it's just somethin' I do to help others out."

I drove away. Made it back to the ranch in time to meet the youngest one

CHAPTER 6

at the bus stop.

Chapter 7

A few days passed before I got an unexpected call from my oldest sister-in-law.

"Hey there Carol," there was a dryness to my tone.

"My brother called yesterday." She got right down to business. "He called from ... do you have a pen?"

"Yes."

"He called from Montana, 406 ... 555 ... 4332."

How does she know I don't know where he is? "From Montana?"

"Yes. Four zero six is Montana, eh."

"Really? Well ... it seems your brother is directionally challenged as well as a liar!" A light huff escaped my throat.

"What do you mean, eh?"

"Well ... he said he was goin' south, you know ... from Colorado. Last time I looked ... Montana isn't south of here."

"Yah. He's not doin' things *right* here eh," his big sister's scornful tone was not lost on me.

"You are right Carol," I said flatly. "He's been blockin' the phone number he's been callin' from, now this Montana part ... it makes more sense now. Thanks for givin' me this number."

"Yah, he told me he's called you, eh, but he hasn't shared where he is. This is just not right, eh! That's why I called," the compassion in her voice could not be denied. "You have a right to know, and you need to know where he is."

CHAPTER 7

"Okay. Thanks for takin' the time to call."

"You and the kids okay, eh?"

"Yeah. We're gonna be just fine. Thanks." *Like now is a time to ask, 'how we are?' Any trust I had for you Carol is wavering. Oh my goodness! What about all of these lies. Lies you knew about. Lies you let your little brother continue to perpetuate. Your entire family helped him lie ... to me! Damn you Carol! Did I misjudge the love I thought had grown between us? Thanks for 'this' phone number, but... you've slept in my beds, you've eaten at my table ... and all you did was let him continue on with his lies! You helped him lie to me!*

The lack of sound on the line must have been too much for her.

"If you need anything, call," she said breaking the silence, was that love or an afterthought.

It took mere seconds for me to depress the keys of the Montana number. A queasiness set in as I heard the ring. Abruptly it stopped.

"Hello," a cheerful female voice came across the line.

"Hello, is Mike there?" I matched her cheerfulness.

"No, he's not in right now. This is Kim, can I help you?" she unexpectedly asked.

"No thanks," I said before I hung up.

The tears streamed down my face before I could set the phone down. *And of course, he's up there with another gal! Efff him. I am **so** done! Where are those effing papers?*

And with that I grabbed a pen and got back to work on the divorce papers.

The next night my mother called.

"Hi Momma. How are you?"

"Doing well, but the more important question is how are you?"

I sighed.

"I'm gonna be fine Momma. I'm gonna be just fine." With a thousand miles separating us, I didn't want to make her worry any more than she already was. "I'm off to file these divorce papers right after I get the kids off to school in the mornin'."

"That's good."

"Yeah, sure it is," I did not sound convincing. My voice muted as my mind raced. "He thinks I'm stupid! I hate that Momma."

"You can't judge yourself by his standards. He's got to make everyone out to be dumber than he is. After all, he's so smart he blocks his calls to you but not to his sister," Mom said with a huff.

"I'm tryin' Momma. I'm tryin'," the tears streamed down my face, I sniffled. "But I feel so stupid," I added in a near whisper.

"Oh honey," the distance could not deny the sorrow in her voice.

"And he's moved up to Montana ... with another lady ... Kim somethin' or another. And ..."

"Well, maybe your sister can help you run a phone number search, find out her name and address, that way you can have him served."

"Yeah, maybe she can," the lack of enthusiasm in my voice was undeniable. "Twelve and a half years Momma... twelve and a half bloody years," a mix of exhaustion, and disappointment weakened my voice. "What a waste of time."

"I know. But you'll be al'right. You'll be al'right."

"But ... I've put so much into this mess. What a waste."

I sat with shoulders slumped while tears of defeat flowed.

Silent minutes passed, except for my sniffles.

"I'm sorry."

"Oh Momma, me too," I said through clenched teeth. "I gotta go. I need to splash some water on my face before I go get the beauty."

The call ended with the promise of talking tomorrow.

Minutes of tears flowed before I could pull myself together. But when I did, I breathed in more determination to stop him from taking advantage of me.

Chapter 8

After I tucked the kids in bed, I dialed my sister's number.

"Hey, mum suggested that I see if you could teach me how to do a reverse search on a phone number and locate the name and address of who Mike is stayin' with ... in effin' Montana."

"In Montana?"

"Yeppers, it seems. I'm learnin' a bunch more about geography, stuff they didn't teach us in that school we went to.... Like Montana is south of Colorado!"

"Guess we did learn it wrong, huh."

"Yeppers!"

"I can do a reverse phone number lookup. What's this Kim's number?"

I gave my sister the phone number. Within minutes she gave me the address and last name of Kim.

"Thanks. I gotta go. I'm gonna put this down as the address to have him served at and get this set of papers filed before the kids come back from school tomorrow. Talk to yeah later."

That night the mental fatigue gave way to exhaustion. Sleep came, it was more a result of weariness than anything else. But slept I did. We all did, Coojoe included.

The drive to the county seat was uneventful. Once parked, I took a deep breath, reminded myself of the multitude of lies and ... *and that Montana crap!* And with that, I picked up the papers and walked into the courthouse.

"Okay, this will need to be served to the Respondent," the gal at the counter said like this was a common occurrence. She explained, "The sheriff's department in the other state can serve him, and don't be surprised if they charge you a process fee."

I thanked her and headed back to the ranch. I used my dial-up connection to accomplish an internet search for the closest Sheriff's Department to the address my sister helped me get. I called the Kalispell, Montana Sheriff's Office, confirmed their address, and found out they charged $35 to serve the papers.

"Thank you, I will send them up tomorrow," I said to the receptionist at the Kalispell office.

I put a check and the court papers in the envelope and out in the mail it all went.

Chapter 9

Weeks passed and each day, when I checked the mailbox, there was no confirmation that Mike had been served.
They must be busy up there in Montana. Breathe. They have thirty days to serve him.

My thoughts raced as a vision of the Kalispell Mountain range filled my mind. As I took a deep breath, I could still smell the fresh crisp Kalispell air laced with pine and grass. I smiled at the nearly 10-year-old memory. It did not last long as the high desert air refilled my lungs on the next inhale. The delay was soon acknowledged with an unexpected call from a deputy.

"Hello ma'am. You've asked us to serve these papers, but I've checked and there isn't a Cody at that address. There's only a Kim and a Mike."

Really! I rolled my eyes.

"Sir, I did put a.k.a. Michael on those papers." *Oh shit. Don't sound so patronizing, you need this guy to help you. Mike... is short for Michael down here... isn't it short for Michael up in Montana too?*

"Oh. Yes ma'am. I see that now. I will try to have these served this week."

"Thank you, sir." *Is it just me who reads papers or what?* I thought as I hung up. *Is the lack of smog in the area affecting your brain cells?* I shook my head. *Be grateful for the forward movement, let it go.*

Ironically, Mike's weekly installment of keeping this wife on the marital chain happened only hours later.

"So I'm thinkin' about puttin' the truck to fire," he said like he was detailing a day's events.

My jaw dropped nearly to my chest.

"What?"

"Yah."

Anger grew within me. Acid bubbled in my stomach. I grabbed a piece of sourdough bread and ate it as we talked.

I guess he hasn't been served yet, 'cuz all he's talkin' about is trashin' his truck.

I lifted the slice of bread to my nose, inhaled the freshness of it as he rambled on. I tried to talk him out of his crazy scheme.

"Well, yah. It's burnin' oil and not runnin' well. Don't you think it's a good idea?"

The bread did little to sop up the ever-increasing acid in my gut.

"No. No I don't!" I took a deep breath and held on to it for a few heartbeats. "You better not do it. You need a way to get around up there." It was then I noticed my wifely heart flipped a switch. I now spoke to him like the stranger he was. "You should just get the truck fixed and stop playin' your games."

As he continued his nonsense, I grew more and more tired of him. Yet I couldn't help but wonder: *Why is he telling me he is planning on setting his truck on fire? Why? Is he serious? Why is he trying to get me to buy into this? He has it insured ... with Cubbie's son.*

"You do what you are goin' to do Michael, but I think you need to rethink what you are talkin' about doin'. I know you need that truck and it's the only transportation you have," the flatness of my tone was a sign the conversation was over.

I grabbed another piece of bread. I paced. The comforting smell of childhood, I held in my hands, did little to quell the ever-growing animosity that boiled in me.

Is he serious? Would he actually *set his truck on fire? Why? Why did he tell me? Why was he trying to get me on board with this shit?* I took another bite of the bread and swallowed it after only a few chews. *Come on bread, work your magic, sop up that acid. Oh shit! Did he insure that truck in both our names? Was it even registered in both of our names?* I shook my head at my own lack of

CHAPTER 9

knowledge. *Why don't I know this? Should I call the insurance agent? Should I give them a heads-up? What if he really does it? I* **don't** *want my name attached to this!*

I picked up the phone and the phone book. Even though it was dark out I dialed the number and, as expected, got the answering machine.

"Hey this is Kathleen. I just want you to know that Cody called and is talkin' about burnin' down the truck we just insured with you a few weeks back. I'm not sure he will do it, but I don't want anything to do with this. I told him, 'It's not in your best interest to do anything stupid.' But I am not sure where his head is at, and I thought it best if you knew."

Well, what is done is done. That'll be quite the message to open the office to in the morning, but... what else could I do? I certainly can't stop him from what it sounds like he's plannin'. I shrugged my shoulders. *Or maybe he won't do it. Maybe.*

Chapter 10

Sunday, a week and a half later, I got confirmation the deputy had served Mike with the divorce papers. But it was a rude awakening. As the sun rose, I was greeted by the comforting sound of hooves hitting the ground. The horses came in from pasture and made their run to the water trough in my unfenced front yard. I stretched.

What a wonderful sound. Who needs an alarm clock when I've got the sunrise that triggers the horses to check in each morning?

It was that check-in that made my heart sing, as the dog stood up beside the bed and laid his head on my chest. Minutes later I walked down the hall, I was glad the carpet helped my bare feet not make any noise. I halted at the children's bedroom door. Soothing gentle breaths were all I heard. I continued to the kitchen and made coffee. As the coffee maker started its daily routine, I gazed out the window above the kitchen sink. Pike's Peak was still there, just where I had left it the night before. But as I scanned the pasture on the other side of the bridge I noticed more.

What the...? My heart pounded.

I retraced my steps to the back bedroom, grabbed my revolver, and made it back to the kitchen to take a better look at who might be parked out on the ranch. Although it was just over seven hundred feet away there was no denying there was an aluminum goose neck trailer and a brown-on-brown flatbed parked there.

What is he doing here? He's supposed to be in Montana!

CHAPTER 10

Adrenaline coursed through my veins. I went to the windows on the other side of the mobile and saw the three horses he had taken with him at the trough, along with their herd mates. My eyes filled with tears at the sight of my chestnut mare. I shook the sentiment off and returned to my vantage point at the kitchen sink. I visually searched the land around the truck and trailer, but I couldn't see him. I rushed to the back bedroom window and scanned the barn area for him. Nothing. I picked up the phone and dialed 9-1-1.

"What is your emergency?" came from a calm female voice.

"My husband is back. He's here! He's here on the property! He's not supposed to be here," I worked to steady my voice.

"Okay, stay on the phone with me. Is this Kathleen?"

"Yes, yes, it is," relief that caller I.D. told her who I was did not settle the quiver in my voice.

"Okay Kathleen, can you tell me what's going on?"

I brought her up to speed on the divorce and the fraud I just found out I was married to.

"I have a couple of officers heading out there now to have a chat with him."

"Okay, thank you."

"Stay on the line with me. Can you safely do that? Can you stay on the line with me?"

"Yes ma'am."

"Do you see him at all?"

"No ma'am. I've looked. I only see the horse trailer, the horses he took with him and ... I can't see him, and I've looked," I heard my voice get higher.

"Have you gone outside?"

"No ma'am. The kids are asleep and...."

"How do you know he's not up by the house and he won't try to get in?"

My heart doubled its beats.

Oh my goodness why did she say that? I don't see him. I told her that! "Oh... no, no I don't see him, and he won't come in this house."

"Why are you so sure of that?"

"Because he knows how well I shoot," I spat out the words with defiance.

"You have a gun?" concern filled her voice.

"Yes ma'am I sure do."

"You're gonna put that away when the officers get there, aren't you?"

I scoffed.

"Yes ma'am and I'm gonna throw on some pants, too, 'cuz I'm still in my nighty."

She kept talking to me the entire time it took for the two cruisers to reach the property and it took a while as we lived about six miles out of town.

"Okay, the officer just said he got to your gates. Can you see him yet?"

"No. Not yet. The gates are on the top of the property," I responded. I continued to peer out the window from my vantage point. "There … I see one of the … nope both of the cruisers cresting the hill. They've made the turn and are heading down the second section of the drive…. They've made the next turn … they're almost to his truck."

"Okay, one of the officers is coming up to see you."

"All right. I need to go put some pants on. Thanks for sending the boys out."

"You're gonna put your gun away too, aren't you?"

I shook my head.

"Of course I am. These boys are here to help me. I don't need to have it out anymore."

And with that she let the officers know I had put my firearm away and it was safe to come all of the way up to the house.

With my satin slip-style nighty tucked in my pants, I met one of the officers at the front door. This helped avoid him having to knock and wake the kids.

"Hey there Officer Brad."

I stood on the top of the steps which helped me remain at eye level with the 6-feet 4-inch-tall linebacker sized officer I had been on a first-name basis with for five years.

"Mornin' Kathleen," he spoke like an old friend.

I brought the officer up to date on what I had learned in the last month,

CHAPTER 10

or so, about the guy we had all come to know as *Cody*, including filing for divorce.

"I think the deputy was able to serve him the papers."

"Okay, so we'll ask him to leave. You want him to take the horses with him?"

"No. I'm not gonna take it out on the mares. I'll make sure they're fed and all, after all, their ribs are showin' a bit."

"You might want to put them up in the barn if you have room. It will keep us from havin' to come out here again real soon," Officer Brad suggested with raised eyebrows.

"Yeah, okay." I shrugged my shoulders.

"You got proof that he's been lying about his name and all? Like a birth certificate?"

"Hmm, I should. I think he purchased one."

A scowl grew across the officer's face. I nodded.

"I don't know if he took that paperwork with him when he went South," I made air quotes as I snarked, "South of Colorado to Montana."

"Okay, take a look and see what you can find. Keep it. Just in case it's needed."

"Okay Brad, I sure will."

The radio squawked.

Brad reached up and pressed the mic button, "Roger that.... Well, Cody says he's not on the property and he made sure he wasn't when he parked there early this morning," Brad repeated what he had heard with his earpiece.

"But the property goes all the way up to the gate. We are the only ones back here once you get inside those gates," I said wide-eyed, Brad nodded in agreement.

"Okay, give me a few minutes. Let me go talk to him. I'll be right back."

A couple of minutes later I saw the truck and trailer on the move – up and out the driveway. Both cruisers proceeded up to the house. I stepped back outside breathing a little easier, as the officers exited their vehicles.

"Okay, we had a chat with him. He agreed to leave the property and he was concerned about the mares, but I told him you were gonna feed the horses," Brad said, in an attempt to reassure me that the kids and I were safe.

"I heard some of the details," Officer Christiansen said as he tilted his head toward the senior officer. I nodded. "You might want to go in tomorrow to the Family Crisis Center there in Cañon City and ask them to help you get a restraining order. Okay?"

His eyes were filled with compassion and an urgency that I could not deny. I glanced from Christensen to Brad whose friendly face had become one filled with concern. They both seemed displeased with how their Sunday morning was turning out, but not because I'd called.

"He shouldn't bother you anymore today, but don't hesitate to call, okay?" Brad urged.

I agreed and they left after many thanks from me.

Before dusk fell, the sun, low on the horizon, reflected off of the aluminum horse trailer, parked on the neighbor's ridge a half mile away. Anger and fear erupted within me.

You just had to make sure you could watch everything we do. Now that you can't park on the property you just had to find a way to let me know you are still here… intimidate me. What a prick!

Chapter 11

"Okay kids, mom's gotta run some errands today," *I hope my struggle to sound cheerful isn't heard by the kids.* "How about I drop you off at school?" Smiles and nods came from my three beauties. "Alrighty then, let's load up an' get goin'."

A glance to the horizon told me the trailer was still parked on the ridge, giving him a vantage point. I swallowed hard and drove off the property. I held my breath for a moment in hopes of refocusing my worries.

"Whatcha gonna do in town Momma?" my son asked.

"Oh Lovie, I just gotta get some chores done, food and the like."

As we neared the railroad tracks, the school bus, which was in front of me, slowed to a stop before crossing. As I brought the Jeep to a stop, I noticed the brown flatbed with its hood up. Mike got out from behind the wheel, eyes focused on those inside the bus. With the kids not spotted, he quickly turned and fiddled with the stuff under the hood as if he were actually fixing something. That was when he saw the Jeep. Looked up. We locked eyes.

What the hell is he doing? Oh, so this is your idea of staying away from your wife and kids as ordered in the court papers you received? The other side of a two-lane highway isn't 100 feet from us, you dumbass.

After I dropped the kids off at school, I drove directly to the Family Crisis Center. I tried the door, but it didn't budge. That's when I noticed the sign on the door: "9 a.m. to 5 p.m."

Not open for another forty-five minutes ... now what? Maybe I should drive back to the ranch. Forget this. Maybe I'm not meant to file any paperwork.

A dull pain, accompanied by an undeniable sharp intermittent cramp developed in my stomach. My breaths quickened. My heartbeats increased. Panic, frustration, and insecurity fought for dominance within me.

The cops can't help me if I don't get this stuff done. You can go get a cup of coffee and come back. I had to repeat my self-coaching more than once ... *The cops can't help me if I don't get this stuff done....*

I got a coffee, only to return at the top of the hour.

"Um, hello..."

"Come on in, I'll be right with you," the brunette welcomed me in.

She motioned to the couch against the wall. Moments passed as I did my best to restrain the anxiety that had given rise to fidgeting. I interlocked my fingers, as I rubbed my thumbs on my palms.

"Thanks for waiting, how can I help you today?"

"I ... I..."

"Oh," she stood and came out from behind the desk, "I'm sorry, can I get you something to drink ... water... coffee?"

I took a deep breath, paused, and shook my head.

"The officer ... Officer Christensen ... and Officer Brad, sorry I don't remember his last name, suggested I come here ... yesterday." As I swallowed my throat tightened.

"Oh, okay. My name is Brenda. Why don't we go over here," she gestured to a desk behind a tri-fold screen, "where we can talk." She patiently waited for me to accept her invitation.

I detailed what the cops said, where Mike parked both at night and this morning to see the kids.

"Has he ever hit you?" Brenda asked.

I focused on my boots as the memory of the first time he hit me came to mind.

"Did you call the cops then? File a police report?"

"No," I shook my head, "yesterday was the first time I've ever called the cops on him." Anguish filled me. *I've screwed up again, haven't I?*

"That's okay. You're not the first nor will you be the last to not call the

CHAPTER 11

cops. After all, domestic violence is about power and control and often we are ashamed or busy licking our wounds an' we don't call." She let the words lay in the air between us. "It's okay. You don't have to have filed a police report for us to help protect you. Do you have kids?"

"Yes." I brought my focus back up to find a set of compassionate blue eyes. "But I don't know what to do, what's next. I've never …."

"That's why we're here. From what you've already shared … I'd like to recommend you fill out a request for a protection order for you and the kids because … we don't know what else he will do now that you have filed for divorce."

"Where do I get the paperwork?" I sighed heavily. *Goodness … more bloody paperwork.*

"We have the packets here … if you think you're ready to move forward."

Brenda sat quietly and watched my every move. My pulse quickened and my palms became moist. I nodded. She slowly reached for a packet in the desktop file divider. My eyes widened.

"Read it over before filling it out. It has a set of instructions with it."

I hope that's what's making the packet so thick!

"And … it sounds like the sooner you get this filed the better."

Is that encouragement … or … urgency I hear in her voice?

I let my palm graze my thigh in hopes the jeans would absorb the moisture before I accepted the packet.

"There's one more thing I want to give you," she said, then raised from her chair. "Suzie, could you get…" she directed her comment to the receptionist who responded by moving to the closet.

As we got closer to the entrance, Suzie returned with a cell phone. Brenda tried to hand it to me.

"This is for you to use."

"But I can't afford a cell phone!" I retreated a few steps.

"No, no don't worry," Brenda attempted to reassure me, "there's no bill. These are donated old phones, and they only dial 9-1-1." I stopped before I bumped into the table behind me.

How's a phone supposed to help me? I live six miles from town. The Florence cops won't come out, they never have. We're considered to be out in the county. It's covered by the Sheriff's Department, and it takes them a long time to get out to the ranch. He's already proven he can show up when he wants to ... even under the cloak of darkness or any other time he wants. I've got that revolver Dad gave me, that's more than any phone can do. And... do we even have cell phone coverage out at the ranch?

"Just take it with you," Brenda urged. "It's just in case."

She stood with the phone and charger in her outstretched hand.

The uncertainty of how it could help me belied the confidence I saw in Brenda's eyes. Reluctantly I reached up and accepted it.

"Make sure you charge it once a day and ... take it with you everywhere. Use it if you need to. We never know when we might need it."

The phone was larger than the palm of my hand. Its curved grey body had a hard plastic cover that flipped out to access the phone pad. I shook my head.

"Don't forget, if you need anything else ... if things change ... if you think you need help getting you and the kids to a safe place ... just give me a call," she added as she handed me her card.

My eyes darted from Brenda to Suzie and back again.

"Thank... you."

I got in the Jeep, more burdened than when I walked in.

Back on the ranch, I fed and watered the horses and then headed to the dining room table to deal with the paperwork. Glad for the helpful instructions which steeled my resolve, I put pen to paper. I wrote in the petitioner, me, and the respondent, him. I checked off – protection from "Domestic Abuse" and "Stalking". I included all three kids so they could be under the same protection as well. As I got to the next section, I took a deep breath and reread the bolded words:

Be specific:
    What was the threat or acts of violence?
    Where did this occur?
    Were the minor children or other Protected Persons present?

CHAPTER 11

Was a weapon involved?

The subsequent section requested information about the "most serious incident" ... and "Any other past incidents of violence...."

Most serious.... Which event was 'most serious'... when I was pregnant or back on the ranch in California?

I began writing about the most recent time.

Late March of 1996 he decided my objection to something was one opinion too many. I was 9 months pregnant. He snuck up behind me and hit me on the back of the head. He hit me so hard that my chin almost bounced off my chest. I had a large bump on the back of my head. Our younger two children, ages 4 and 2, were only about 15 feet away. This happened at our residence —

1234 Hwy 67, Florence, Colorado. Weapons — his fists.

The four lines on the front of the form were not enough space to tell what he did, so I got a blank piece of paper and continued.

February 1990. Location – the family ranch in Tehachapi where we trained horses. Mike got mad at me ....

The memories flooded my mind.

Something slammed into my thigh, just below my hip joint. I glanced down to see the metal curry comb fall to the stall floor. Not sure where it came from, I peered out the open stall door to find Mike. He stood about twenty feet away, in the arena attached to the barn. He stared at me.

Adrenaline surged, mixing with my blood like never before in my twenty-seven years. My eyes widened with fear. Self-preservation took over.

He stood squarely. His jaw rigid. His eyes focused tightly on me.

I need to get out of here!

I checked again. He had not moved a muscle. Although he was staring at me, he appeared ready, ready to attack again. Yet he stood like a statue, an angry statue.

I could see the arena panels to the left. I initiated my escape with a brisk walk. As I exited the stall, I leaned the pitchfork against the wall. Thankful for my long legs, I made it to the panels with only a few strides. In one swift movement, I raised my foot to the second rung, grabbed the top rail, and swung my leg over it.

Before I could get over the top rail, Mike had closed the distance between us. My forward movement was abruptly stopped. He pulled me backward. My grip on the top rail was lost. He pulled me off the fence and whirled me around. I landed on my feet. We stood face-to-face inside the arena. It took a moment for me to realize that both of his hands were around my throat. More adrenaline surged through my body.

We now stood, all of his 6-foot 2-inch frame which loomed over my 5-foot 7-inches, connected by his long-outstretched arms and his hands. Hands that encased my throat. I could feel his large palms and long fingers all the way around my neck. I attempted to move. With little effort, his grip stopped me. There was a glare of wildness in his eyes that I had never seen before – in him or in any other human being for that matter. He looked like a stranger. Like an unknown angry stranger had embodied my husband of seven months.

What's next? What is he doing? Why is he…? Why hasn't he let go of me? Why does he have his hands on me? Why are his hands around my throat? You need to let go of me! What do I do? He's ….

It was difficult to come up with a full rational thought with this guy who stood in front of me with pupils as small as pinpoints and a flat expression. A guy who kept a hold of me by my throat. *By my throat!* My thoughts competed for clarity with the loud thump of the blood that pumped within me. It seemed to reverberate through my bones. The whoosh, whoosh, whoosh, and thud-dah pounded in my chest as it blocked out all other sounds of the ranch.

"Let go of me," I demanded through clenched teeth.

He was silent. He just continued to have the look of a wild animal. Crazed. Waiting to strike.

How am I going to get him to let go of me? What would make him release me? Release me before he hurts me more? He's so much bigger and stronger than me. His arms are so long. His hands … so big. How am I …? My mind rallied. *He's a man…I could kick him. Maybe I can get him to protect himself and let go of me.*

"Let go of me or I will kick you in the nuts," I said after quiet moments

CHAPTER 11

passed.

I need to get him to let go of me or…. It's like what I'm saying doesn't matter. It's like he can't even hear me. A bead of sweat rolled down the center of my back. *What has happened to him? Where has he gone to? Why can't he hear me?*

I stood still and watched him. Unsure what to do. Sweat dampened my pits. My tongue stuck to the roof of my mouth and my breath quickened as he continued to glare as if he was looking through me. I no longer recognized the man who stood before me. He was now a stranger, one that camouflaged the man I thought I loved.

What have I done… to deserve this? Why are his hands still locked around my throat? What if he tightens his hands? Oh my god! He could choke me out at any moment. How do I get him to let go?

Minutes of silence dragged on in this standoff. I tried the only thing this 27-year-old newlywed could think of, I repeated myself, more forcefully this time.

"Let me go … or I *will* kick you in the nuts!"

A couple of additional tense moments passed and out of the blue, he calmly took his hands down from around my neck. Silence rang in my ears. We stood, motionless. Him with his hands at his side, still looking through me. I did not wait around for an explanation. I climbed over the arena panel and escaped.

I included all of this on the request for protection. But that was not all. As I put pen to paper, I wrote:

His verbal abuse started in 1989, in public, in front of my friends. And it continued whenever he felt the urge to give me a tongue lashing intended to bring me down a notch in confidence. He moved us frequently, for example – twelve times in the first five years of our marriage. The moves took me farther away from my family, from California to Kentucky, and onto ranches with fewer and fewer people around.

My hands started to shake as I remembered the last time he threatened to hit me.

How stupid is he? I wondered then and now. *He never seemed to care if the kids could hear him threaten me.* I shook my head. *He never cared if the kids were in the room playin' or watchin' TV. He would just spew his nasty words.*

I got up from the table and poured coffee in my cup. As I drank the dark liquid, I forced myself to think positively.

He was nice... at times.

Like the time we went out dancing on a break between horse shows in Spokane, Washington, the first month of our marriage, in 1989. We two-stepped well together and he seemed to like it when I was able to keep up with him as we polkaed around the dance floor.

He did buy me that beautiful chestnut mare. But he took her from me... to hurt me. He knew I loved her. Just like he did in Kentucky. My positive thoughts were not sustainable. *He made me give up my Gunny. Don't forget. I don't have my Gunny anymore either. He convinced me to sell my personal mount. One that loved our kids – because everything is expendable... family, pets, people. He was my black. I was his human. Gunny loved me and the kids.* I swallowed the lump in my throat. *I could trust Gunny with the kids. I wonder if Gunny will ever forgive me for selling him. He wasn't expendable.*

The clock declared it was 11:49. I took a deep breath as thoughts of picking up my youngest at the bus brought a smile to my face. I gathered up the papers, put them in the makeshift office cabinet, and headed up to the gate, coffee cup in hand.

Chapter 12

I was able to go back to the courthouse and file the papers the next day. "Umm," I said, as I stepped up to the counter. "I was told to bring these papers here and file them?" my words were soft, timid, and unsteady.

"Okay," the gal said. She reviewed them quickly. "Come back here tomorrow at 8:30. Come to courtroom B. The judge will see you then."

The woman date-stamped my paperwork.

That night I made sure the horses had full water buckets so all I would have to do is throw feed to them in the morning.

After I took the kids up to the bus stop – with hugs and kisses and all – I fed the horses in the barn and ended up in front of the closet.

"What to wear. What to wear?" I said as Coojoe looked up at me. "What do you think boy?"

My hand landed on the blue and white large-print floral nearly ankle-length dress. The softness of the cotton fibers comforted me.

"Well boy," I said to the dog as I pulled the dress off of the hanger, "I guess this'll have to do. After all, I don't need to be worryin' about what I'm wearing, huh."

I guess the days of figure-affirming office-style suit skirts, blouses, and pumps are gone. I sighed at my reflection in the mirror. *Guess this maternal body will just have to do.*

A frown grew on my face – at the realization of how much my life had changed since that last time I wore this outfit.

I slipped the country dress over my head and let it slide down over my hips and belly. *The belly that grew three beauties. Tried to carry four ... but grew three beautiful babies,* I reminded myself as the heaviness of the full skirt caused the hemline to bounce and rebound back up toward my knees before it settled at its full length. After I pulled on my pantyhose, I slipped my feet into my low-heeled ankle-high lace-up brown boots. I fidgeted with the short sleeves and pulled them to their full lengths over my deltoids.

"Okay Coojoe, outcha go, it's time for me to go."

He hesitated. I reached down and stroked his broad head.

"You can't come with me, Coojoe. Not today. Maybe when I go up to get the kids."

My protector relented and escorted me to the Jeep before he found some shade.

~~~~****~~~~

"Please come up to the table," the judge invited.

I pushed the low gate open. The hinges complained sharply and echoed loudly in the library-quiet courtroom. Two empty tables awaited me. I glanced up unable to hide my wide-eyed confusion.

Which table does he want me to go to?

The judge motioned for me to take a seat at the table on the left.

"I see you have filed a request for protection for you and your children," Judge Lawson said.

I nodded.

"Please respond aloud so this can be on record," the court reporter announced.

"Yes, sir," I added to my nod.

"I've read your request, and I am granting you a temporary, two-week, restraining order. Because this is a domestic violence request, we usually have a sheriff's deputy serve this on the respondent. I will want to see you back here in two weeks," the judge paused, looked down at his calendar, "on

CHAPTER 12

October 22nd, at 8:30 in the morning."

He handed some papers to the clerk.

"Ah, okay. Thank you, your honor." I sat still. Sweat beaded on my brow. *Now what?*

"If you would like to wait in the gallery the papers will be ready in about ten minutes," the judge added with a gentle tone.

"Thank you."

I rose and took a seat in the back row of the empty courtroom as the judge left the bench and returned to his chambers.

Wow. I took in a deep breath, held it for a moment. *That wasn't as bad as I thought it would be. Brenda was right. I guess Mike wasn't supposed to be here. Right, he doesn't know I've requested this. Guess it's the best way to listen to someone who is afraid... without the horse's backside in the courtroom. I sure am relieved he wasn't here. He's gonna be pissed off even more.* I shook my head. *Mike, you should have respected the other paperwork and stayed away.* I sat up straighter. *You've pushed the wrong woman for the last time.*

I wiped the palms of my hands on my thighs, glad my cotton skirt would remove the dampness.

I'm glad I wrote all of that stuff down. No matter how stupid I feel, sayin' that all out loud. Seein' it all laid out on paper sure makes a girl realize... what I never needed to put up with.

I'm glad the cops are goin' to serve him, 'cuz he's moved the trailer and I've no idea where he is... well, at least the truck and trailer were gone from the ridge this morning. Where would he go? Who would let him park that rig on their property? Trisha? Richard? He wouldn't go to Richard. Mike most likely still owes Richard money.

I sneered at the memory of when Richard told me he had loaned Mike money ... and offered that I could 'repay the loan by having sex with him.' *Who did that fat ass, Richard, think he was! Who would be willing to have sex with him to pay for a husband's debt? I sure hope to hell that Mike didn't suggest I would!*

I wonder who else I'm going to bump into in town just to be told Mike's made yet another deal that I don't know about? I sighed. *Oh, stop worrying about it.*

*It's not your worry anymore. He's not **your** worry anymore. This shit stopped being **your** worry when he left, and that date is on the divorce paperwork. But it's a small town, he won't be far away. It's such a small, bloody ass town.*

The bailiff came toward me with the papers in his hands.

"Keep these with you at all times. It's even helpful if you make copies so you can have one with you at all times. Like in your purse, at work, in the house, in your car, etc. If he breaches this restraining order, call 9-1-1. You need to call each and every time he breaches. We can't help protect you and the kids if you don't help us know when he violates the restraining order." His kind eyes held mine. "Okay?"

"Thank you, sir," I nodded as I spoke.

As I headed back to the ranch, I felt a sense of accomplishment. But it was short-lived. I couldn't help but notice his brown flatbed parked on the knoll of the only side road off the highway we lived on. It gave Mike a direct view of our gate. My stomach lurched in my belly.

If he's got binoculars or a rifle scope ... he'll be able to watch the comings and goings of this ranch from there! I sighed as the joys of my recent success evaporated at the sight of his truck. *Maybe the cops will be able to serve him soon. Maybe the cops can serve him right there, in his bloody truck!*

The mile and a half of my own driveway was long enough for me to decide to make a call to let the sheriffs know where they could find Mike. A couple of days later Officer Brad stopped by the ranch to let me know Mike had been served.

Chapter 13

The next two weeks remained pretty quiet, but that could have been because I limited my time off the ranch. October 22nd we both showed up in court. I had hoped to get into the courtroom first to use timing as an extra buffer, but as I pulled into the small parking lot, he was already there. Waiting. The brown flatbed was backed into a spot with the nose of the truck strategically pointed toward the entrance. Our eyes met. He glared in my direction.

"Your intimidating look is not going to work today. I've had enough of you! I'm done with you and your B.S.," I said emboldened by my determination to be free of him and his pack of lies, even though I knew he couldn't hear me as we sat in our own vehicles twenty feet apart.

Can you go through with this? I looked down at my lap, I did not want to see his face anymore. *Yes. Yes, I can.* I coached myself while I put my car in park. *Oh God, I'm glad he can't hear my timid voice. You can do this. Get going... before he gets out of his truck.*

I got out of the vehicle and walked rapidly, in hopes I would reach the sanctuary of the courthouse without tripping. Once inside, I slowed my pace the closer I got to courtroom B. As I opened the door, I noticed the post – we were eighth on the docket. My shoulders dropped.

Eighth? I let out an exasperated breath. *I wonder how long this is gonna take today?*

Once safely inside, I chose a seat in the row closest to the front. This time

I sat on the left, more confident that that is where the judge would look for me. Minutes later, Mike walked in and found a seat, on the right, a few rows back. The court was called to order after the bailiff did a rollcall of sorts.

"Your honor, cases one, five, and six are no-shows. Cases two and eight ... both parties are present and case numbers three, four, and seven are waiting for counsel to show," the bailiff announced after the judge took the bench.

"Very well," the judge said. He moved some files to his left. He handed them to his clerk. "Let it be shown that the following cases are no-shows and dismissed without prejudice." He called the other case up first.

I wonder how this is going to go. I reached up and tugged on my sleeve. *Will the judge ask questions?* My skin began to feel itchy. *Will he ask me questions?* Absentmindedly, I scratched my left arm. *Will he ask Mike questions? Will he be fair?* A tightness grew in my throat. *What lies will Mike tell today? Will the judge believe me ... or ... will Mike's lies work on him?* I shifted in my seat.

It was then I heard the judge kindly question the petitioner in the case ahead of us.

"I see you were granted a temporary restraining order, a couple of weeks ago. And the respondent was served." Both parties nodded. "Miss Sanders, do you feel a need for this restraining order to remain in place for another six months?" the judge asked.

Miss Sanders shrugged her shoulders and remained silent.

"Miss Sanders is your neighbor no longer a threat?" the judge queried. "If everything has quieted down, we can be done here with no further action."

"Your honor," the respondent interjected. "I have moved from that location,"

"Okay. Miss Sanders, if you agree that your neighbor is no longer a threat, because she has moved, we will dismiss this case. Is that what you would like?"

"Yes, sir," Miss Sanders finally spoke. And with that the case was dismissed.

That seemed pretty easy. He seemed kind. He asked his questions with kindness,

CHAPTER 13

even when she hesitated. He didn't bark at her. Breathe. I breathed in deeply through my nose. *It's going to be okay. Breathe.* I let the breath out through my mouth, slowly. I crossed my legs and smoothed my skirt on my lap.

But what if the judge says no? What if he denies this order today? How am I going to get Mike to stop trying to control my every move? Will Mike be able to come back out on to the ranch? I uncrossed my legs, pumped my heels a few quick beats, and crossed my legs again.

Moments later the judge called our case.

"Number eight, case number CV201-10-109 Walton verses Walton. Mrs. Walton, please come up and sit to the left." The judge motioned toward the table he had me sit at before. "Mr. Walton, wait until she is seated, and you can come up here on your right."

I sat. When the hinges of the wooden gate announced Mike's entrance my body tensed. My shoulders drew in and my back rounded. My jaw muscles tightened. I interlaced my fingers and focused my eyes on my cuticles.

"Mrs. Walton, I have read your paperwork submitted…. Mr. Walton did you submit a response to the Temporary Restraining Order - TRO?"

"No," Mike answered.

I brought my eyes up, surprised.

What? No telling the judge I'm lying? No stories to tell the judge?

"Since you didn't submit anything in writing…" the judge looked squarely at Mike as he spoke, "… is there anything that you would like to tell the court?"

"I don't understand why she filed for this," he said in a pathetic abused puppy style of voice. "I just don't get it."

I rolled my eyes. I sat up straight, my back stiff. I waited for Mike to enlighten the judge, but silence filled the courtroom.

"Do you have *anything* else you would like to let the court know?" He waited for Mike to respond, but Mike just shook his head from side to side. "Sir you need to speak up and respond verbally because the court reporter can't take down shakes of the head."

"No," Mike said, shoulders slumped.

What? Nothing to say. No dramatic flair to go with you denying that you hit me ... like you did the last time you hit me? No making me out to be a 'crazy bitch'. Humm, guess you don't think the judge is okay with you puttin' your hands on me. Humm!

My arms tensed and my hands became fists as we sat in silence. I watched the judge quietly flip papers back and forth.

"The court has read and heard from both parties relative to the petitioner's request for the protection order. The court has found sufficient evidence to grant the TRO," Judge Lawson said as he handed a file to his clerk.

I don't know what I felt more of – disbelief in Mike's lack of pushback or relief in the judge's ruling.

"The court will be granting the TRO for cause. The terms of the initial restraining order remain in effect until February 22nd of next year.

"Mrs. Walton," the judge spoke with a soft tone, "the clerk will get you a copy of this order. You may wait in here. Mr. Walton," an undeniable sternness filled Judge Lawson's voice, "you will wait outside the courtroom and a bailiff will bring you your copy," the judge commanded.

I waited for Mike to exit the courtroom, but he hesitated. Out of the corner of my eye, I saw the bailiff take two steps toward him. It was then that Mike turned and left the courtroom. I looked up and the bailiff smiled. There was a kindness there. I did my best to mirror his compassion. I mouthed 'thank you' before heading back to my seat in the gallery, as the next case was called.

"Are the counselors for the next two cases here yet?" the judge asked the bailiff.

There was a continued exchange between the bailiff and the judge. Fifteen minutes later a deputy came up to me.

"Mrs. Walton?"

"Yes."

"The clerk asked me to bring this to you." He handed me a copy of the extended TRO. Kindness exuded from him as he looked down at me, he continued, "I've given him a copy. He's already left. It's safe for you to go out now."

The bailiff waited for me to rise up from the chair.

CHAPTER 13

"Don't forget … if he breaches it … report it," he said now that we were looking squarely at each other.

I nodded and we shared a light grin.

"I will. I promise. Thank you. All of you."

As I made it to the front doors of the courthouse, I couldn't help but scan the lot to make sure his truck was not out there. A sigh escaped my lips with my relief to find it gone. I made it to my Jeep just in time as tears started to fall. I hurried to sit behind the wheel. The tears became sobs. My shoulders trembled. I lost track of how long the crying went on, but I let the tears fall.

Finally, I reached up to wipe my eyes. I shook my head as my watch came into my blurry view....

I can't believe I've been sitting here so long.

I sniffled and blinked. My eyes cleared. That is when I noticed there were fewer cars in the lot than when I came out of the building.

Refreshed by my tears, I glanced at my watch again.

Oh good, I still have time to make it to the bus stop to get Bella.

It took more effort to reach up and turn the key in the ignition than anticipated.

Wow. Who would have thought I could be so exhausted and yet … a smile grew on my face as I exited the parking lot … *filled with relief and gratitude? I'm glad that's over with and… worked out so well.*

I turned the Jeep right and headed back up Highway 50 East and took the back roads that would lead me home. Instinctively, I kept a lookout for Mike and his truck.

I wonder what he's got hidden up his sleeve. I gripped the steering wheel as I made my way down the driveway. *Why didn't he fight back? Why didn't he say more in court? Is he giving in? Is he taking me seriously now?*

Softly, I pushed down on the brake pedal. The vehicle came to a stop just past the mobile home. I put it in park and glanced over at the barn.

I never would have thought it would have taken so many others to help me to get to this point. I sighed. *Reality is, I never thought it would ever go this way. Who would have thought it would have taken so long and so many people showing me the way?*

Chapter 14

The call waiting beeped in my ear as I told my mom about the proceedings.

"I've gotta 'nother call mum. Talk to you later."

"Okay, bye."

"Hi, it's Cherri. Jessie's mom."

"Oh yeah, hey there Cherri."

"Jessie said, 'Emma told her that her daddy had left.' I wanted to let yeah know that Cody's moved into the trailer park here 'bout three trailers down from the kids and me, on the main road. He made it clear he was here, makin' sure as many people were payin' attention to how *difficult* it was for him to park that big horse trailer beside the mobile home. The one that has a long front part, that attaches to the bed of the truck instead of off the back, at the bumper."

"Oh, the gooseneck trailer," I injected.

"Oh, is that what you call it. Yeah, the gooseneck. Then he acted like he had oh-so-many talents that the rest of us didn't have, because he successfully parked that thing," she sarcastically said. "I think it's 'cuz he saw Jessie and wanted her to be able to tell the kids where he was."

"Oh, thanks. I appreciate the heads-up. By the way, Cody's not his real name … it's Mike."

"Huh? Why'd he lie 'bout his name?"

I quickly explained the name thing.

CHAPTER 14

"Really?" She chewed on the new information for a while. "Well then, I'm glad I called you. You've always been real helpful to me. It's the least I can do."

I couldn't help but remember the desperation in her eyes when she told me, a year or so back, she had to get permission from the judge to have her tubes tied at twenty-five, 'because every time I've had a kid, he gets me pregnant again real quick. He won't let me take birth control and he refuses to use condoms. I've had eight kids already. I can't go havin' anymore.'

The judge must have seen the hopelessness in her eyes, like I did, because he granted it without the husband's permission. I scoffed to myself.

I shook my head as I remembered having to get Mike's signature before I could get my tubes tied when I was thirty-two.

*Why is it that any man should have a right to tell me if I can or **can't** take control of my own reproductive organs! I understand makin' me wait thirty days to make sure I didn't change my mind but havin' to have my husband sign off on it, like my reproductive organs are his property... is... archaic!*

My outrage surprised me as it erupted, again, just as it did five years ago.

"Yeah. He's stopped askin' if I'm pregnant again," she sighed. "I get to get my teeth fixed now!" Her excitement was undeniable. "The doc said havin' so many babies so close together's what damaged my teeth."

Wow... looks like I dodged a bunch of bullets when I said 'no' to Mike when he told me he wanted more kids than his dad – which meant thirteen kids or more.... I shook my head, momentarily ridding myself of **that** memory.

"That's great. I'm glad you moved forward with having your teeth worked on."

"And I'm lookin' into startin' classes in Cañon City soon."

"Well, things are lookin' up for you. I'm so glad. You and those beauties sure are worth it."

"Yeah. Thanks …. Well, if I see anythin' goin' on down there, I'll give yah another call."

"Thanks. And thanks for this head's up."

I dialed our buddy John's number.

"Hello?" he said in his regular kind voice, a kindness that I had come to count on over our ten years of friendship.

"I just got the location for the gooseneck and Mike that you asked for last week."

"Let me grab a pen."

"Yeppers." I gave him the information I had.

"Thanks. I've already contacted someone down there. I will have it repossessed this week. Can I have them bring it out to your place and can you store it there until I can drive down and pick it up?"

"Sure," I nodded. "He's not allowed out here anyways, not with the restraining order, so it should be safe out here."

Will he come out here though? Will Mike breach the restraining order and try to take the trailer back?

"Okay, I will let the guy know. Thank you. I will talk to you later to make arrangements to come down and pick it up … or sell it from there," John said. "Thanks for helping me get the trailer back."

"Sorry 'bout this John," I said as if I was the one who broke some agreement with him.

"No worries. I had no idea he had plans to leave you and the kids behind when I loaned him the money for that trailer. He's not keepin' his end of *any* bargain acting like he is. He can't just up and leave you and the kids with no income, run off, and expect no one to be pissed. It's just not what you do when you have a wife and kids," John said with a gruffness to his voice I had not heard before.

The repossession was completed, and the trailer was dropped off beside the house within twenty-four hours. That afternoon Cherri called me again. "He's pretty pissed off," Cherri reported. "He called the cops and everythin'. He was pretty loud as he was tryin' to stop the guy from takin' that trailer."

"I bet he was. Guess he didn't expect that to happen," I said as I paced in my living room with the phone to my ear.

"Yeah, I wasn't the only one who Cody made sure could overhear most of the situation. The Repo Guy who was here to get it was really nice. I heard that guy tell the cop, 'He can get his stuff out of it, but he needs to do it now. I was just hired to repo the trailer, as you can see.' And the guy was

CHAPTER 14

handin' the officer some papers. The cops got Cody to calm down and they let Cody get his stuff out of the trailer before the guy left with it," Cherri explained.

"That's pretty interesting. Thanks Cherri."

I glanced out my window at the gooseneck trailer and smirked.

"I gotta go, the baby's cryin'. Talk to you soon."

Cherri's call wasn't the only one I got that week. My neighbor – who was renting our single-wide next to me – called, within a day, to report that she too had information.

"Jimmy bumped into Cody in town today. He said Cody was pissed off that someone stole his horse trailer or something like that," Loral said.

"Nah. No one stole anything from him. The guy, our buddy, who loaned Mike money for the trailer repoed it," I attempted to help Loral get the facts straight.

"You mean that one that is parked out by your house? That trailer?"

"Yeah. The guy who owns it will be comin' down from Idaho to pick it up soon."

"Oh, Cody's gonna be pissed off when he finds out it's out here!"

"Well now ... since he's not allowed out here on the ranch, due to the restraining order I was just granted, it won't matter. Plus, who's gonna tell him our long-time friend has parked the trailer out here?"

"I don't see why you got that restraining order on him," Loral shared her opinion. "He's not a threat. He's just angry," the naive twenty-something added.

"Well," *pity she's so innocent, but I'm sure that's what Mike's counting on ... "* what you **don't know** is his seemingly idle threats are not so idle. I know, personally, he follows through on all of his threats."

"He says he's never threatened you," she defended him.

"He has," my body tensed. "He does it so no one else hears it," my jaw muscles tightened. "I'm not the only one. I've watched him do it to others for years. He makes a threat and like a snake he waits for the right moment. He's been willing to wait a long time before he reminds someone he has it out for them, that he hasn't forgotten. He lets his 'I'm gonna get you' comments add up. You've only known him for a couple of months – *and you haven't pissed him off yet* – but ... after twelve years ... I know." I shook my head. "He's threatened me, many times.

"He's just playin' you and Jimmy as he tries to get info out of you about what's goin' on out here. I bet he says he's never hit me either, but he has...." I shook my head even though my neighbor couldn't see me. "Watch what you say, will yeah? Because you can put the kids and me in danger."

I tired of defending my own need for protection. Protection that this young girl was not privy to but seemed to have her own opinion of.

He's at it again. He's found someone to feed his line of crap to and she has no idea what game he is playin' and how he's usin' her as a pawn. Just what Mike was counting on.

I ended the conversation by nearly hanging up on her. It was time for me to lean on the one thing I've learned I can count on... a strong cup of coffee.

Chapter 15

That weekend Sally, the mother of my son's best friend brought her two boys out to the ranch to play with the kids. A visit with another adult, over coffee, invigorated me.

"You know your husband was under investigation for arson when your house burnt down last year?" Sally said, unexpectedly.

"Wha ... wha ... what did you just say? And how do you know this?" My stomach became queasy.

"Yeah. Didn't you know I was in insurance?"

I shook my head, "No," and sat down across from her at the table.

"Yeah. There was a *big* investigation of him."

"Why didn't you say ... anything?"

"Well, I couldn't. I wanted to, because our boys are so close, but it was an active investigation," she disclosed.

I reached for my coffee cup, and steadied the cup with both hands as I brought it up for a sip. My mind raced.

Mike, investigated, arson, our home, the flames, my babies!

"And so," Sally's voice helped me refocus, "when they couldn't prove that he set the house on fire, they had to pay the claim," she explained. "That's why it took so long for you to get a check."

So, what the kids said was true! They didn't do it! I always knew they weren't putting matches in the space heater. How the hell does someone put effing matches in an electric heater that's in your kids' bedroom and blame it on your kids! And then start a fire ... on effing Christmas day ... when your family is home?

"You didn't know about the investigation, did you?" she asked with a softer tone of voice.

"No. I mean, I remember the insurance guy comin' out to the ranch. He asked me some questions. I remember Mike sittin' in the guy's truck for a while... they were talking, but that's it." I swallowed the lump in my throat. Silence fell between us as I did my best to wrap my head around this new information. Minutes later I looked her in the eyes, "Wait ... wait, you said, '**he** was under investigation'. You said ... '**he** was'...." My heart beat faster.

Sally nodded her confirmation.

"... You didn't say **we** both were... Why wasn't I?"

"Oh, you were," a half-smile graced her lips, "just like all homeowners are when their home burns down," she assured me, "but for a short time." Her gaze softened as she tilted her head. "The investigation quickly became focused on him."

"What an effing asshole! I remember when he said he 'found matches in the space heater that was in Ethan and Emma's room,'" I shared with air quotes for emphasis as I shook my head in disbelief.

My mind filled with the memory of Mike calling me into the back bedroom, a couple of weeks before the house burned down. He pointed out two unburnt matches on the ledge of the portable space heater. The matches were just inside the protective small-gauged screen.

Adrenaline raced through my body.

Oh my god, how did those get there? They weren't there this morning when I woke the kids. And the kids have been out in the living room with me until now! Plus, I turn the heater off after the kids are dressed and out with me eating breakfast in the kitchen. What's it doing on now?

It was then that I noticed the match heads were not close enough to ignite. I was consumed with the safety of my kids and overlooked the lack of logic to what my husband was showing me. I could see the matches couldn't come in contact with the bright orange-red heating elements because the insulators on the base prevented *anything* from being able to easily touch the lowest heating element. Plus, it's designed to shut off if the heater gets knocked over. I remember ensuring that before I allowed it to be placed in

CHAPTER 15

our kids' bedroom.

I *had* unplugged the heater immediately and called for the two oldest kids to come into the room. I looked around the room for a matchbook and pulled open the dresser drawers. Found nothing. I searched in the closet. Still nothing.

Where did these matches come from?

Mike was angry and accusatory as he interrogated the kids. He wouldn't let the kids even speak as he told them how they *must* have put the matches in there, including how and when *they* did it.

I didn't like how he was *telling* the kids what they *must* have done. He told them he was certain *they* did it. In hopes of softening the blow to the kids, I asked similar questions in a kinder tone of voice. The kids still denied putting the matches in there.

"He reprimanded the kids. Blamed it on the kids!" Nearly frozen in my seat, I continued my recount and Sally listened intently. "I remember the fear on Ethan's face that day. He said he didn't do it. I believed him." I focused deep into my lap as the guilt of being played by Mike, even then – especially against my own kids – washed over me. "I remember not knowing where the kids could've gotten the matches from." I frowned. "I mean, the kids hadn't ever played with matches before! They didn't even have access to matches when Mike smoked because he used a lighter. And he always kept his lighter on him … in his pocket.

"And I didn't think Emma did it either," I chanced a look at Sally in the eyes, "but I guess I figured it must have been one of the kids …. After all, I'd never imagine a parent would put their kids at such risk. What the fuck? Who the fuck would do that?" A new sense of anger emerged – with a vengeance.

"I'm sorry Kathleen," Sally diverted her eyes to her cup. "I'm sure glad I told you."

"Me too. I had no idea!" I shook my head, teeth clenched, fists scrunched tight.

"I was beginning to make Christmas dinner," I rambled on as my memories, from ten months back, came flooding in. "I realized I needed another pan… to cook dressing… or was it yams in….." I mumbled because details were lost. "So I went up to the storage trailer … up by the barn. The dogs were escorting me."

That must have been when he did it.

" I remember hearing an unfamiliar poppin' noise … the dogs heard it too," I shared. "I looked out at the barn… saw nothing out of the ordinary. So, I went back to searching through boxes. I found the pan and heard the sound of breaking glass, a lot of glass. I peered out through the trailer's window this time, back toward the house … that's when I saw the flames. They were lapping up over the roof, out of the back bedroom windows of the double-wide …. Ethan and Emma's bedroom windows!" My eyes widened with the memory of the hungry flames. "I remember dropping the pan." As I swallowed, even now, my throat felt dry, like it was on that Christmas day. "I ran, ran faster than I thought was possible, back down to the house."

The 600 feet felt so far away as I tried to get to my beauties. I don't think I've ever run that fast. Ever.

"That must have been so scary."

"It was." I glanced up. "As I got closer to the house, looking for the kids, Mike and Ethan were the first I saw. As I turned from them to go into the house, I remember asking, 'Where are the girls?' and him saying, 'They're in the truck.'"

I remembered… even then … *in the truck… I haven't been out of the house that long….* I turned to look for my girls. There they were, Emma holding tight to Bella. Both with terror-filled eyes as the flames destroyed our home and everything, including their special gifts from Santa, and the handmade cross-stitch Christmas stockings their grandmother had finished in time for this special day. Able to confirm the kids were all out of the house, and safe enough, I was able to take a deep breath and regroup.

I shook my head in disbelief.

"Ironically, it was then I noticed a light snow had started fallin'. Stupidly, I remember looking up and wondering … hoping … if it was enough to put the fire out. But we know it wasn't."

CHAPTER 15

I diverted my gaze from Sally to the tree outside the replacement house. I felt a need to see my children yet continued to share more details with my friend.

"And after I was able to check and make sure the kids were okay, Ethan stopped me …. 'Mom, I'm sorry. I tried to get your Christmas present, but Dad stopped me from going back in there.'" Tears welled in my eyes, today, months after the fact, as my son's downturned mouth and sad eyes filled my mind. My breath caught in my lungs – then and now.

"Mike even tried to make it sound like he went back in to get stuff… how brave he tried to sound," my voice became gruff as hatred burned within me. "He got his spurs," I half-heartedly laughed as I stared out the window. "He told me about the burns on his head. He said, '… It was from the aluminum roof melting….' What the eff?"

Sally pursed her lips as she listened.

How would he get burns, from dripping aluminum … on his head … if he wasn't back in that bedroom?

Chapter 16

Hours later the kids happily yammered for supper. I was able to make a box-inspired goulash and salad.

"Hold on you guys. Go wash up while I finish making the salad dressing," I said to the threesome who headed down the hall.

Giggles filled the air as each jockeyed to be the first into the bathroom. Minutes later they settled around the table, eager to eat.

"Please God …" I started to say as they reached for their forks.

"…Please God," we all said in unison, "bless these gifts that we are about to receive through the bounty of Christ our Lord, amen."

"And thank you Lord, for keeping these beauties safe all this time," I added under my breath as we all smiled. I nodded my approval for them to eat. "Did you guys have a good time today?"

"Yeah. Thanks for lettin' 'em come out mom," Ethan mumbled with a mouth full of food as he looked up from his supper.

"I'm glad they were able to come out," I paused with a fork full of salad ready to satisfy my taste buds. *It's so nice to see you smile son. It's been so long.*

I continued to watch him and the girls as they ate. They were more relaxed than I'd seen them in a long time. Too long.

Later, as I tucked each of the beauties into bed, I hugged each one a little tighter. Okay a lot tighter than the night before. My lips lingered on their cheeks as I kissed each one goodnight.

"Love you son." Ethan reached up and embraced me.

CHAPTER 16

"Night Mommy," Emma said.

"Nigh' mom...my," Bella barely got out as her eyelids closed.

Before I exited the room, I felt lightheaded. My vision became unclear. I stopped and tightly gripped the door frame, just as my knees buckled.

Oh God. Please not here, not in front of them.

I took a deep breath, recovered enough to turn out their light, make it out of their room, and safely walk down the hall steadying myself periodically with a hand on the wall as I went. As I fell into bed, fully dressed, the tears came, relentlessly.

I can't stay here. We can't stay here. I can't keep the kids here, it's not safe! Not with the realities of what Sally.... My tears became sobs. *He's not going to give up! He's gonna continue to make good on his threats! He's not taking 'I'm done with this marriage' for an answer.*

I tried to catch my breath, but as visions of the flames out of the back of the kids' bedroom flared up in my mind again, breathing became difficult. I gasped. I rolled into the fetal position – my knees drawn tight to my chest – as the memories didn't stop. The wide eyes of the neighbor and 'I've already called 9-1-1,' the fire truck speeding down the driveway, the snow falling harder, the red-orange glow of the metal walls of the mobile... and how I could distinctively see the framework of the walls through the fire as I followed the fire truck down the drive, the cop cars, Officers Brad and someone else, the lady from the Red Cross, the solemnness of the firefighter as he gingerly carried a coffee table book to me, presenting it to me. 'We were able to save this, sorry we couldn't save more.' The fear in the girls' eyes, the pity in the eyes of the hotel's desk clerk. Although I wrapped my arms tightly around my legs and rocked myself – comfort evaded me.

He could've killed us! He could've killed any one of the kids! He's lucky no one got burned. Scarred for effing life! What a stupid ass! I screamed into my pillow. As I rocked, my fear grew, and my anger resurfaced. *I can't stay here. It's so unsafe here!*

The dog must have heard my scream as he nudged me with his nose and then laid his chin on my rib cage when I didn't respond. Minutes stretched. Finally, I reached up and stroked his head. He refused to move. I steadied my breath without wiping the tears. Exhaustion washed over me, and I drifted off to sleep.

The next day the sound of the horses coming in from the pasture, at sunrise, woke me. I sat up. Coojoe glanced up from his spot beside the bed.

"It's okay boy," I said in my morning hush.

I rubbed my eyes to rid my lashes of last night's tears. With eyes open, I blinked in an effort to focus. I took notice that I was fully dressed, shoes and all. I shrugged my shoulders.

"Guess this saves time this morning," my sarcasm was lost on the dog as he tilted his head.

As I swung my legs over the edge of the bed, I listened intently for the kids. My reward was the soft in and out breaths of my three.

Morning chores dragged on as I tried to let the normal repetition sooth me. But the sight of a white cruiser coming down the driveway ended all that.

"Come on Coojoe. Let's go to the house."

We walked to the house and waited for the officer. I stood at the kitchen window, watched the cruiser slowly come up the long drive. My mind raced.

Why are they coming out ... today? Are they coming out to ask me more questions? Did Sally talk to them yesterday? Is he here because Mike's causing trouble ... in town? Did Mike breach the restraining order ... at the school?

My coffee did little to settle me this time.

The dog got up and went to the door. I followed and opened it as we both heard the cruiser pull up and the car door shut.

"Hi Officer Christensen."

"Hello, can I come in?"

"Sure."

I updated the officer on the restraining order he recommended I get.

"Yes. Yes, that's what I'm here about." The officer chose to stand just inside the threshold. "Were you able to find some of Walton's paperwork you mentioned to the other officer?"

I nodded.

CHAPTER 16

"Do you want them?"

"Okay. Good. And no, take them into the Florence PD as he's under their jurisdiction now, because of where he lives." Officer Christensen scribbled in his notepad. He lifted his eyes but found a spot on the wall to stare at instead of looking at me this time. "Isn't there somewhere you can go? Somewhere to keep you and the kids safe?"

"I... I..."

"You guys are just so far out here. It takes us so long to get out here. I feel like we can't protect you," he said in a somber tone. "I just think you'll all be safer *not* out here by yourself. If you are somewhere he can't get to you... you'd be safer."

"I don't know ... I'll check." I shook my head.

"Don't you have family you can stay with?" unease laced his words.

"I do, but not in this state. They're out in California...."

"All right." He tucked his notepad back in his breast pocket and stood squarely. "I can't tell you to leave the state with your children, but I really do think you need to go."

I gazed over at him and noticed he was now studying my every move.

"I understand sir. I hear you. I will see what I can do. And I promise to call if he comes out here. I promise."

"Okay. We'll keep an eye on him too."

Within an hour the phone rang, caller ID was something I'd learned to rely on.

"Hello there Claudia."

"How are the quilt blocks coming along?" she asked.

"They're comin' along. I've been able to get ten of the twelve flowers cut out for the applique blocks," I allowed myself to relish the pleasure of working with fabric as I surveyed the stack of large scraps of fabric I needed to finish cutting. "I think I will be able to get these last two blocks done soon and I'll be able to send them to you so you can sew 'em together. They're gonna make a pretty display in your quilt store."

With small talk out of the way, I filled my friend in on my visit with Sally and the officer.

"Well, since my dad and the other cops I've known don't make those type of suggestions without good reason, we need to get you and the kids out of there!" Claudia said with a sense of urgency.

"But I've got five head of horses out here. The two you purchased, my mom and dad's two, and the kids' mare…. How'm I gonna get them moved out to California? And I'm sure this Jeep won't make the trip, and where will we stay? He knows where my folks' place is, we used to live there, train horses out of there … it wouldn't be safe there either." I couldn't help but notice the octave changes in my own voice. It sounded strange, to me, as it got higher – higher as my heart rate increased and uncertainty grew. I shook my head. "I don't see how I can do this. I can't move. All of the kids' stuff and the kids … I …."

"Well, maybe you can borrow John's trailer," she offered a viable solution. "It's still at the ranch, right? I mean, he hasn't come down to get it or sold it yet, right?" she asked.

"Right."

"Okay, do you think he'd mind you using it to move and get safe?"

"No… I guess not. I can ask, I guess, but what good would that do? I don't have a truck to pull it with."

"No, but I do. I can bring out both of my trucks and my two-horse trailer. We could put all of the stuff you and the kids want to take in the trailer and transport the horses that need to come out here in John's gooseneck trailer. It's just a thought. Maybe you can call him, ask him. And if he says yes, the earliest Gary and I can come out is Thanksgiving weekend. But we could do it."

A dizzying determination fought against my timidness.

"You give him a call," Claudia urged. "I'll talk with my husband and get someone to cover things here and we'll talk tonight."

Chapter 17

"So ... I called John. He said, 'No problem.' And he'll worry about selling the horse trailer in California, later, after the kids and I are safe. He figures he'll get more for it out there anyways," I attempted to add some cheer to my voice, as I settled into bed.

"He probably will," relief that one hurdle had been overcome, was undeniable in Claudia's voice.

"Thanks for the suggestion that I call him," I sighed and shook my head. "I guess I just wasn't thinkin' straight ..." the exhausting confusion of today's changes came across in my voice. "Are you sure your schedule can handle you guys coming out here? I mean, who's gonna run the quilt store for you?"

"Yes. But I usually close it Thanksgiving weekend anyway. The upside is this'll give you a couple of weeks to get the packing done," Claudia sounded upbeat. "Do you think you can get it done?"

"I will have to, won't I?"

"I guess so, but it should be easier as you can concentrate on the kids and you, now," she encouraged. "By the way, you and the kids can stay here, with us. It's a private community. He won't be getting back here."

"I do remember there's only one way in, but..."

"Yes, and it's a pretty tight community, we know when someone is where they don't belong," she tried to reassure me.

"Okay." *But is it more secure than his warped sense of determination?* I shook my head. "I ... am ... tired of this B.S. I just think it would be best for us to not be out here." I shrugged my shoulders. "Well, here we go again. Another move. I guess I don't get to live anywhere, any...where... for more than five years."

I half-heartedly chuckled, to myself.

"Go. Sleep well. You have a lot of packing to do," Claudia encouraged.

"Okay. Night." My head sank heavily into the comfort of my pillow. *Many things to get done tomorrow. First sleep... then ....*

The next morning coffee helped me focus on a multitude of things I needed to accomplish. Close to the top of my list was taking paperwork into the police department as Officer Christensen requested.

"I... I have some paperwork I've been asked by a sheriff's deputy, or two, to bring in and share with you." I handed the officer the manila envelope. Unsure of the next move, I just stood there.

The sergeant pulled the papers out of the envelope addressed to "Cody Walton."

"It seems it's a fake birth certificate," I explained, "at least I figured it is fake since I just found out that there are ... like ... twelve lies on our marriage certificate," I frowned as I heard the words come out of my own mouth. "So, this is a lie too."

Quiet minutes passed as he examined the light teal paper, the order booklet, and the invoice. The officer looked up.

"Who's writing is this? On the cover of this booklet?"

"It's Cody's," I filled him in on what I'd learned weeks ago about the guy I'd married.

"And I thought this was just going to be a simple custody issue," Sergeant Adams said as he shook his head, accented with a light chuckle.

"What do you mean?"

"Well, he was in here yesterday complaining about not being able to see the kids. But *this* changes a lot." A light smirk graced his face. "What made him purchase this birth certificate?"

"Um, when he broke his back and was applying for SSDI, he needed it. I remember him sayin' he'd lost it and his mum didn't have it." I shrugged

CHAPTER 17

my shoulders. "He said he would get one from the county he was born in, just like the lady at the Social Security office suggested. And a few weeks later, it showed up."

"I need to keep these, if you don't mind?" the officer said as he lifted the paperwork. "I can give you a copy of it all if you'd like?" he added, as I hesitated.

"Okay. And yes, I would like a copy of them."

"Go ahead and sit over there, if you don't mind, while I get you copies."

He unlocked the back-office door and disappeared.

What the hell is going on? Mike's whining to the cops about not being able to see the kids? I shook my head. *No wonder Christensen wanted me to get this paperwork in here. When Mike said he got his birth certificate ... I had no idea he bought a fake one!*

Minutes later Officer Adams returned to the lobby.

"I did some checking. This is definitely *not* a real birth certificate. He purchased it from a known company that has been identified to specialize in making and selling fraudulent paperwork."

"Fake documents? Purchased? Not from the county he was born in?" My mind struggled with what I'd come to know over my twelve-year marriage and the reality of what I'd learned only days ago. "Oh wait... he wasn't even born in Texas," I reminded myself aloud.

"No. And there's no such place as 'Lookit, Texas,'" Adams said as he waited for it all to sink in.

"Lookit, Texas isn't even a real place?" dismay filled my voice as I shook my head. "Well, there's another lie to add to the pile."

"I'm going to look into these fake documents and the company he purchased them from. It may take a while, but I promise to look into them." Adams swiftly changed the subject, "he said you won't let him see the kids. What can you tell me about that?"

"Judge Lawson granted me a restraining order and I've filed for divorce...."

"Which has an automatic restraining order in it too," he grinned at the additional information. "He said something about an upcoming holiday program, at the school."

"How does Mike know about the kids' school performance?" I inquired.

"He must have gone by the school."

"Hopefully it's when the school was closed and the kids are not there," I quipped.

Officer Adams raised his eyebrows.

"I guess… he could come to the holiday performance, tomorrow. But only if he stays on the other side of the auditorium." I wrung my hands together.

"Are you sure?"

I peered up, wide-eyed. "I think it would be good for the kids," the quiver in my voice betrayed my braveness.

After all, it will be the last time they see him … for a while.

"Okay, I'll let him know he can show up tomorrow for the performance, but he must stay away from you and the kids. He must stay on the opposite side of the auditorium from you." The officer extended his hand as I rose to leave. "Don't worry Miss, we'll keep an eye on him."

"Okay," I said. "I hope I've made the right decision," I added, in a near whisper, as I left to get packing boxes from the grocery store two doors away.

Chapter 18

I opened my purse and checked to make sure a copy of my temporary restraining order was in it.

Okay, breathe. It's gonna be all right. Breathe. The darn paperwork hasn't escaped since you put it in there two weeks ago, nor since you checked it an hour ago, or checked it ten minutes ago for that matter, I chastised myself.

I closed my eyes, inhaled deeply before I forced the air out though my mouth.

"You ready to go in and see your sister sing something?" I forced cheer into my voice as I made small talk with Bella.

"Yeah!" the five-year-old said with enthusiasm as she unbuckled her seat belt and climbed over into the driver's seat. "I get out with you."

It was more of a statement than a request for permission, which made me smile as I got out of the Jeep first.

As we walked into the elementary school, I looked for his truck. My neck and shoulders tensed as I did not see it. Walking through the lobby I greeted the school secretary behind the counter. The bounce in Bella's steps helped me focus on her instead of the 'what ifs' as we entered the gym that doubled as an auditorium.

Oh good, we aren't the first ones here.

The acknowledgment kept my pulse from doubling.

"Hey Lovie, we're going…"

I winced as I heard his all-too-familiar heavy heels hit the wooden floor.

Shit! I tried to swallow the lump that blossomed in my throat. Bile threatened to rise up into my mouth. *I should have brought antacids!*

Just past the fold-out bleachers, I saw him as he walked in. My eyes widened as the brim of his grey Stetson preceded him. All of a sudden, forty feet away wasn't far enough away. He hesitated and then turned in Bella's and my direction. My hands found my youngest's shoulders. I took a step back and pulled Bella to me. She willingly followed my silent communication with a relaxed body. I bumped into the wall, too close to make a retreat. My body stiffened. My pulse quickened. My eyes darted left.

Is there enough space for me and Bella to hide under the bleachers?

Just then, out of the corner of my eye, the tan of Officer Brad's uniform shirt came into view. He stepped into the auditorium without hesitation, walked past me, and strode in front of the bleachers to confront Mike. He glanced away from us. Officer Christensen walked in the other door, the same one as Mike had. Christensen joined Brad and they strode to their target. It was then that my breath stopped catching in my throat.

I stopped my retreat as I watched the officers approach Mike. He clenched his jaw as the officers spoke with him. He kept his eyes forward and away from us. As the officers turned to leave, both made eye contact with me. Brad nodded his head as a smirk appeared on his face before he stopped near the bleachers, on the far side of the room. As the officers stood, they made small talk with other parents. Mike stood against the far wall of the auditorium.

Do they have kids here or are they just staying around to let Mike know they're still watching him?

Minutes later the noise in the large room increased as teachers directed students where to sit on the hardwood. Miss Emma didn't have to look around much to find her sister and me. We shared a smile before she glanced around the room. Next to come in was Ethan's class. He noticed his father first. Smiled. And then he found my kind expression awaited him. The youngest waved at her siblings.

Thirty minutes later and a few flapping turkey wings – enacted by second,

CHAPTER 18

third, and fourth graders – the hall erupted with a round of applause. The smiles on the children's faces made me forget, for a moment, that he was there. That is until some kids rushed to their parents for hugs, including Ethan and Emma. I couldn't help but notice that their father exited without hesitation. He let the other parents become a buffer between the officers and him as he walked closest to the wall on his way out.

Chapter 19

"I guess choosing what to take and not to take's gonna be easy," sarcasm dripped from my words, as I stood in front of my closet. I frowned. "Since most of what I want to take burned up last year with the house." Anger raged within me. I reached up, pulled the few dresses and shirts – hangers and all – down from the rod before layering them in the cardboard box.

I miss that red satin shirt that I loved to wear at Christmas. Focus, focus. That kind man said this would happen. I worked to change my focus from what I was missing, but I was struggling. *He warned you,* I reminded myself, *that even years later to expect to reach for something, a shirt or whatever, and feel like you've misplaced it long before you remember it burned ... and it's only been not even a year yet.*

"Expect to get frustrated because you can't remember where you put something," he had kindly told me, "I remember there were moments when I thought I'd misplaced something I just knew I had. Somewhere." Compassion filled the grey-haired and bearded man's eyes as he tried to prepare another fire victim for things to come. "It took me a while, as I'm sure it's going to for you too... to you remember you lost "it" in the house fire," he had explained.

All of that is gone. Gone. That horse's backside made sure of that. I looked down, away from my new-to-me clothing. My hand-me-down tennie-runners came into view as tears welled. I shook my head .... *You can do this.*

CHAPTER 19

You can find another shirt to wear that you'll like. Or you can make one yourself. You'll get a new pair of shoes, too ... one day. Don't worry about it.

I was more than appreciative of the generous donations that came from around Colorado and as far away as California than I felt I could ever convey, so I worked to refocus.

A turn and two steps were all it took before I lifted the light metal drawer pulls.

Leave out a pair of jeans ... okay maybe both pairs, that's all I need to keep out, and just a couple of shirts. Undies, socks, I guess I can pack most of these. I can wash what I need to in the sink. It's only a week or so until we leave. Leave for good.

With most of my room packed I set the boxes in the closet. The doors slid shut and I headed to the bathroom.

I found packing easier as the days went by. Little by little. Only the essentials remained out. I stacked boxes of our belongings in the corner of the living room.

Clouds had moved in, just like the weatherman said it would. The single-pane windows and the sliding glass door were letting in the chill. The chill that forty-degree nights brought to a mobile home.

"Momma needs to get this house warmed up, huh?" I said to my beauties as they sat on the couch focused on the TV, the girls cuddled together under a quilt.

"Whatcha gonna use to warm up the house Momma?" my son asked.

Oh my goodness, what am I going to use to warm this house for my babies? Not a lot of propane left in that tank. Last I checked it was about five percent. I don't want to buy more. Don't want to waste what money I have on that. Don't know if the heater even works? I do have the fireplace. Yes! The fireplace! What am I going to do for firewood? What am I going to use to cut wood? Did he leave me a saw? Why didn't I think of this before... like in the daylight?

I headed toward the door to see what I could find when a solution for tonight's fire came into view.

Well, well, well, I grinned. *All of these years. All of the horse show winning we did ... what a waste of effort.* I paused. I read the inscription on the trophy plaque hanging on the wall in front of me. And then I looked at the trophy above that. *That was the show we got offered $25,000 for the mare ... and* **he** *turned it down! Even after we both agreed to sell her! We could have used that money. Maybe that was a lie all-along too. I think he only wanted people thinkin' he was a success, instead of being a success. These are **my** trophies too. All the hours in the saddle, training – both horse and human – getting clients to trust us with their horses, grooming, caring for and competing with the horses... side by side* with him*!*

"Okay Lovies. I've got it," I said triumphantly as I reached up and took one of the oak trophies off the wall. "Grab some of that newspaper and I'll get some matches."

I circled around through the kitchen and located a matchbook before I met my son in front of the fireplace.

"Okay Lovie let's crumple some newspaper," I instructed as we prepared the paper kindling.

The oak plaque nestled easily on top of the stack of rumpled newsprint. Both lay cradled in the wrought iron log holder. I drew the match head across the striker strip. The promising scent of sulfur wafted up. I touched the flame to the paper in numerous spots. It was then I noticed the small lever for the flue. I slid it from side to side a few times. A metal clunk told me when it was in the shut position. The flames licked up over the edges of the dark stained eight by ten wood flat. As the flames increased, knowing they needed air to live, I knew I had the flue in the open position.

I grabbed two more of the Scottsdale Championship plaques off the wall. With an unsteady hand, I separated the protective chain screen. A bit of guilt and sadness washed over me as I laid them in different directions.

"I paid the entry fees for these classes," I said through clenched teeth low enough to be the only one who heard me. "And I put out the blood, sweat, tears, not to mention a broken foot – when It's The One stomped on it," I scoffed under my breath as I laid the proof of our successful horse training business on the flames. "I paid for them! They're at least half mine. I own the horses too. I can burn them!" I encouraged myself. "Plus, he shouldn't've left me with no way to take care of our kids."

CHAPTER 19

My smile grew as the oak released its hidden warmth.

After all, I snickered, *these damn trophies were* always *more important to him than we were!* I giggled as the flames slowly devoured the wood. *I will look for the saw and scrap wood in the morning.*

A squeak came from the front door hinges.

"Momma, here's this saw thing." Emma offered the skill saw she held with both hands. "Will this work?"

I relieved my beauty of her heavy treasure.

"Thanks Lovie!" I wrapped my other arm around her. "Where'd you find this?"

"In the barn!" she said with much glee.

"This is great," I smiled wide. "We'll grab up scrap wood tomorrow and we'll stay warm for the next week and a half without issues." I grazed her cheek with a kiss.

Oh my goodness, I thought I was going to have to use a hand saw. What a blessing. This is great! I bet he didn't mean to leave this behind. He'd never leave something behind that'd actually help me. A giddy chuckle escaped my lips. *I can go find wood as the coffee is brewing tomorrow and warm this place up for the kids before they go to school. Yes!*

Chapter 20

I rolled over, peered at the red numbers on the digital clock – 6:00 AM. "Well, I guess it's time to get that coffee pot makin' its magic while I go out and make fire," I said to the dog. Minutes later, "Extension cord, check. Coffee brewing, check. Saw, check. Now all I need is the wood," I said to Coojoe as he escorted me out into the front yard. "Okay boy, it's time to go find some wood."

I climbed through the wires of the fence that separated the barn from the house pasture.

"Oh look Coojoe, smaller pieces of wood! I shouldn't have to cut those much, maybe even just break them with my foot. And make some kindling, real kindling."

As I turned into the smaller metal barn that currently doubled as storage, I saw a loose two by six.

"Sure am glad I let the power company put in that security light!" I patted the dog as I peered in the shed. "It will help me make sure we don't take any spiders with us, huh!"

Gloveless, I grabbed the wood.

Sure hope no Brown Recluses or Black Widows are on this wood.

I flipped it over as I pulled it into the barn aisle. Satisfied I was safe, I headed back toward the house, paused along the way to pick up a couple of other scraps.

His sloppy habit of leaving things where they lay may just work for me this

CHAPTER 20

week. My jaw tensed. *Positive. Drop that. Let it go. It's all gonna be better. One week, that's it. Find something positive. Now!* I demanded of myself. *This is good for me and the kids. It's going to make it much easier to warm the house as this Second Summer gives way to Winter. I sure hope the weather holds off like it has for the last eight years in November.*

I cut the plank in uneven increments, a small pile developed, kindling included.

Just enough to take the chill off the house for my beauties. I can always cut more later.

With an armful of firewood, I went back into the house, escorted by Coojoe, of course. By the time the kids got up, the chill of the morning air was just beginning to give way to the heat of the fire.

"Do you need help with finding wood?" Emma asked as she ate her breakfast.

"Sure Lovie, you guys can go wood-hunting after school today."

Smiles grew on both the girls' faces. The boy just stared up at the fire.

I don't think he likes fire anymore, even when it's in the fireplace.

My heart ached at how some of the simple pleasures in life had been taken away from my oldest. Taken away by his father.

Wonder if he thinks his father started the fire too?

I sipped my coffee as I watched my son evaluate the safety of the flames he saw.

Who needs breakfast, I have a full serving of dread here this morning? Didn't think this fire would upset 'im or any of 'em for that matter. Damn.

"It's safe Lovie," I said so only Ethan could hear, not wanting to interrupt the girls' chatter.

His eyes widened and became full pools of fear. I reached over, drew two fingers along his jawline.

"It didn't start in the fireplace." I half-smiled, half-frowned.

He blinked the waiting tears away and resumed eating his cereal.

"We'll make sure to take the nightlight with us to Claudia's. I'm sure she won't mind if we plug one in ... okay Lovie?"

My attempt to reassure my boy seemed to fall on deaf ears as he finished breakfast in silence. I couldn't tell if he was satisfied that I was going to let him continue on with his newest tradition since the fire – a nightlight in his room at the age of ten – or if he was looking forward to leaving this all behind too.

Chapter 21

I watched two trucks come down the driveway. Butterflies danced in my stomach. I glanced to my right as a stack of boxes held a limited definition of our life. As the trucks made it around the curve, I turned and headed for the front door.

"Come on Coojoe. It's time to say hello."

Coojoe and I stood out in front of the house waiting for Claudia and Gary to pull up.

"Hey there," I said cheerfully as I walked to the first driver's door. "How was the drive?"

"Not too bad," Claudia said as she turned the truck off. "Who's that?" she asked with an unsteady cheer in her voice, she looked at the Rottweiler who kept step with me.

"Coojoe. Hi Gary," I added as my friend's husband exited the second truck. I patted Coojoe on the head. "He's pretty friendly, once I let him know yah'll are okay."

A snicker accented my smirk.

"Hi Coojoe," Gary said in his deep baritone voice. He bent at the waist to make his six-foot beefy frame seem less threatening as he presented his hand, palm up, for Coojoe's inspection. The dog sat down beside me, and Gary moved forward and embraced me. "How you doin', sis?"

"Okay," I monitored my voice to downplay all that had happened of late. *I don't want others to worry about me. Them here ... shows they are worried enough.* "It's good to see you. Thanks for comin' out here. I know it's a long drive from Cali to here, especially on a holiday weekend."

"Well, Claudia's been keepin' me up to date on what's been happening here since you stayed at our house this summer. It's the least we could do for you and the kids," he smiled.

Claudia was out of the truck now, Coojoe sniffed her hand. He didn't block her access to me, hugs were shared.

"Thanks again," I said in her ear. "I can't believe you came all this way."

"Well, it was the best time to come get you and the kids. I don't think it's going to get any safer waiting for another weekend or month. It's best to get you guys out of here, to a safe place. And the sooner the better. Just like the deputy suggested."

"Yah'll want to walk around a bit, or do you want me to start loadin' the truck?"

"Yeah, let's, let's see whatcha built here," Gary said.

"I could use stretching my legs a bit," Claudia quipped.

"Okay. The ranch property starts down there…" I donned my best tour guide voice as I pointed back down the driveway, "…just about where you started up the hill. The house that burnt down was there, by that lone power pole. Somehow …it survived." I shook my head and shrugged my shoulders." We walked toward the barn. "We put a shedrow barn up here because it was flat."

"How many stalls?" Claudia asked.

"Five stalls in each section, ten all together. We do use one as a tack stall, but we were supposed to make that single-wide there into our tack room," I lifted my chin to point to the white mobile home Mike had brought in about six months ago. "We've got the arena off the back side of the barn. It runs along the full length of the stalls."

"What are those tires for?" Claudia asked as she pointed to the far side of the arena.

"It's our round pen."

"Hum," a bit of intrigue interlaced her skepticism, followed by a silence that hung in the air.

Does she get it? Do I need to explain it? No. She should know. She's claimed to have trained horses before..... She should know the uses of a pen smaller than an arena.

"You've put a lot of work into this place," Gary complimented.

"Yeah, we have." A mix of pride, accomplishment, and sadness tainted my sigh. "There was only cactus, mostly that Cholla and Cow Tongue cactus, buffalo grass, and dirt when we got here."

"You put all of this in?" Claudia said as she looked around.

"Yes. From the well to everything else you see. Except for some of the cross-fencing. It's changed over the years… like this metal barn used to be down about where that last turn is before coming up to the top here." I turned my focus out to the pasture. "We had to put the bridge in just to get the first parts of the house in." I scoffed. "The first single-wide got stuck in the creek and they had to hire a guy with a big tractor to get it out! It was a bit of a cluster fuck as the spring storms were already hittin' the mountains and Mike had said it had started rainin' just before they got it out. The trickle of the creek became a torrent, almost like a flash flood, before they left the property. We had to wait a week before we built a bridge so we could get the second single-wide in."

We all focused down toward the creek.

"Guess we should of figured somethin' was up when the bank of the creek was six plus feet above the creek bed." A chuckle escaped my throat.

"One summer, during an evening storm…it sounded like a constant rolling of thunder. Curious, we put jackets, boots, and hats on… the kids were asleep, and we walked down to have a look at the creek." I accented my light sarcasm with air quotes as I said 'creek'. "I couldn't believe all of the water coming down! It was well over the bridge, nearly up to the pasture on the far side." My eyes widened as my mind filled with that loud, powerful, ominous sight. "You know, it was about four feet above the bridge you see there. All that water pushing rocks, dirt, and brush south. It still amazes me, all of that power, the potential for destruction."

I'm gonna miss this place, the summer storms … and the rainbows. A smile graced my lips. *The double rainbows. One always brighter than the other, but the lighter one always showing up.*

I surveyed the landscape up from the creek and saw a few of the horses in the pasture across the way. That's when Pikes Peak came into view. The snow-capped mountain had held a constant vigil for the last eight years. At over fourteen thousand feet tall it was easy for it to loom, protectively, as a constant element in our lives, over many lives of Colorado inhabitants even if it was seventy miles away.

Maybe I'll be back to see you. Maybe tomorrow won't be my last sight of you... my pretty Pikes Peak. I sighed.

"How many acres do you have here?" Gary asked.

"We own the eighty acres up here, but we have use of the two thousand within the fences."

"Wow!" Claudia responded.

"Bet that helps keep down on feed costs," Gary summarized.

"It sure does. Plus, we checked, years ago, this Buffalo Grass has a good protein level!"

"So were are all of the horses? Didn't you say we were bringing six back with us?" Claudia asked.

"Five. We only need to take five. They're out in pasture. They'll come up shortly. I can call them up if you'd like, so you can meet the ones you bought before Cody, I mean Mike, left –

Tall and Paint In Time."

"Well, who are these pretty girls?" Claudia said as she swooned.

"It's The One is the pinto, WA Silken Rose – Rosie is the bay, and Cee Cee is the chestnut," I answered.

"Are we taking these three with us?" Gary asked.

"No," sadness filled my voice. "Those are the ones Mike originally took with him when he left us. And then let loose on the property, a couple of Sundays ago, when he parked his rig on the other side of the bridge. You know, the day I had to have the deputies escort him off. I can't afford to keep these mares, even if their registration papers show they're mine, like Cee Cee or even if they are registered to both of us, like the other two. I just don't have the funds. I'm gonna be stretching it to get the payments on the land made until the divorce is finalized."

CHAPTER 21

And hopefully, I get awarded the farm, so I can sell it.

"But as angry as I am at Mike, I refuse to take it out on my mares. I am making sure they are fed and fed well … at least while I am still on the ranch," a mixture of regret and defeat rang in my ears. "I'm just keeping them up here in the barn, as the deputies asked me to. Plus, I can fatten them back up a little, as they came in with their ribs showin'."

I lifted my fingers up to my mouth and whistled loudly. The small herd of horses could be seen out in the pasture.

"Come on, let's go meet your two new horses. They'll be up here, at that water trough," I pointed, "before you know it."

We walked back toward the mobile. Moments later the thunder of their hooves reached my ears. Claudia and Gary glanced around. Seconds later five horses rounded the house. They slowed down to a trot, circled around the front yard, and stopped at the water tank. Excited to be called up to the house they pranced around and blew air out their nostrils.

"This dapple grey is your Tall, WA Walking Tall to be exact. And this pinto filly is your Paint In Time."

A smile grew on Claudia's face as her eyes began to twinkle with glee, childlike.

"I know you'll like Tall. Him being a champion cow horse and well broke," I continued the introductions.

She grinned as we all eyed at the well-built fifteen-two-hand Arabian gelding.

"You can start riding him when you get him home to Tehachapi."

"I'm looking forward to that!" Claudia crooned.

"I'm pretty sure Mike's been up on Paint In Time's back, but she's green broke and we'll need to do some work on her, after all…" I looked over at Gary, "we all know everybody's got a different definition of 'green broke.'"

We shared a chuckle.

"Okay. We can do that at my ranch," Claudia said unable to hide her excitement.

"This dark bay is Mister, and the bay and white pinto is Cueball. These are my mum and dad's colts. And hello my beauty," I reached up and stroked the liver chestnut mare's face. "This is Molly, the kids' mare. I just can't see leaving this sweet beauty behind." Molly nuzzled my neck. "I can't have the kids lose everything just because I know it's not safe to stay here anymore. They need something that they recognize. She's going to go to my folks' place, with their boys, until I can afford feed for her. But at least the kids will have 'er."

Claudia busied herself with an outstretched hand. She introduced herself to her new horses. Gary, Molly, and I stood in silence.

"Hey, I need to go up and get the kids. They all get off at the same time today, half-day, with the holiday tomorrow. Let me take you inside so you can sit in there and wait. I only have to go up to the end of the drive."

We all went inside the house.

"Wow, that smells delicious. What're you cookin'?" Gary asked.

"I did a turkey for us. I figured we needed a proper Thanksgiving meal, even if we were leaving on the holiday." I turned to face my friends. "It's the least I could do for you. Make you a good meal."

"You didn't need to do that!" Claudia said.

"I know, but I had the turkey given to me and ... we might want traveling yummies!" I brushed off the accolades. "There's coffee if you want. Cups above the maker. Sorry. I need to run." I grabbed up my keys and headed to the Jeep.

I only waited minutes for the bus to pull up, for the last time. I got out of the vehicle as I anticipated the bi-fold door's opening.

"Hi Barb. I wanted to thank you for all of the times you've looked after my kids. It's been nice to know I could trust that they would get to and from school safely," my throat tightened, and I had to force out the last few words.

She cocked her head, smiling, but an undeniable light confusion washed over her, translated in her eyes.

Ugh, I hope she didn't hear that catch in my voice.

I shrugged my shoulders, wanting to not alarm her.

"'Tiz the season to start saying my many thanks." I smiled graciously brushing my sincere comment off to the season before looking at the

CHAPTER 21

ground.

When the kids aren't here on Monday, Tuesday, Wednesday or any other day from now on, hopefully, she will remember how thankful I have been for her over the last five years.

My threesome clomped down the bus stairs, hugging me as they passed.

"Have a good holiday," Barb said cheerfully.

The kids turned back toward her, "Happy Thanksgiving," they said in unison.

"Happy Thanksgiving Miss Barb," I rolled my lips up hoping she didn't see the tears beginning to well in my eyes. We headed for the Jeep. "Okay, up top you guys."

The kids climbed in.

Chapter 22

"Who's here?" Ethan inquired as we pulled up to the house and he saw the unfamiliar vehicles.

"Claudia and Gary. They just got here, a little bit ago," I answered.

We got out of the car. Once in the house, introductions and hellos were exchanged.

"Oh great, you got coffee," I cheered.

"Are these few boxes all you've got packed?" Gary said with a hint of concern as he pointed to the six boxes in the corner.

"Oh no sir," I said cheerfully. "I've already been packin' the front of the gooseneck trailer." A proud smile graced my lips. "You wanna go see?"

"Yeah."

Gary and I went outside while Claudia got acquainted with the kids she'd heard so much about.

"Because Cody ... I mean Mike," I corrected myself, "took everything *he* wanted when he left ... leaving me and the kids with what he didn't think was important...." I opened the door to the nose of the trailer. "I don't have too much. I mean, I don't know how long we'll be gone ... and..." I sighed, "... at the end of the day, what essentials *are* there in life."

I let the statement hang in the air.

Mainly since the house burnt down, along with much of what I would have **wanted** *to move with me anywhere I went!*

CHAPTER 22

Anger flared within me. Anger for Mike and the burning down of the house I'd been suppressing.

"There isn't a lot of room in here is there," Gary said trying to bring a bit of cheer back into the day. "We do have room in the two-horse, you sure you don't want to put these boxes in there? This trailer will be going to our ranch and weren't you planning on leaving this bigger trailer at your mom and dad's?"

"I am planning on that. Yes."

"Okay. Well, we can put this stuff in the two-horse, that way you guys can have access to your stuff at our house." Gary smiled graciously. "Let me move the smaller trailer over here. We can transfer this stuff quickly and... if there's not much else, we can fit it all in there."

"There's not much else. Less than a dozen more boxes," the sadness I heard in my own voice brought an ache to my heart. "I tried Gary." I swallowed a lump in my throat. "I didn't want to hold us back from leaving and getting an early start tomorrow, so I've been packing for days. I do have to return the emergency phone tomorrow on our way out though," I informed him.

"Do you have to go far?"

"No," a half-hearted shrug of my shoulder accented my response. "It's about fifteen, twenty minutes away."

"Why don't you go ahead and return it now?"

"I'd rather wait until tomorrow morning if you don't mind," concern filled my eyes.

I rubbed my thumb back and forth across the side of my index finger.

"I don't trust him, let alone the cops out here don't trust him either. Add to it the folks renting that other mobile," I tilted my head to my left, "they aren't here, they're at her mum's for the holiday and ..." my voice quivered.

"No worry girl," Gary placed a hand on my shoulder, "tomorrow is fine. Why don't you let me move these trailers around and we'll move the boxes shortly? Go, have a cup of coffee."

His smile was comforting.

"Okay. Thank you."

Gary not only moved the smaller trailer closer to the front of the house, but he hooked up the other truck to the gooseneck and we were all set for finishing up the packing and leaving.

"Hey, I'm gonna go out and help move some more boxes in the smaller trailer. You guys need to make sure there's not anything else you want to take with you. You can bring it out here in the living room. Go on. Make sure Momma didn't miss anything real special, 'cuz Momma's not sure when we might be comin' back here."

The threesome trotted down the hall to their room.

"You want to stay in here and rest or…?" I said as I crossed the room to pick up a box.

"No, I'll come on out with you," Claudia said. "Let me get that door."

We made it out of the house before she got to see I had already started packing.

"Wow. You did all of this?" she asked.

"Yes ma'am. I didn't want yah'll to have to wait any longer than necessary. 'Cuz I know we need to get home to Tehachapi, so I don't cost you any additional downtime."

"I think it will be best if we have them put their stuff in this trailer in case John gets that trailer sold real quick," Gary informed his wife. "'Cuz I think that will sell fast out there. I might even know someone who might be interested."

We transferred boxes and sewing machines into the small trailer.

"You taking any tack with you?" Claudia asked.

I frowned.

"Don't tell me he took that too?" she quipped.

"Yeah. He took both of the good saddles and left me with … well … an old one."

"Of course," she scoffed.

"I already have my bits, reins, spurs, and headstall in the trailer, in a box. You never know, maybe I can get one or two horses in training while I'm out there," my uncertainty was accented with a half-smile and raised eyebrows, "It would sure help pay the bills."

With all of the things settled in the trailer, I went to the barn and laid out

CHAPTER 22

halters and lead lines for five horses. Cee Cee was at her stall door hanging her head out over the bottom of the Dutch door. She watched every move I made.

"Whatcha doing sweet girl," I said as I walked over to her stall.

She lowered her head smelling my outstretched hand. She softly closed her eyes and breathed in deeply. I stepped closer and wrapped my arms around her neck as I leaned my forehead against her cool hair. I stroked her neck.

"We've come so far. You used to be so scared to even be in the barn. Remember?"

Cee Cee brought her chin in tight to my back embracing me.

"I wish I could take you with me girl, but…" I didn't try to hold back the tears. "I'm gonna miss you girl," I said between ragged breaths as I buried my nose in her mane and neck.

I inhaled her smell hoping to never forget it before I quickly pulled myself away from my mare. Minutes later I was back at the house checking on dinner.

"Is there anything I can do to help you?" Claudia asked.

"Nope. I'm almost done here," I said as I put the sautéed onions, mushrooms, celery, and oysters in the pot of cornbread dressing. "It shouldn't be long."

"Do you want us to go out and feed the horses Momma?" Emma asked.

"Sure Lovie. That would be great."

"She feeds the horses for you?" Gary asked.

"Oh yeah." I smiled widely. "She's been doing it for years. One time, I had a migraine and had fallen asleep on the couch here, and I woke to a note on the table 'Don't worry about feeding mom, I'm doing it.' I got up and peered out the back bedroom window and there she was throwin' feed to the horses in the barn."

I couldn't help but grin wide, even now.

"And when she came back in, she put her hands on her hips after I thanked her and said, 'Well, what's an 8-year-old supposed to do.' She was glowin' with so much pride I didn't even go out to check to see if the horses had been fed enough. I figured we feed them well enough daily that even if she fed them light, they'd survive."

I smiled and made eye contact with Gary.

"I did go out and check to make sure she got the stallions' doors fully latched, but not until after she went to bed."

He nodded his appreciation.

"And what about the other horses? You gonna bring them up and feed them?" he inquired.

"Oh. No. Not tonight," I said stirring the mixture. "They will be up in the morning at sunrise, and I will catch them then," I assured him. "Claudia said she'd go in with me in the morning to return the cell phone to the Family Crisis Center and then we will be able to leave. Plus, that way they can settle in and eat in the trailer as we go."

"All done," Emma announced as she entered the house.

"Okay Lovie." She came into the kitchen and wrapped her arms around my waist, squeezing lightly. "Thank you dear."

I leaned down and kissed her on the top of the head.

"Go wash up and tell the others it's dinner time, please."

Minutes later everyone was sitting around the table.

"I wanted to thank you." I looked over at the kids and corrected myself. "No, *we* wanted to thank you," the kids and I smiled, "for coming out here and helping us move."

A solemness could be felt in the air for a moment.

"And we wanted to have a Thanksgiving meal too. So, let's eat up and get a good night's sleep as we've still got a bit of work to do before we can leave tomorrow," I said before saying grace.

Gary carved the turkey, and I served the dressing, green beans, and yams as small talk eased any tensions.

Chapter 23

The next morning, the last morning really, the horses came in from the pasture at sunrise, right on schedule. It startled my friends.

Guess they forgot that I told them the herd would come up at sunrise! I grinned ever so slightly as I patted Coojoe on the head.

With my boots on, I headed out the door to greet the herd. I opened the storm door slowly, gaining just enough room for me to squeeze out without hitting Molly with the door. Coojoe shadowed me.

"Good morning girl. Let's get you in the arena and get you a treat," I said as I stroked her face. Placing my hand under her jaw I pulled lightly, and she fell in step with me. "Come on you guys."

I glanced over my shoulder at the others at the water trough as I walked to the panel I had left open to the arena.

Once in the arena I slipped into the barn aisle and grabbed a couple of flakes of hay. Walking out far enough for those at the water tank to see me, I called to them again. It didn't take much convincing for them to join Molly and me in the arena. I made five piles of alfalfa before locking them in. After going to the stalls and feeding the horses that were staying behind, I haltered the ones going to California today. I left the lead lines on the ground, just outside the arena. I walked toward the house, but I couldn't do it. I had to stop and pet the mares I was leaving behind one last time.

Sometimes I wish he hadn't come back. Wish he didn't make me say goodbye to you girls a second time.

I swallowed the lump in my throat as I stopped at the first stall.

"You're a good mare. I'm gonna miss you It's The One. Thanks..." I said caressing her face. "It's been my pleasure. You had a sweet mum and I miss your dad, but ..." I sighed deeply. "I'm glad I got my first cow-horse win on you girl."

"Love you pretty lady."

I patted the pinto on the neck and walked to the next stall.

Only two more to go. Damn I hate this part.

"Hey there Rosie."

The bay filly turned away from her food, greeting me at the door. She looked at me with her doe-like brown eyes. Such comforting kind eyes. Her velvet soft muzzle made contact with my neck, just above my collarbone. I brought my hands up and stroked her cheeks. Before stretching my arms up to her neck, behind her ears. I embraced the mare in silence. After all, what is there to say to a mare that followed in her mother's hoofprints and let any and all kids up on her, even before she was 'broke to ride'? She complimented her breeding always exhibiting the best parts of her sire too, Gunny – my personal mount.

"Bye Rosie," I whispered and then kissed her on the muzzle.

I swear they know something is up.

I didn't stop at Cee Cee's stall. I just let her eat her hay.

I blinked the increased moisture in my eyes away as I walked back to the house. I stared at all of the boxes carefully stacked in the trailer, bit my lower lip, nodded, and released a sigh. Coojoe's muzzle bumped my thigh. Without looking, I reached down and pet my protector.

I'm sorry Coojoe, I can't even take you .... My jaw clenched. *Shit! I feel like such a traitor. You're not going to understand why I left you behind. I bet you go up to the bus stop, looking for the kids too. Damn! So much effort into my life, this ranch, my dog, my friends. I loved learning to work with you. I loved how we learned together.* I smiled remembering the everyday training on-leash we did. *It sure paid off. And now, now that we are a matched pair, we walk together in stride no leash needed anymore ... I have to leave you here. Here!* I crouched down beside my dog wrapping my arms around him. *I am asking so much of*

CHAPTER 23

Claudia and Gary, putting the kids and me up on their ranch. They have a dog. Mom and Dad, well, they have their dogs. And ... I sniffled and buried my nose into his black coat as my chest tightened.... *and, that bastard better take care of you. Maybe, maybe I will get custody of you in the divorce. I sure hope so.* I hugged him tightly.

"Come on, let's get some coffee," I said as if he drank it too.

I began cleaning up the dishes. I scraped bits and pieces of last night's dinner in Coojoe's dog dish. He watched attentively.

"He looks like he's ready for his big meal too," Gary said.

"Good morning, yes," I responded. "Yes, he knows he deserves a helping of leftovers."

I grinned as I looked down at my patient dog.

"Are you up to coffee this mornin'?" Gary nodded. "Okay, let me grab the cream for you."

I handed Gary the cup of joe, and the carton of cream, as he settled at the dining room table.

"So where would you like me to put the bales of hay?" I asked. "I would like to take a few bales, for the trip over."

"Yeah, Claudia and I are thinking we might need to stop at a hotel tonight. So that would be a good idea."

"Right."

"Not sure how far we will get."

"We usually make it on over to Gallop, or thereabouts, and depending on when I can get us a civil standby... we can make an earlier getaway."

"Don't worry about it. We'll leave today. Claudia never has the store open this weekend and she's closed on Mondays. We'll get back with plenty of time to rest," encouragement filled his voice. "How about the kids and I load up some bales of hay while you and Claudia take that phone back and then... all we will have to do is load up the horses and go."

"If I ever had a big brother ... I'd'a loved him to be just like you Gary."

As my smile grew, I lifted my coffee cup up to him and took a sip of my dark liquid. Moments later Claudia joined us. And the kids came out of their room next.

"Ethan you will be bunkin' with my son, Thomas, in his room," Claudia said trying to change the melancholy mood into a cheerful one."

I tilted my head toward Miss Emma as she hugged my neck.

"Where will we sleep," a timidness filled her voice.

Claudia opened her arms wide.

"Well, you and Bella," who walked over to Claudia's open arms, "... I have a bed ready for you upstairs too, on the pull-out bed. And your Momma can stay in the room she stayed in this summer when she was at our house. Do you remember her telling you about it?"

The girls nodded. Even though they didn't know the details behind me staying with Claudia and Gary, hiding really. It was the only way I could get away from Mike's daily calls, after he sent me to my parents 'because I was ... what did he call it... falling apart.' When in reality it was my mind and body's response to the forced sleep deprivation their dad orchestrated that culminated in me hiding in the kids' room in a ball of tears on July fourth.

"I think you will like it," Claudia continued. "We have barn cats who love to be brushed and we have a dog, too."

"Is that why we can't take Coojoe?" Emma asked with a pouty bottom lip.

"Yes, Lovie. Plus, we don't know how long we'll be at Miss Claudia's and Mister Gary's," I tried to explain. "Here..." I got up, "why don't you guys eat," I said, pulling the bowls, cereal, and milk out. "Here's some spoons too."

The kids ate with little conversation. Sadness hung in the air like a deafening silence.

I need to make this move a much more positive thing. It's time to pump this up.

"Okay you guys, did you find anything else Momma forgot to grab out of your rooms? Remember I'm not sure when we will be back to the ranch and all, so we..."

"No Momma we've got it all. All of the good stuff," Emma piped in.

"Good Lovie. I am glad to hear that. And in just a couple of days you will get to see grandma and grandpa too."

"Why aren't they here now?" Emma asked.

"They are at a horse show," I said looking down at my lap.

CHAPTER 23

"They ... they didn't," Claudia, I could feel her eyes upon me. My jaw muscles drew bow tight. "They didn't understand this was the best weekend and they had plans. But ..." a new cheer entered her voice, "you will be able to see them next week. I'm sure!"

That seemed to satisfy the kids, as smiles graced their lips, and they continued eating.

Chapter 24

"Hi. This is Kathleen Walton, out on Highway 67. I'm looking to have a civil standby this morning," I said to the deputy on the non-emergency line.

"And what do you need this for?"

"Well, I just think it will be best." *Will she say no?* "We've had some trouble out here. Plus, it's been recommended by the ladies at the domestic violence office that I have an officer here, to keep the peace, between my ..." I swallowed the lump that had built in my throat, "... soon-to-be ex-husband and me. I have a restraining order and it would just be best to make sure we can leave the ranch without incident."

I hung up the phone as I turned to face Claudia and Gary.

"Okay, so they can't get a deputy out for another hour or so. We'll go drop off this phone at the office and then, by the time we get back, all we'll have to do is load the horses and head out." I tried to keep the cheer in my voice. "Hey kids, will you help Gary move some bales of hay over to the truck and trailer so we can feed the horses while we're on the road?"

They nodded.

"And Ethan... if you wouldn't mind, would you grab up a few of the water buckets too?"

After dropping the emergency phone at the Family Crisis Center, we headed back to the ranch. I pointed out places I'd come to find interesting and where I'd found joy here.

"So, as I said, the Royal Gorge is off to the west and this is our Cañon

CHAPTER 24

City," I reported. "This beautiful set of buildings make up the Abbey. The kids and I have been going to church here."

"All of the way over here?" Claudia asked. "Is this the closest Catholic church?"

"No. There's one in Florence. But a few years ago, the Bishop of Pueblo, as we were told, instructed his priests to give a sermon in which they told us all 'If you are a single parent you need to give your kids up to a two-parent household. Because they could raise them better.'" I shook my head. "It was shortly after Mike had a heart incident and surgery ... and I felt that the parish was telling me that if my husband *had* died, I would not be worthy to raise my own children." I frowned. "So, the kids and I get up fifteen minutes early and we drive a bit farther to attend the Abbey services. The nuns love the kids," I added.

"I bet they do. They must find it a treat to have respectful children come to church."

"Yeah," I said as I turned down the side road. "I like it that a bunch of the old, retirement-aged priests seem to be being taken care of there too."

"What's over there?" Claudia pointed to the buildings at the base of the hill.

"Oh. I believe that's the women's prison," I answered nonchalantly. "We have like fifteen levels of prisons around here in the county, including the federal one."

After stopping we turned East.

"Here's the lumber yard we got the slab wood and rough-cut planks from to build the barn."

We drove in silence as we passed hay fields, scattered with bales. I could almost smell the sweet aroma of the once fresh-cut alfalfa. The Aspen trees, that flanked the fields and butted up to the rambling Arkansas River, had already started dropping their leaves. The light breeze made the few yellow, orange, and red foliage, not ready to take flight, dance. They made me smile. The road quickly became the main street of the town we'd called home, all three blocks of it. Dragonflies felt like they were taking flight in my stomach as I glanced left and right. Watching for him. The last thing I needed was for him to find out we are leaving today.

Oh my god! Is that him?

My eyes locked on the figure with the black cowboy hat. My heart pounded, my breath caught in my throat, my muscles tensed. I gripped the steering wheel so tight that the skin over my knuckles lost all color. He stepped away from his truck, and up onto the curb.

Shit it's him!

I looked away, staring down the narrow two-lane street with cars parked at an angle to the curb on either side.

"Oh, please don't look over here, please!" I whispered under my breath as my stomach knotted and became queasy.

My tense body readied for a fight, but I was unable to move. All I could do was watch him.

"Don't speed up. He'll notice. Let him just walk into that bowling alley. Act like you're not even here," I coached myself in a near whisper.

As he reached for the door handle, he paused.

Don't look back. I quietly urged him.

"Lord, don't let him see the reflection of the jeep in the glass door, keep looking forward. Just walk in! If he stays here at the bowling alley, we might not have any trouble with him," I said aloud as we drove by.

"Oh, was that him?"

"Yeah."

I took a deep breath and held on to it for a couple of heartbeats.

I kept driving down Main Street until I could turn right on Hwy 67. Once across the railroad tracks I pushed the speed limit for my last trek to my driveway.

"I hope the deputy gets out here soon. It would be great if we could get all loaded up before Mike gets done having breakfast, or whatever he is doing at the bowling alley."

Chapter 25

With the green panel gates near the highway still open, through their welcoming open arms. I accelerated down the straightaway. Kicked up a light cloud of dust as I did. Only slowed the vehicle a little where the driveway changed directions. Slid the Jeep to a stop. Parked past the water trough up by the house.

"Oh look, the hay's all loaded. And I see Ethan's gotten the water buckets too," Claudia announced with cheer.

A hesitant smile graced my face.

Great. That'll help. This'll save us time. When's that cop gonna get here?

Leaving the keys in the ignition, I exited the vehicle like a bullet, forcefully shutting the door behind me.

"It won't be long," Claudia said, as I came around to the passenger side of the truck. She patted me on the arm. "We'll be able to get you guys off this ranch and to safety."

"But we need to get going," a curt tone laced my timid bark.

The kids and Gary started walking over from the barn.

"Thanks you guys!" I said as I wrapped my arms around my beauties.

Within minutes we were joined by a white cruiser.

Well, here we go. It's now or never and never is not the answer for me.

"Hello," Officer Patel said as she shut the driver's door. "One of you requested a civil standby?" she asked as she surveyed the three adults and three kids.

"Yes. That'd be me. I'm Kathleen," I said with an outstretched hand.

"Thanks for coming. We're all ready to load these horses and then we'll be leavin'," I explained.

"And where is he?" she said with raised eyebrows.

My skin tingled as my muscles tightened, I was ready to bolt. But instead, I took a deep breath, and I stepped closer to her. I kept my voice low to avoid the kids overhearing and asking questions. Coojoe flanked me to my right.

"We just came through town and saw him and his truck over at the bowling alley."

I bit my lower lip.

"Okay. That's what I thought I saw too."

We shared a smile.

They seem to be still watchin' him and the other cops must have filled Patel in on what's been going on here.

"You takin' all of the horses and the dog?" she inquired.

"No ma'am. We're just takin' the ones in the arena. Two belong to my folks, two belong to my friends here, and one ... one is the kids' mare." We both smiled at the last mention. "I'll leave a note for the renters ...if they don't show up before we leave."

I cocked my head toward the single-wide mobile.

"They can contact Mike and tell 'im he has to come out and feed his own horses, the ones he originally took with him when he abandoned us, and the dog."

I frowned as I reached down and pet the dog on the head. The officer's eyes followed my movement.

"There's only so much I can take with me ... to a safe house," sorrow lay heavy on my words. I grimaced as I focused on my dog. "He'd better take care of this old boy too," an undeniable aggression tainted my words.

Moments passed and Officer Patel let me gather myself before I donned a brave face for my children and friends. Steeling myself with the thought of not having to look over my shoulder all of the time, I stood tall, looked the officer in the eyes, gently smiled, and turned to get the horses.

"It shouldn't take me long to load these seasoned horses," I said, making

CHAPTER 25

small talk as we walked toward the back of the trailer.

"That's good. 'Cuz all I'm gonna do is stand here and watch," she said with a light smirk as we stopped at the back of the open trailer.

"We're all loaded to go, except for the horses. We didn't want to waste your time, nor take too long should *he* have gotten wind of us leaving ... like from the renters," I added.

"Do you think they went into town to tell him of your plans?" the officer asked as she repositioned herself so she could see around the end of the double-wide and down the long driveway.

I scanned over my shoulder and back down the driveway too.

Shit! Shit! Shit! Did Patel see something? Is he coming down the drive?

I searched the horizon and the top of the driveway. My eyes darted back and forth from the crest of the drive and the spot closest to the gate.

I can't see anything.

I willed my ears to hear. Nothing.

Wait. What's that? It's a truck. Shit!

My eyes widened. My pulse quickened. I winced at the thought.

I can't wait to see if that truck is comin' this way.

"Let's get these horses loaded! I need Walkin' Tall first as he's the heaviest, then Mister, Cueball, Molly, and lastly Paint-In-Time."

"The kids wanted to help, while you were gone, so we ... they all have halters and lead lines on," Gary informed me as we opened the arena panel. "Plus, I knew it would get us out of here faster."

"The quicker we get out of here and on the road, the better," I added. "Guess they want to leave too, huh."

Lord, it sure must be time to get us out of here. Now let's just do it without Mike showing up, please.

"Yeah. This is a good thing, all around. Let's get movin'."

I took hold of the lead lines draped over Tall's and Mister's backs.

"Come on boys."

They fell in step with me as the slightest tension reached where the halter lay behind their ears. I paused momentarily as I watched back out the driveway. I let Emma, waiting near the trailer, take the lead for Mister as I walked Tall into the trailer.

"Easy son," I said, not because he was becoming antsy, but rather out of force of habit as I worked to move and get this part of our getaway completed.

Even as I latched the divider to the back wall, the horse did not make any unnecessary movements.

"Okay. Let me have Mister," I said to Emma as I walked to the back of the trailer. "Toss me the lead Lovie, it's okay."

I nervously glanced back out the drive, but not wanting to waste time I caught the end of the lead. The bay horse stepped up into the trailer without additional encouragement.

"Thank you, boy."

"Here's Cueball," I heard my son say.

"It's a good thing you guys thought to put the leads on them while we were in town. You know how mischievous Cueball can be and how much he likes to play!" Ethan and I shared a knowing smile.

"Do you think he'll be a problem to load?" Claudia asked, knowing it would delay us.

"No. Not with his buddies already in the trailer."

I stepped to the colt's shoulder and with a light pull on the lead line the pinto gelding stepped with me. Before I could get him secured in his stall the mares were being staged, at the ready, behind the trailer.

Teamwork. Both the horses and the kids. Thank you, God! I'm almost done. Just a couple more and I will have these kids out and on our way to safety.

My heart rate increased with anticipation.

Within a few steps, I was back at the trailer's opening. I glanced at Patel. The officer stood, arms crossed focused beyond me, on the driveway. I reached up and tucked the end of the halter more securely into the buckle before asking the mare to enter. I stroked her neck, and she brought her muzzle in toward my side.

"It's all good girl," I spoke softly trying to not telegraph my unease. "I know it's been a couple of years, but it's just like last time. It's just another trailer ride sweet thing," I said assuring her as I gathered her lead in my

CHAPTER 25

hands.

I just don't have the luxury of letting you get used to the idea of getting in the trailer. Please load up quick and easy. Please Molly!

I heard the soft hum of another engine. I swallowed but the muscles of my throat tightened and struggled to comply with my forced request.

Focus Kathleen. The cop will take care of that.

I turned and took a step away from the mare. She followed me up into the trailer before any tension came onto the halter.

"That's my girl," I crooned.

Within a few steps, Molly's chin was close enough to the ring that I was able to run the lead up through it and tie a quick-release knot. While I wanted to slam the divider in place, I did not want or need to scare the horses.

Slow down next to this mare. Don't scare her.

I forced myself to gradually make my moves. My hand lingered on her hair – down her neck, to her withers, and along her back. It calmed the growing panic building within me.

"Okay, girl," I spoke softly as I swung the divider into place.

Molly blew a relaxing breath out her nostrils and seemed to settle in with ease.

"That's my girl."

I extended my strides and quickened my steps as I went to take the pinto filly's lead. The officer stood with arms still crossed and a smile now graced her face.

"This is going pretty easy," she said not hiding her surprise.

"Yep."

I took hold of the end of the filly's lead.

"This is the last one."

I smiled at the filly, hoping she would load just as easily as the others.

Did I just see a green SUV? Is the neighbor coming up the drive?

My palms and pits dampening, I swallowed hard.

"Up top girl."

I lightly wiggled the lead and the filly stepped one hoof then the next in the trailer. She mimicked her mates and positioned herself in the last stall. "Wow, you made that look easy. You didn't even take ten minutes." Officer Patel's smile was tainted with a hint of disbelief. "I thought I'd be here for an hour or more!"

"*They* make it easy. And they make me look good sometimes." I allowed a light nervous chuckle to escape my throat. "I'm grateful it went without a hitch."

Moments later, after securing the last divider, I stepped out of the trailer. Gary and I closed and latched the back doors. As I came around the trailer, I didn't see the renter's SUV.

Was I hearing things? Was I seeing things? Is he hiding on the other side of the single-wide?

"Okay kids. I'm gonna make sure you haven't left anything behind and we're gonna be heading out shortly," I encouraged.

"I want to thank you for comin' on over today," I said to Patel. "It would've been all bad if he'd gotten wind of this...."

Acid bubbled in my stomach.

"And I *think* he *could have* talked with the renters. She's usually here all mornin' and their car *was* here when I went off the ranch earlier and ... now ... it's not ... and I'm not sure if they've told him that my friends are here with trailers," my voice cracked, as did my confidence, as a surge of urgency continued to build within me.

"I'm glad it went quietly," Patel said as we walked back to her cruiser. "I'm gonna wait and drive out with yah'll."

"Okay, we're just gonna be a minute or two."

Chapter 26

I went in the double-wide for one last look around. As I walked down the hall, I heard the door hinges complain. My jaw tightened, but I didn't bother to look back.

I know we needed to get going.

Once at the end of the hall, I glanced around… the donated mattress, no box spring, lay on the floor, the sheets the only remnants of life here. With a quick turn I made sure nothing I wanted or needed was in the master bathroom.

And the soaker tub that never got used. I sighed.

Seeing nothing else left out that I needed to take with me, I started back up the hall pausing at the kids' bathroom. I laid my hand on the door and pushed it open just enough to see there were no boxes left behind in there either.

Next was the kids' room. Nothing. I stopped in the kitchen. I gazed back at the dining room table we had eaten so many meals at.

How long will it be before we eat at this table again? Will we ever eat at this table again? I liked having the table right off the kitchen. We were just getting used to the new-to-us double-wide. Will the table even be here when we get back?

Too many questions for me to tackle today. I looked away.

"Are you sure you don't want help cleaning up these dishes before we leave?" Claudia asked.

"Um…" sadness tainted my voice as the gloominess in the air filled my lungs.

I absentmindedly moved a pan from the stove to the sink. Moving forward, I reached for the handle on the refrigerator. Little effort caused it to open. I stared at the leftovers.

"It wouldn't take long."

As I heard my friend's voice my mood changed.

"No." I said flatly.

I turned around, shut the door behind me. The dirty pots and pans on the stove top came into view. Anger flared within me.

"I don't care if I leave this place a mess."

Blood pumped faster through me, tainted with soured adrenaline.

"He made our lives a mess. Moved us all the time. Shit, in these twelve years we've never lived anywhere for more than we did here. He usually uprooted us only after twelve months or so. Always making me drive substandard vehicles, so I'd get stranded. Always movin' us farther and farther away from family, friends, and towns. Leavin' it up to me to deal with the companies when we couldn't pay our bills," I was rambling.

"He walked away not caring one bit about the mess he left me with. To be cleaned up or dealt with in whatever way I could. He designed it so I would be stuck here. Here… where he figured he had total control of me. And him out there doing… God knows what, with God knows who. He just left it all behind, so he can clean up this effing mess, this mess, for a change!"

The image of leftover unattended food with fuzzy mold filled my mind. *It'll be a mess worth cleaning up when I get back here, if he leaves it like it is. Just leave it here. Make him wonder where and what we're doing. Just walk away. Like you'll be back… later … tonight. But not!*

I walked over to the cabinet, grabbed a piece of paper and pen, jotted down my folks' phone number and *in case of emergency call here.*

"Tah hell with him. If he doesn't come back right away, then," a half-hearted smile graced my face, "It'll be an even bigger mess." I cocked my head with daring bravado long absent from my personal confidence.

Claudia smirked as I walked through the living room toward her. When our eyes met, I shrugged my shoulders and smiled even wider.

CHAPTER 26

"I'm just gonna go put this note in the door of the single-wide and then we can go."

It was then that I heard a vehicle coming up the driveway, getting closer and closer to the house. I stopped. Claudia and I, both wide eyed, locked eyes with each other.

Shit that could be him. Shit. Shit. Shit.

I snatched up my purse before heading out the door with Claudia in tow. Once down the stairs I saw the renter walking toward me. My quickened breaths slowed a little.

"What's going on?" Loral asked looking at the police car.

"The kids and I are heading out."

She shook her head.

"I don't get it. He's not a threat to you."

I rolled my eyes as my heartbeats increased.

"I know that's what you think. But I've known him longer than you. A lot longer." *Like 12 years longer.* "I know he makes good on his promises, they aren't just idle threats." *And oh, how he's made promises. Promises you haven't heard. Promises I was the only one meant to hear!*

I shook my head recognizing naive futility when I heard it. I thrust my note toward her.

"Here's the phone number to my parents place."

"Is that where you're taking the kids?"

"I..."

My eyes widened and the muscles in my jaw clenched tight.

Why is she asking. She didn't ask before. Is she gonna tell Mike? Oh Hell no! No, don't tell her. Remember, the ladies at the Family Crisis Center said, 'Don't let anyone, here, know where you are going.'

"No. It's just where you can get a message through to me. Plus," I let a false sweetness come into my voice, "I don't want to put you in any danger, by knowing where the kids and I are. 'Cuz he'll push you until you tell him where we are and what you know ... and that wouldn't be positive for you. Just know, if you need me, you can call my folks and they'll let me know I need to call you."

I looked at the officer standing at the ready, beside her car. With a nod and then peered back at Claudia. I jerked my head toward the trucks.

Enough is enough. I need to get out of here!

"The older kids wanted to ride with Gary. Is that okay?" Claudia asked as we fell in step together. "It would help keep us all less cramped in the trucks."

"Sure…" I said with a smidgen of trepidation as I stretched a welcoming hand out toward my 5-year-old. "Come on Lovie, we're gonna ride with Claudia."

As I helped Bella up into the truck, I looked back at the older two. An uneasiness filled their wide eyes. I braved a smile holding their gazes for a couple of moments. I forced a bigger smile and mouthed, "I love you" before getting in the truck.

"We're gonna follow Gary and the horses out, okay?" Claudia announced as she fumbled for her keys, dropping them.

She struggled, stretching her wiggling fingers toward the keyring that lay on the floorboards just out of reach.

"Sure. Do you want me to get those?" I said in a rush as Gary had already started down the driveway.

"Nope," she grunted as she stretched her hand even further toward the keys. "Got…'em." A sigh of relief escaped us both.

"Gary and I already chatted about the route, and how it won't take us back into town where Mike is. We'll actually be headin' east out Highway 67 'til it crosses Highway 50. We've planned the route to get down and across the 40 most of the way," I shared as we headed out the dirt drive, the white cruiser pulling up the rear.

Bella wrapped her arms around my waist, and snuggled in tight to me as I buckled the seatbelt around us both. I stroked her sandy-blonde hair.

"It's gonna be okay Lovie."

Her grip tightened.

"I promise Lovie," I softly said with determination.

Chapter 27

The gooseneck trailer, which was in front of the truck I was in, was maneuvered through the gates and onto the street. Out to my right lay the pasture, the ranch I called home, until today. I sighed in defeat.

A smile interrupted my melancholy as I saw that Juniper bush. There it stood, like a protective sentry. The snowstorm that ended up being called 'The Blizzard of October '97' filled my mind. All of that snow and our truck – out of gas.

"Trisha said she'd meet me at the gate in about an hour and she didn't mind picking up a pack of diapers for Bella. So, I guess I'll ride up there and meet her." I remember saying as I pulled my husband's heavy insulated coveralls up over my three other layers of clothing.

"Take the "old man" up there. He'll take care that you make it up and back," Mike instructed as I headed out the door to the barn.

I grabbed Spangle's bridle, my saddle, and a pad before heading to the last stall in the row.

"Hey there, Spangled," I said just before swinging the saddle up on to the lower half of the Dutch door.

He peered over at me. I unlatched the door and entered the stall.

"Sorry son, we need to go to work." I saddled him. "Sorry it's ice cold," I said as he lipped the frigid steel of the bit, before taking it into his mouth. "Good boy."

I slid the bridle up over his ears.

Spangled stood patiently as I hefted my cocooned body up into the saddle. I moved him closer to the stall door. Cued him to sidestep enabling me to open the door without getting off of him. We headed out into the storm.

With the snow hitting us from behind for the first half mile, while cold, wasn't as bad as I thought it was going to be. But as we made the first turn on the driveway the wet flakes were hitting us head on.

"Oh son, this's gonna be *fun*," sarcasm dripped off my words as I reached forward patting him on the neck with my well-gloved hand.

I evaluated the long section of the driveway we were heading up as he walked.

"You think we should stay on the driveway or cut across to the gate?" I said as we neared the top of the knoll.

As I finished my query, which was said as much for me as for him, I must have transferred some of my weight in the saddle because Spangled moved his head slightly off to the right. He carefully chose a path diagonal to the driveway, cutting the distance and hopefully the time we'd need to be out in this weather. When we got near the gate the wind had changed directions. It was blowing continuous, beautiful – almost blinding – cold, white lacey particles that had a brutal softness as they reached the limited exposed skin on my face.

"Son let's huddle behind that bush. It looks big enough to help block the onslaught of snow… at least a little bit. Plus, this way, we will be able to see Trisha when she pulls in the drive. Don't want her gettin' stuck out here in any mud or…" I examined the accumulation, "or the snow."

I lifted the reins, laid them along the left side of his neck and brought my leg in so my calf made contact with his ribcage. Once situated, I pulled the knit cap down over my ears.

Minutes passed – ten, then twenty. When my mind wasn't flitting from reviewing my class assignments and children waiting for me, and hopefully a hot cup of coffee in front of the fireplace, I hummed Amazing Grace to pass the time.

"She shouldn't be too much longer."

CHAPTER 27

I pulled the collar up on the canvas coveralls, to better cover my neck, and we waited. The generous bush protected the horse, but I wasn't so lucky. I started to shiver.

"Five more minutes son. We really do need those diapers. Bella is down to three or four, possibly less by the time we get back to the house. If Trisha doesn't show up soon, we're gonna head back. And get better prepared to head into town, just you and me.... And this bloody storm."

The 18-year-old horse stood at ease with slacked reins and his head down, letting the Juniper do its protective best as the wind changed direction and swirled the one-of-a-kind bits of frozen rain around us. As the wind frequently altered directions we were being hit from all sides.

Not wanting to miss getting the diapers I let the wait stretch, but not much longer as the wind-chill was getting to me and Spangled.

I lifted my gaze from Spangled's ears to the open gate. The fence line came into view. Hints of the highway, that I knew were there ... before, now gone. The dirt, the thirty feet I knew lay before me was now indistinguishable. Visibility was down to about ten feet. I reached down and picked up the strips of leather.

"Come on Spangled, maybe she couldn't make it out here from town."

My teeth chattered as we turned to go back. I adjusted the silk scarf that was covering most of my face.

Last thing I need is another bout of bronchitis.

While I would have loved to get back to the barn in ten minutes, letting the family's steed choose his steps wisely was more important. After all, if he slipped on snow or ice, he, or both of us, could get hurt and I'm not up for that. Fifteen frigid minutes later, as Spangled began making his way up the incline in front of the house, I saw Trisha's brown car parked in front of it.

What the...? How long's she been here? Why didn't we see her? I shook my head in disbelief as frustrations flared inside of me. *Why didn't she wait up there for me? We agreed to meet up at the gate. What if I'd walked, instead of gotten a horse?*

Once back in the stall I uncinched and pulled the saddle off of the horse.

I pulled the glove off one hand so I could get a couple of fingers under the leather that lay behind his ears. He opened his mouth, released the bit. I wrapped my arms around him.

"Thank you Star Spangled for being someone I can trust to do what I need you to do."

The click, click, click of the ball turning in the hitch brought me back to today. Claudia pulled the truck and smaller trailer out onto the highway. My heart beats slowed. My fingers shook as I continued to stroke the strands on Bella's head.

We're leaving so much behind, including the bones of ….. Goodbye Star Spangled. Goodbye so much. I promise … I won't forget.

Chapter 28

We pulled out onto the highway, and I saw the reflection of the deputy's car in the side mirror.

Our protective sentinel. An uneasiness stirred within me. *I'm glad she came out today. I'm glad Mike didn't!*

I breathed a sigh of relief. It was momentary.

We passed the road, Mike's favorite perch, where he could spy on the kids and me. I hunched my shoulders and tucked my head. Looking out of the corner of my eye, I snuck a glance.

No brown truck! Phew. I lifted my head and released the air my lungs held. *Oh Lord, please don't let him leave that bowling alley... please! Please let us get out of town without him knowing. Does he know?* My heartbeats nearly doubled. *Oh God. Please don't let him try to stop us. Please!* I looked down at my youngest who was still cuddled-in tight.

"It really doesn't look like it holds prisoners," Claudia remarked, breaking the silence.

"I know," I said as I looked at the buildings that made up Level-One, then "The Camp" of the prison I had taught at. "Some people even thought these were new office buildings," a light huff escaped my throat.

"Guess they forgot to read the signs!"

"Right! Or noticed the razor-sharp concertina wire along the tall double fences."

We shared a lighthearted chuckle as we got closer to the large brick planters that flanked the driveway. The well-placed letters distinctly announced the campus' purpose – Federal Correctional Complex.

Next, Claudia slowed the truck as our freedom train reached the railroad tracks. Out of force of habit, I looked both ways. The song: *I'm Movin' On* by Rascal Flats came out of the speakers and the lyrics rang true, oh so true.

Only one more block. Focus. Try not to think of… the friends I'm leaving behind…. The kids can't even say goodbye to their friends. Damn it!

My cheeks heated up. My jaw clenched tight. I shook my head, chased the thoughts away.

"We're gonna turn right up here and head out of town," I shared with Claudia.

Minutes later, as we neared Highway 50, a brick farmhouse, the large out-buildings, and hay barn came into view. The pages of my memory fluttered as if tickled by the wind. The flooding of remembrances came again.

My mind looped on the memories of me being stuck in that car. The vehicle that Mike just **had** to purchase.

"If John and Carol can drive around in a Mercedes with windshield wipers on the headlights then you *will* drive in a Mercedes too," I could almost hear Mike saying.

I shook the multitude of unpleasant memories that rushed in, and Mike's insistence in having *his* wife drive *that* car.

After all, he didn't care if the Mercedes ran well. He just wanted to be able to brag to his family members that he too had one for his wife to drive. Drive around in for no one in his family to see ….

I pushed away those thoughts. Thoughts that surged frustration back through me.

I smiled at the positive memories.

Damn. Sure have enjoyed livin' here.

Moments later Claudia was following Gary and his rig onto Hwy 50 West. The officer drove past us and got on the highway heading East.

Thank you, Lord. Thank you for allowing us protection. Please let Officer Patel know I really do appreciate her. And Officer Brad and Christensen too. You've

CHAPTER 28

sent my beauties and me great soldiers. Thank you. Amen.

The next thirty-seven miles could not have gone by fast enough.

As we got close to Interstate 25, Claudia asked more questions, taking me out of my gloom.

"And what's that up there?"

"Oh, that's the University of Colorado. That's where I've been goin' to school."

Bella lifted her head to see the concrete buildings that sat up on the hill.

"All the way out here?" Claudia added.

"Yeppers, five days a week for the last few years. By the way, we'll be gettin' on the freeway, here, just past this signal."

Putting forty miles between Mike and me did little to ease my worries. I searched the passenger side mirror, again, to see if his brown truck was back there. Nothing. I looked in Claudia's side mirror. My eyes darted back to the passenger side mirror, back to the driver's side!

Oh shit! Is that a brown truck behind us? How did that guy pull up on us like that? Sweat beaded on my brow. *Shit. The driver's got a cowboy hat on. Shit. Is that effing Mike?*

Claudia slowed to navigate the onramp. Within seconds, the driver of the brown truck put his turn signal on, changed lanes, and drove past us, continuing under the overpass as we got on the freeway.

My heart skipped.

"Wow! I thought that was Mike in that brown truck for a fat minute!"

Chapter 29

Five hundred thirty miles, seven hours, and a few fuel stops later we pulled into a motel parking lot at Gallop.

I opened the trailer feed door for each of the horses. Emma extended her hand as Tall stretched his neck out to greet her. His muzzle made contact with her palm.

"Good boy," I cooed.

By the time I got all five windows opened Gary and Ethan were back with buckets of fresh water.

"Thank you, son ... Gary.

Holding up a bucket we allowed each horse to drink their fill.

"Momma..."

"Yes Emma."

"We gonna feed 'em?"

"You betcha. Momma's gonna fill the hay bags."

"Can I help?" Emma's soft request warmed this tired mom.

"Sure Lovie." I eyed an empty water bucket.

"We've got this," Gary offered up. "We'll go fill the buckets and offer them more while you feed."

Ethan and I locked eyes and shared a smile.

"Thanks guys."

"That way we can go get a bite to eat sooner," an enthusiastic Claudia said, as she came around the truck. A tingle of rejuvenation could be felt in the

CHAPTER 29

cooling air.

"Okay!" the cheerleader, in me, encouraged. "Let's get these critters fed so we can eat!"

Emma and Bella fell in step with me. We headed to the back of the trailer. "Let's take these up to the truck bed, okay girls!"

I laid a couple of hay nets in the outstretched arms of my girls – upturned lips and wide glee-filled eyes were looking back at me.

I lifted both girls up onto the bed of the truck. Claudia had her pocket knife at the ready and cut the orange strings.

Emma inserted a couple of delicate fingers between the first two flakes of hay, and my beauty pulled them apart. I opened the macrame bag wide enough to accommodate the wedge of alfalfa. We repeated this cooperative unrehearsed dance until we had enough to feed all of the horses. Bella held the cinching strings in her hands to the first bag. Pride emanated from her as the 5-year-old was able to do her part.

"Okay, let's give these out," I said.

Bella stepped forward. I assisted her then the older down. Each helped carry at least one of the flakes back to the horses. Bella did more dragging than carrying but the results were the same.

"Here you go." I lifted the netted sack through the portal. Tall took his first bite before I got the bag secured. He pulled his head back, eyes wide, with hay protruding from his mouth. "It's okay Tall." I stroked his face. "I know you're hungry."

A few pats from me later he relaxed and started chewing. I climbed down off the running board and picked up the next bag of feed, drawstrings offered up by Emma.

"You think they'll be okay out here?" Claudia asked as I served the pinto filly.

"Yeah." I stroked Paint-In-Time's dark brown and white forehead. "I'll check on them again after we eat. If it's chilly I'll close up these doors. They've all spent a night in the trailer before."

"Okay. It's time for us to eat," Claudia cheered.

"Where's Ethan?" Only finding the empty buckets by the trailer tires, my eyes widened. My head felt like it was on a swivel as I visually searched for my son between the cars and the motel. My feet felt like they were in cement, unmovable. "Girls... do you ... do you know where your brother is?"

There was no response.

Did Mike follow us? Oh my God, did I miss something? Why didn't I keep a better eye on my son? Did he grab up the boy? Shit! I don't see a brown truck. How could I have missed him?

I continued doing a visual search of the parking lot as my lungs sought air more rapidly.

"He's most likely with Gary," Claudia offered up.

Most likely my ass!

As dusk fell it challenged my ability to clearly see.

"I'm sure they went over to get us a table."

"How long ago?" I heard my voice crack. Not waiting for her to answer I walked to Claudia. "We can leave those buckets here. I need to see my son! Make sure he's okay," my voice strained as desperation accented my words.

She looked up and saw the panic in my expression. Claudia nodded.

I scanned the parking lot toward the diner.

I need to see him. Confirm he's with Gary. Oh, how I hate this ... is he safe?

As we walked across the parking lot, I scanned the windows of the restaurant. Still not seeing my oldest I reached for my girls' hands.

"Let's go eat!" I forced cheer into my voice.

I need to get my kids all back together. This trusting our safety to others isn't working for me. How am I going to do this? Where is my Ethan?

Once through the doors, I glanced around. I saw Gary and the back of a boy's head.

There's Ethan... it's Ethan isn't it? Doubt bumped into my maternal instincts. *But that's not his jacket. It's my Ethan ... right?*

Walking to the table I tried not to rush. I extended my strides. Dropping my daughters' hands, I reached out.

It's got to be my son!

My palm stroked the hair on his head and my heart relaxed as he looked

CHAPTER 29

up. I leaned down and kissed him on the top of the head. My lips lingered a little as I breathed in the scent of him.

"Hey Lovie. I didn't know you came over here."

I pulled up a chair beside him. Bella chose the chair to my left and Emma beside her. Claudia and Gary sat at the other end of the table.

Dinner was ordered all around. Limited conversation was needed after a long day.

"I got you guys a room with two queen beds," Claudia announced as we waited for the waitress to bring the bill.

"But I don't...." A feeling of dread filled me.

"We didn't ask you to stop with us tonight," Claudia's words came softly.

"We know if you were drivin' you'd drive right through, sleep on the side of the road," Gary's words rang true.

"We all need to rest. So ... I got you and the kids a room too," Claudia added.

"I don't know how I'm ever going to repay you," I said, timidly as I looked up at my friends.

"Come on Lovies," I said. "Momma needs to check on the horses before we go up to our room." We all walked back toward the trailer.

"Momma, you want me to grab our bag?"

"Yes Ethan. Thanks. That would be great!" I beamed with pride as my boy spoke.

My son walked around to the sleeping compartment of the gooseneck, opened the door, and retrieved our duffle bag. I checked on the horses. A couple were still eating.

"They didn't have two rooms together. I hope you don't mind being a couple of rooms apart." Claudia handed me a key ring. The oblong plastic keychain indicated we would be in room 145. "We'll just be a couple of doors down."

My smile was full of appreciation.

Minutes later I put the key in the lock and opened the door to our evening accommodation.

"Okay my Lovies." We walked in. "It's time for some sleep. Is anyone tired?"

"Nope!" Bella chirped.

Chapter 30

"I'm a kind of tired, Momma," Emma plopped on the closest of the two beds.

"Can we watch some TV?" my son asked, holding the remote control.

"Sure Lovie." I yanked my feet out of my shoes, collected up the kids', lined them all up, and paired them together in the small closet. "You guys pull your jeans and fold them up, put them in these drawers, please." I pointed to the dresser under the TV.

Emma wiggled out of her pants and socks. Her eyelids appeared heavy as she folded and tucked the garments in the drawer. Bella was already under the covers on the bed near the bathroom. I removed her socks and pants before tucking her in.

"Just keep the sound down, okay Lovie?"

My son smiled and nodded as he flipped channels.

"Thank you." I tousled his hair. "Will you be okay if I jump in the shower? The girls are asleep."

"Yeah Momma."

"You want a shower first Lovie?"

"Nah."

We shared a smile as I checked the chain and lock on the door.

"I won't be long."

As the shower ran, so did my tears. But not for long.

Suck it up. Go out. Get some sleep. You're not home free yet!

I toweled off, put my shirt and shorts on, and joined my beauties.

Ethan had moved up to lean against the headboard next to Emma.

"Whatcha watchin' Lovie?"

"Texas Ranger," my son said with cheerful confidence.

"Nice choice!"

Before the end of the hour, Ethan had melted down into the bed beside his sister. I tiptoed over, made sure they were both under the covers, and relieved him of the remote. I checked and rechecked the locks on the door. I paused and drank in the tranquil beauty of my two oldest before sitting up beside my youngest and channel surfing until an episode of Law and Order gave me some comfort.

My eyelids grew heavy while the characters of the show kept vigil as we slept.

Chapter 31

"Yah'll get dressed and maybe Ethan will help you brush your hair," I directed toward my youngest. He nodded. "Thanks, Lovie. I'm gonna go feed and water the horses so we can get on the road."

Ten minutes later the kids were petting the horses. Molly was hanging her head out the feed door, finding just as much comfort in contact with her humans as we were with her.

"Let's close up these doors and then we can eat some sinkers on the way out this morning," Gary shared.

"Really?" Emma asked with a smile as I nodded.

I latched the feed doors. We divvied up the doughnuts, cups of caffeine, and cartons of milk!

Come lunch time we were at Needles filling up the trucks and refueling our bodies.

"Next stop, the ranch," Claudia said with much fanfare.

"Hey Ethan, do you want to go to your grandma and grandpa's with me to drop off the two horses?" Gary asked.

Ethan looked at me for permission.

"You can if you'd like. I'm not sure if Gmaw and Gpaw are back from the horse show yet, but…"

A cheer-filled glint occupied my 10-year-old's eyes.

"Hey Emma, why don't you jump in here with us girls and we'll go to my ranch," Claudia encouraged. "That way we can go feed my horses and get the pasture ready for the ones Gary and Ethan bring back with them."

The excitement of the new adventure translated into a bounce in Emma's steps. Within a few hours, Claudia was showing the girls around the barn. She introduced the girls to the horses, cats, and a dog. Next, it was a tour of the house.

"Your brother will sleep in here with my son, Thomas, and you two will sleep out here on this pullout. Your mom will sleep right in this room." The girls inspected the upstairs rooms. "And here's the bathroom you guys get to use."

Downstairs again with my three beauties back with me, I called my folks.

"Hey Momma," I let the answering machine take a message for me. "I know you and Dad will be home late today and you might notice you have an extra bay and pinto on the ranch. Gary and Claudia decided to let the kids have their mare here with them. We'll talk in the morning. Love you. Night."

This was a good move. A calmness washed over me. *We will be safe here.*

Chapter 32

The next morning, I woke to footfalls coming up the stairs. My body tensed.

"I thought you might need this," Claudia said dropping the volume of her voice as she noticed I was not alone in bed. She stood with a cup of coffee in her hands. "I thought you'd get to sleep alone," she eyed the three kids in the bed with me.

I shrugged.

"They needed their mommy, I guess." I smiled undisturbed by the fullness of my bed. "I'll be right down."

Claudia left the cup on the dresser. I slipped out of bed while the beauties continued to sleep. We enjoyed a couple of cups before the kids came downstairs.

"So, kids who live at my ranch," Claudia explained to her pint-sized guests, "they help with the chores. Which means we'll all get up, feed the horses, and clean the pens each day, twice a day." She glanced at each of the three. "We'll also share in the reading of this devotional each day too," Claudia said as she held up a book.

Bright eyes and acceptance were on the kids' faces.

"And you have to make your beds before you come downstairs. Did you do that this morning?" Three sets of wide eyes told her they hadn't. "Okay, head up there now that you are done with your cereal and make those beds. We've got to get going to the quilt store and we can't go until we feed the horses. Once you kids get into school you will help with the evening and weekend cleanings, but this morning you can help anyways."

And that began our daily routine.

An hour later we had stopped at the quilt store and one of the ladies, Starr, who befriended me last summer came into work.

"Kathleen's got to enroll the kids in school ... do you mind?" Claudia motioned to the three beauties sitting at the table.

"No. Go." Starr encouraged.

Within the hour Claudia and I headed to the school.

"I need to enroll three of my kids in school."

The secretary handed over a couple of sets of papers.

"Bring them back, tomorrow. There's a lot to fill out," the brunette said, kindly. "Where are you coming from?"

My eyes widened as panic set in.

How much do I tell her? Is it safe to tell her? Do I lie? I don't want to lie, but ... they need to know where the kids went to school before ... don't they?

"Um... Colorado."

She looked up, big-eyed, and pushed words out through her jovial giggle. "Oh, you're going to laugh when it snows out here." She air-swatted at an unseen nuisance. My brow knitted with confusion, but she didn't know I'd lived in this town before. "My husband's from there too. He laughs ... 'cuz we get an inch or less of snow and we close the schools down for the day."

Her light chuckle and playful admonition was welcoming.

What a great lady to have here at the front desk.

"Um... I have a restraining order...."

The secretary stopped laughing but retained her soft expression.

"The kids and I are ... in..." I swallowed, but unspoken words stuck in my throat. "Well ... their father doesn't know we are here," the words came out in a near whisper.

"Oh. Okay. Let me get the principal," she said as she turned and walked out of the area.

Moments later a woman with shoulder-length auburn hair came down the hall. Her outstretched hand preceded her. We shook hands.

CHAPTER 32

"Hi Mom. I'm the principal here. Could you come back to my office with me?"

I nodded and followed, but not before I glanced back at Claudia with wide eyes. I bopped my head sideways, silently asking my friend to come with me. She rose from the chair and fell in step. The principal motioned for us to sit before she shut the door. She sat behind her desk.

"How can I help you?"

After I explained my children's plight and showed her my restraining order – she read it, made of copy of it, and agreed to help me keep my children safe.

"The only people allowed to pick up my kids will be myself or my friend here, Claudia."

Accepting my admonishment, she attempted to assure me the kids would be safe while in her care.

The principal gave us a tour of the school. Showed us where the kids' classrooms would be.

"And the playground is fully fenced with a teacher or an adult monitoring the kids when they are out here. Would it be helpful if we put the kids on the lunch program until you get settled?" she offered.

"Yes." I nodded. "It would. I haven't even thought that far ahead. We just got here yesterday. I do appreciate all of this," I added as we got back near the school entrance.

Next, we drove to the school bus office.

"You sure Starr won't mind the kids being at the store with her?" I asked. "I just hate imposing on…"

"No," Claudia interrupted me. "She loves having the kids there. She understands. She knew we were comin' to get you. All of you."

I sighed as we got out of the car. Once inside the bus-barn, I had to explain things again.

"So, I have two kids that need to be picked up … we're over at Hart Flat, but we have some special circumstances."

I put the restraining order on the counter.

"Okay. Here are the times the bus picks up at that stop," the gal on the other side of the counter jotted the times down. "The same driver does the pickup and drop off. I'm gonna let you tell her personally about this, okay?"

"Thank you."

"See, they'll help you keep the kids safe too," Claudia said as we got back in the car and headed back to the quilt store. "And you can meet the bus driver this afternoon because I set my store hours, a long time ago, around my sons' school hours."

The doors of the store were locked promptly at 3:30, and we were at the bus stop in Hart Flat within fifteen minutes. After the students disembarked, I stepped on the bus.

"Hi," I introduced myself and presented the restraining order.

"Yes. I'm Miss Carol. The office said I'd get to meet you today," she said with an upbeat tone as she reviewed the papers.

I smiled, but it was short-lived.

"No one, absolutely no one may pick up my kids, nor can they be released to anyone except me!" the Momma bear came out in the gruffness of my voice.

"Yes ma'am," she attempted to assure me. "I'm the driver for the morning and the afternoon bus. I will *not* let them go with anyone else." She glanced at my stiff posture, softened her tone even more and added, "I promise."

"Okay." I studied her face, her body posture, and her sincerity. Quiet moments passed. "Thank you." I backed down the bus stairs. "Okay," I reached back and motioned to the two oldest, "Ethan, Emma, Bella … this is Miss Carol, your new bus driver."

Introductions were made and the kids agreed to be on time in the morning.

"See you tomorrow, seven-thirty!" Miss Carol encouraged.

The next morning, I escorted my beauties up to the bus stop. Emma chose to sit in the seat behind the bus driver, Bella beside her, Ethan a few seats back. I stood, rubbing my damp hands on the legs of my pants, watching the yellow-orange transport take my kids away from me. My stomach wrenched. I almost lost my morning coffee and toast. I forced a slow breath of cool mountain air into my lungs. I crouched, lowered my

CHAPTER 32

head, and concentrated on measured breaths.

Oh God, please let this be a good idea. Please let these eleven miles be safe miles each day.

I repeated slow steady breaths until my lightheadedness subsided. Standing back up to my full height my steps toward the borrowed truck were on unsteady legs.

They should be okay. He doesn't know where we are... God please! I silently pleaded as I drove the mile back to my friends' ranch.

Once back in the house, I clung to Bella, having her finish her breakfast on my lap at the table.

"More coffee before we go feed?" Claudia offered.

"Sure."

Ten minutes later I helped Bella put on her pink cowboy boots and we were off to feed the horses.

Chapter 33

The two older kids convinced me, with a little help from Claudia, that walking to the host house from the bus stop was okay. The reality was, the kids and I had done it a couple of times. Bella, who I picked up daily because she was only attending school half-day had walked the distance with us. They knew the route. There was only one street.

"Okay Lovies."

"You can go up to the porch and sit in the chairs if you get here before we do," Claudia's voice was filled with cheer. "Or stay down in the pasture pettin' your mare."

Smiles came from the two older kids as a bit of relaxed freedom was being revisited. They seemed to miss it too.

After closing up the shop – Claudia, Bella, and I jumped in the truck and headed for the 5 Heart Ranch. We passed the bus stop, there were no kids waiting for us.

"They probably got here a few minutes early and the kids are walking," Claudia offered up.

"Right. That's what's happened…." I nervously said as Claudia turned onto the private road. "… They've already started walking." I forced the corners of my mouth up into a smile.

I let my eyes dart back and forth as we drove.

A quarter mile down the street … "They're probably at the house already,"

CHAPTER 33

Claudia said.

I chose to believe her, but I kept looking for my beauties. Half a mile in, there was still no sign of them. I felt my face get flush. My palms became damp. As she pulled into the long drive, I released a cleansing breath as I realized I was glad to be *home*. My eyes searched the pasture off the right side of the driveway.

Maybe they're with Molly. You know how much they love their Molly... and she loves them. I'm really glad we brought her.

Claudia stopped the SUV at the barn.

"Let's feed and clean now," she said.

"Ah, okay." My pits dampened. *Why isn't she worried about the kids? Did she see them, and I missed getting a glimpse of them?*

I pulled my attention away from Molly's pasture because I saw Molly but no Ethan and no Emma. Concern flashed in my eyes.

"They're probably up at the house."

"But they can't get into the house. They don't have a key," my words rushed out.

"Oh, but they can sit on the porch. Remember? They were going to sit on the porch if they got here first?" Claudia consoled.

My wide eyes showed I was not convinced.

"Yeah.... They're probably up at the house. You're right."

As I stepped out of the truck I lifted my fingers to my mouth, placed my index finger and thumb under my tongue, and blew. I stood still anticipating a "Yoo hoo" from my Emma, as she couldn't whistle yet. But the oak trees seemed to absorb the sound I made.

My entire body heated up as my eyes widened and panic set in, emanating from every pore.

Maybe the ex-reserve cop recognized the fear. Maybe she smelt it. Maybe she instinctively felt the maternal pangs.

"Let me drive up there," she jutted her chin up. "Maybe Gary was here when they got home, let them in, and they're watching cartoons. Or maybe we beat the bus home and they're walkin' back now."

I helped Bella out of the truck shutting the door behind me. As Claudia pulled away, I whistled again. Louder. Longer. Ensuring my shrill could be heard a mile away.

Nothing!

Oh my God! Where are they? They MUST be up there! They've got to be.

I saw the SUV come to a stop in front of the garage. I heard the door's distinct sound of metal-on-metal clank shut. I looked back up the drive, toward the street.

Oh, please be right. Come on beauties, come on! Come on down the drive! I glanced back up at the house. Squinting, I tried to see the porch chairs. *Darn it.* I climbed up on the second rail of the oil pipe fencing. *I can't see them from here! They're up there. Right?*

Bella had climbed through the pasture fence and was busying herself with Molly's lovin'. I attempted to busy myself with feeding the horses in the barn. But I didn't get far. Within minutes Claudia was driving back from the house.

"Come on! Jump in! Both of you," she nearly demanded.

Bella and I hurried to the car.

"What? What's up? Where are the kids?" acid erupted in my stomach like a rapidly boiling pot of water. My esophagus burned as I rattled off my questions and she floored it, cresting the top of her driveway.

"They weren't inside."

My pits released moisture as adrenaline mixed with my blood.

"I saw there was a message on the answering machine. It was from the Tehachapi Police Department."

It felt like my stomach lurched into my throat. I gagged. Sweat ran down the center of my back.

"They won't release them to anyone but you!"

Claudia drove down Clear Creek Road with purpose, getting us to the freeway as fast as she could. Once on the freeway, she accelerated, surpassing the speed limit.

"Okay…" I fought to be rational. "I'm glad they won't release them to anyone but me, but what do you mean? What happened? Why are they at the police station?"

CHAPTER 33

"I don't know, but the message said, 'Your parents are there but they won't release them to anyone but you.'"

"Are they okay?" I wrapped my arms around my youngest as we rounded a curve, and I fought the centrifugal pull.

"I guess so. They didn't say anything about them not being okay. So, I am guessing they are okay." Her uncertainty did not breed confidence in me.

"Did they say what happened? Why they are at the police station?" I repeated in frustration.

Claudia shook her head as she exited the fifty-eight without slowing down. Within three short minutes, she pulled up in front of the station, right behind my mum and dad's car.

I jumped out of the vehicle before it was in park.

"Stay here Lovie," I instructed my youngest.

I grabbed the handle and pulled open the glass door. My parents, wide-eyed, were standing in the lobby.

"Where are...." The older kids stood up and came around the wall. "Are you okay? What happened?"

An unbridled fear emanated from Emma's big brown eyes. Ethan silently stood there. His blue eyes shrouded in confusion, his face showing little emotion.

"He's here!" Ethan said with a subdued angry voice.

"What!" I embraced my older two as I stared at my folks.

"Hello. May I help you?" I heard a protective female voice. "Are you Kathleen?" the gal from behind the counter asked.

"Yes. Yes. I'm their mum, Kathleen. These are my children. What happened? Please!"

"Let me get the officer." The lady picked up the desk phone. "Officer Smyth, the children's mother is here." She returned the receiver to its base. "It'll be just a moment, ma'am."

I nodded. Seconds later the side door opened, and an officer emerged.

"Mrs. Walton?"

"Yes." I presented him my driver's license as I spoke which he inspected. "What..."

His kind smile reassured this Momma, which aided the panic to subside.

"It seems when the bus driver pulled into the turnaround at Hart Flat, your husband was parked in it."

My eyes widened in an unrestrained silent horror. I pulled my two in tighter and the blood rushed past my eardrums. It was so loud that if the officer had spoken, I wouldn't have heard him.

"The driver didn't let the kids off the bus. She said that your daughter let her know that was their father. She said you have a restraining order against him...."

My jaw clenched. Swallowing was difficult.

"Yes," the tone of my voice telegraphed my fear. "Do you need me to get it? It's out in the car."

"You did a good thing," the officer encouraged as he shook his head, "...showing that TRO to the bus driver."

Oh my God. I thought it was a long shot. Just a precaution. Just crossing my "T"s and dotting my "I"s! I never thought he'd have the balls to come out here!

I struggled to smile.

"Tha...thank ... you. Thank you for holding on to my children," the words finally made it out of my throat.

"Glad we could help," the officer sounded genuine. "You can take them home with you now," compassion dripped from his words.

"Thank you, both of you." I made sure I was able to make eye contact with the receptionist and softly repeated, "Thank you."

She nodded and smiled.

The kids and I walked out of the small office still holding on to each other. My parents followed us out. We all stopped beside the SUV. Claudia rolled down the passenger window.

"Sorry. We tried to pick them up for you," Dad explained once we all came to a stop.

"But they wouldn't let us. They wouldn't release them to us," the hurt of being denied access to her grandchildren was evident in my mother's voice.

"Showed 'em my badge and all, but they said they could only release them to you," Dad shared.

CHAPTER 33

Relief came over me, filling every cell with each inhale.

"Yeah, I instructed the bus driver 'to release the kids to no one but me.'"

"Well, she stuck to it!" the grandparents said in unison.

"I'm sure glad they took me seriously." Relief continued to grow. "Thanks for coming out Mom and Dad."

"We're glad to have done it. Glad to be here and sit with the kids while they waited," my mother said. "We weren't going to leave them here by themselves! No way. No how," she was lovingly emphatic.

If eyes could hug, my parents were wrapping us in their love.

"Let's go home.... Back to the ranch. Get something to eat." I finally released my grip on the kids and opened the back passenger door. "Up top now," I encouraged.

After shutting the door, I hugged my parents repeating my gratitude before kissing them on their cheeks.

As we drove back to the 5 Heart Ranch – that now supported four more hearts – we avoided discussing what happened. Claudia turned on a local country music station and spoke about the horses.

"So... when we get back to the ranch, you guys can help us feed and clean!" cheer filled her voice.

"Okay," Ethan said, gloom present in his voice.

I reached back and took his hand.

We finished feeding the horses and cleaning the stalls before heading up to cook dinner. I think there was more to the feeding and cleaning than just the necessity of being caretakers of the horses. I think Claudia knew the healing properties of focusing the kids' attention on something that will love them, unconditionally. The horses.

"You guys wanna head up and do your homework and I'll get dinner started."

"Okay Momma," all three said in near harmony.

Oh the beautiful sound of all three of you tonight. Oh my God... it almost wasn't so!

My head swirled. My vision blurred. I clutched the counter, steadied myself.

"Can I pour you a glass of wine?" Claudia asked.

"Yes, I think I would like that."

I opened the refrigerator and pulled out ground beef, then walked over to the pantry and pulled out the box of helper. Twenty minutes later, Gary walked in from work. Quick greetings were exchanged before I walked up to get the kids.

"Hello my beauties," I said as I reached the top stair. I received three smiles. I added, "How 'bout yah'll wash up and come on down for supper."

Light chatter was enjoyed about the positive things within each of our days. After finishing our last bites, the kids passed me their plates, one by one.

"Why don't you let us do the dishes tonight," Gary offered.

I hesitated but acquiesced after taking notice of Gary's intense stare. The kids and I headed upstairs for showers and cuddling.

"Momma's really proud of you," I told Emma as Ethan jumped into the shower. "You okay Lovie?"

Emma plopped beside me on the couch. Fishing her arms around me. I returned her tight squeeze, not letting go until she did minutes later when we heard the water stop on the other side of the bathroom door.

"Okay, get ready Emma, you're next," I pushed cheer into my voice.

"What about me?" Bella turned away from the TV and asked.

"You're third, Lovie, after Emma... all right?"

"Okay Momma," Bella gleefully said as she scooted closer to me, filling the now empty spot for minutes on end.

"Do you want to help me pull your bed out Bella?" I asked as I heard the water in the shower. She nodded.

We pulled the couch cushions, exposing the loop attached to the bed frame. I pulled it and the bed unfolded easily. I smoothed out the sheets and covers, fluffed the girls' pillows. Minutes later, with Emma done in the shower, I took Bella in and helped her make sure she cleaned behind her ears. With showers completed, I tucked the girls in bed.

Thank you, God, for helping me keep these beauties safe today. Thank you for all whom you put in our path that helped achieve this goal today.

CHAPTER 33

And with that I kissed each of them on the forehead and turned out the light. My son and I went into my room.

"Sit down Lovie."

I patted the bed. He climbed up and leaned against the headboard. I plopped down beside him.

"We're gonna be okay Lovie."

He leaned into me as he let the tears fall.

"I'm sorry Lovie." I wrapped my arms around him as he sobbed. "I'm sorry you got so scared today … sorry you got scared."

He snuggled in tighter. It took minutes, but his breathing shallowed and he fell asleep.

Chapter 34

"It might be a good time to get a cell phone now," Gary kindly stressed as the adults congregated in the kitchen the next morning.

"I guess it *is* time to get one. I'm just not sure I can afford it. It's an expense, like we talked about this summer, that I've not ever put in our budget."

"They're much more affordable than you think," Claudia encouraged. "Plus, it's something that'll help keep you and the kids safer."

I stared at the throw rug, trying to count the fibers.

"Okay," with a coffee cup up to my lips, defeat laced my words. I sighed. *I hate this. Him and his bull shit. Making it so I have to go spend money on a bloody cell phone instead of using it to put food on the table!*

My shoulders slumped.

"I'll take the kids in to school this morning and go get a phone before I come into the store." A frown settled on my face. Making eye contact with Claudia I added, "You said I should be able to get one for about fifty a month?"

"Yeah. Try Verizon over by Albertsons."

The kids trampling down the stairs brought me out of my fog.

"Got your jackets?" I asked my trio. With nods all around I got up from the table. "Go get your shoes on!"

I rose and grabbed the keys off the small hook to the new-to-me car my dad was letting me drive.

CHAPTER 34

"See you later," I said, over my shoulder just before the kids echoed, 'byeee.'"

We piled into the car and belted up as we headed out the driveway. The eleven-mile drive went by fast. We sang along with the radio and kept the mood light. Laughter erupted from my son as I changed the words to a Dixie Chicks song. Playfully I raised my eyebrows, a couple of times, and gave him a cheeky smile.

It's so nice to see him smile!

He looked at me, as I sang on, to see if I would continue to change any more lyrics. Ethan's smile widened as I did not disappoint.

"Okay we're here...." I timed as I pulled up to the curb outside the main entrance of the school. "Want me to walk you in?"

Ethan looked over at me. His blue eyes were clear and determined. He shook his head.

"Na ... oh," Emma's tentative voice gained strength as she finished the, now, two-syllable word.

"Okay. Keep your chin up guys. Momma will be at the quilt store, just a couple of blocks away. The secretary and principal have the number." The trio hesitated. "I'll be back to get you. Just wait for me. Together!" My instructions were met with wide eyes. I pointed. "Right there at the top of the ramp... okay?"

My oldest glanced over his shoulder at me and nodded. I patted his hand which lingered on the passenger seat.

"We've got this."

I smiled fostering confidence.

He didn't hide his concern from me.

"You make sure you've got Emma before you come this far... okay Lovie?"

His head bobbed his affirmation.

I pulled him close and kissed his cheek. Emma and Bella got up and alternated positioning themselves between the front seats giving me kisses.

"Bella, I'll be back to get you at about noon. Have a good day my loves," I barely got out before the car doors clicked shut. Frozen like a statue, I sat until my threesome rounded the corner into the main hall of the school.

I headed to the phone store. Minutes later I found a parking spot in front of the vendor, only to find they would not be open until 10 a.m.

Well shit. Now what? I drummed my fingers on the steering wheel. *Hum. I need to burn about an hour. I guess I could go get some coffee.*

I put the car in reverse, backed out, and mindlessly headed for 5 Heart Quilts.

I can go to Circle K and get a coffee.

A few doors before the Main Street shop, I glanced up and noticed a familiar dark green SUV coming toward me, through the intersection. My heart pounded.

No! It couldn't be Jimmy's car? Could it?

I scrutinized the front of the car. The distinct white and green Colorado license plate fired up the acid in my stomach. As the vehicle got closer, I white-knuckled the steering wheel. All of a sudden Mike and Jimmy were right beside me. Me heading east. The guys heading west. Only the twelve inches of the double yellow lines separated us.

Mike looked over the top of my grey four-door sedan, as if he didn't see me. His eyes and attention were focused on the large wall of windows of the store.

I barely stopped at the white line of the crosswalk twenty feet away. But as soon as I did, my foot went from the brake to the gas. I floored it while reaching beneath the front passenger seat, retrieved my revolver, and set it on the passenger seat. Before getting to the next block, I moved the firearm up onto the dash as I navigated the curves of the street.

Oh my God! Oh my God! Oh my God!

The faster my heart raced the faster my car went.

Wait…think. You can't just keep driving. You need to call the cops.

I took my foot off of the gas pedal and found the next street to turn around in as I forced myself to focus.

But where do I go? Where's safe? What's open? The feed store!

I whipped a u-ie, headed back down Main Street, and I turned the first chance to get over the railroad track. I pulled up, put my gun inside my

CHAPTER 34

waistband and got out of the car, pulling my shirt down over it.

"Hi Randy." *Did my voice quiver? Shit.*

"Hi!"

"Can I use your phone? To call the cops?"

Randy eyed me with concern yet walked over behind the counter. He handed me the handset.

"Hello, what is your emergency?" the 9-1-1 operator asked.

"I just saw my soon-to-be ex-husband. He's here! In town. With the neighbor.

They are here from Colorado! I have a restraining order!"

"Okay ma'am where are you located?"

"Here, at the feed store on Mill Street in Tehachapi, right off the freeway," my words came rapidly.

"Okay, are you in a safe place?"

Ryan could hear both sides of the conversation. He nodded.

"Yes. The guy at the feed store says I can stay here for a bit."

"Okay. I am sending an officer over to you right now. Don't go anywhere."

"No ma'am. I'm not goin' anywhere," trepidation filled my voice.

"Okay, Miss Kathleen, the officer is almost there," she tried to keep me calm.

Chapter 35

As the black and white cruiser pulled up, compassion filled Ryan's blue eyes.

"The officer is here," I said into the receiver.

"Okay. I am going to hang up now. The officer will help you," the 9-1-1 operator explained.

"Thank you, ma'am."

"Did you call for some help?" the officer asked as he pulled open the glass door and stepped inside.

"She did," Ryan said pointing at me.

After taking down my name, birthdate, and other personal information I offered the officer my temporary restraining order. He inspected the pages, wrote down the case number, and then handed them back to me.

"Why don't you tell me what's happened today."

"I was driving down Tehachapi Boulevard ... by the front of the 5 Heart Quilts store. I looked up to see Jimmy's dark green Geo Tracker. Jimmy's one of my renters from Colorado. I saw my husband behind the wheel of the Tracker. Jimmy was in the passenger seat. Mike didn't seem to see me..."

The officer frowned and squinted.

"I've changed my hair cut and color," I explained. *God, I never thought I'd be one of those ladies... one of those who had to change their appearance ... to hide in plain sight from her husband.* "Plus, I was driving a car he's never seen

CHAPTER 35

before."

The officer's face relaxed and he raised one eyebrow.

"He was focused on looking **in** the quilt store. It was like he was casing the joint."

"Okay. Where did you say the kids were?"

"At Wells. Wells Elementary," I informed as I pointed in the direction of the school as if it was just down the street instead of over half a mile away.

"Okay." He turned his focus toward the storekeeper. "Can she stay here for a few more minutes... until I check to see he's not still around?"

"Oh yeah. She can stay in here."

The officer exited the building and took his car toward Main Street.

I paced. Back and forth, back and forth frequently looking out the store's window.

This must be what a caged cat feels like.

"I'm gonna go now. It's been like fifteen minutes."

"You sure?" he did not hide the concern in his voice.

"What if he didn't find 'im ... and he forgot to come back. Brushed it off and all?" I speculated.

"Kathleen ..." Ryan came closer but not too close. "...I don't think that happened. He looked like he was taking this seriously."

I restlessly walked around the aisles of the feed store.

"How about some coffee?"

My ears and mood perked up as he poured. Twenty-five minutes later the cruiser was coming back in the driveway.

"Well, I found him," the officer said.

My eyes grew wide. I gripped the counter to steady me. The shop owner stopped stocking the shelves and came closer.

"He was parked outside the school. In that green Tracker, with your neighbor," there was a sternness to his voice.

My throat tightened. Air caught in my lungs.

"I had them get out of the car. I searched it. He has no weapons. I let him know I am aware there is a TRO against him. He tried to tell me, 'I'm just here checking on the welfare of my kids.' I told no one travels 1500 miles with a car seat and an extra man in the car … just to 'check on his kids.'"

Oh my God! He's here to take them! I wasn't overreacting! Oh my God!

"So, is he still there?" the words rushed out of my mouth.

"No ma'am," he made sure we were looking squarely at each other before he continued. "I told him he couldn't stay. If he did, I'd have to arrest him for breaching the restraining order. I stayed around until I was sure he wasn't coming back as well." The officer reassured me.

My breath slowed. My shoulders dropped slightly. It took a bit, but I was able to come off the edge of panic. The officer stood with me like a sentry, standing protectively in the void for me and my kids.

"Do you have the number to the Domestic Violence Shelter?"

"Yes, sir. I've already put a call into them. They said …" I swallowed, "… if I needed to get safe, to call them."

Daunted by the unknown territory I was about to embark on overwhelmed me.

"Okay, well … it might be good to call them and see if they can get you in, today," he encouraged, compassion cushioned his words.

I noticed his soft stern eyes held mine. I nodded.

Wow, these cops don't like him either! But at least I guess I'm not in trouble for bringing the kids here! Taking them out of state. Even though the court papers said not to leave the state… the cops out here… they seem to understand…. They're supportive of my view on this mess – me not feeling the kids and I are safe with Mike around.

Minutes later the officer and I pulled out of the driveway, heading in two different directions.

It's after 9:30. I'm just going to the quilt store. I need to call the lady down at the shelter.

"Well, did they let you look at the phones and put one on my bill?" Claudia said as I walked in the back door.

"No, they weren't open."

"What's wrong?"

"He's here! He was casing the store. He was rousted outside the kids' school," my voice wavered.

CHAPTER 35

"Come sit!" She motioned to the chair. "Tell me...."
I filled her in.

"Why don't we go get you that phone now, or after Starr gets here, just in case a customer shows up." Claudia braved an encouraging smile.

"I need to call the shelter first."

My friend nodded. I picked up the handset and dialed the number listed in my notebook. Claudia sewed a few pieces of fabric together.

"Okay. You'll have a spot for the kids and me...tomorrow? Yes. Three kids. One boy... oh ... yes, that is us. I did call yesterday. Yes. He's still here." I filled the gal at the shelter, in on the morning's events.

"Are you in a safe place right now?" There was an urgency in her voice.

"Yes. I am at work."

"Okay. What's the number there?" I gave it to her. "Okay, let me call you back in a bit. I have some checking to do down here."

I hung up the phone. Claudia and Starr were both wide-eyed.

"So can they let you guys in tonight?" Claudia's impatience and protectiveness rushed her words.

"The lady isn't sure, but she said she'd call back in an hour or so."

"Well, let's go get you a cell phone."

"You really need one now!" Starr added.

I nodded in agreement. But before we could get out of the store the phone rang.

"Okay. You'll have a spot for the kids and me... tomorrow? Yes. Three kids. One boy.... Oh, yes, we're the ones in Tehachapi.... A motel in Tehachapi. Yes, ma'am, I know that location. Are you sure? They'll have a room ready for us? And tomorrow. I'm to call you at the same number," I repeated the number she had given me. "You'll tell me where to meet you. Not you. Oh, someone who will lead us to the safe house. Yes. Okay. That makes sense."

"Tell her you will be calling from a cell phone, a new number," Claudia kibitzed.

"Yes, my friend will be putting me on her cell phone plan in the next hour, so I will be calling you from a cell phone number. Thank you. Thank you

155

so much. I will see you tomorrow. Thank you."

"So they can't take you guys tonight?" Claudia's impatience won out.

"No." I shook my head as I set the handset back on the sewing table. "They don't have enough beds. They have arranged a hotel room for us, here in town."

I puckered my lips, twisted them into a crooked frown.

"So I'm gonna go tell the principal that the kids won't be in school for a bit."

"Let's go get you a cell phone first! Starr's here. She'll look after the store for a while."

Compassion filled Starr's eyes.

"Okay," I conceded.

"Plus, you said that cop ran Mike off, so the kids are safe at school!" Claudia encouraged.

"Yeah. You've got a point," the quiver in my voice was steadied by determination.

We headed out the door. Getting into Claudia's vehicle. I interlocked my fingers to minimize my fidgeting as she drove the half mile.

"I want to add a line, but to a separate account unless she can get one for herself," Claudia spoke up before the guy behind the counter could even greet us.

Within forty minutes we walked out of the Verizon store, me better able to protect the kids and myself... well, more efficiently at least.

"Okay, so when we get back to the quilt store you can program our names and numbers in your phone and *then* go to the school," my friend instructed me. "Plus, we need to call Gary."

I nodded.

But I really just want to go get the kids. And hide.

My palms felt damp again.

Later, as I drove up to the school, I surveyed the area for that green Tracker. Not seeing it I pulled to the curb. Before shutting the car off I looked around again.

CHAPTER 35

No green SUV. Wait what's that?

I turned my head over my shoulder to see a green pick-up truck pulling away from the boulevard stop behind me. It didn't stop at the school. My grip on the steering wheel relaxed, ever so slightly.

Oh my God, that scared the hell out of me! Calm your shit down Momma. The cops got rid of Mike for a while.

I put the car in park, turned it off, and entered the school. My strides were long which helped me cover ground quickly.

"I'd like to speak to the principal," my matter-of-fact tone telegraphed my insistence without me needing to raise my voice.

Minutes later I was sitting in her office.

"I want you to know that my kids will be missing school for a while. Starting tomorrow. I don't know how long they will be gone. We're heading into another safe house."

"Oh!"

I explained this morning's events, including the one outside the school.

"Well," she sat back in her chair, swallowed hard, and then continued, "well, your husband was here, in the office yesterday."

My jaw went slack. My eyes widened. I scowled at her.

"Wwwhhaatttt?"

"Yes, he asked if the kids were here at the school."

"And you told him they were here?"

"Well, he has a right to know they are here."

My brow furrowed and I squinted.

"You know we are here to keep the kids safe… right? You know the cops rousted him this morning right here outside the school… right? He had another guy with him and a car seat!" My jaw clenched as I waited for her lame explanation. "I want my kids, now! We have to get to another safe house because I trusted you! I trusted you to help me protect my kids and you effing told him where they were!"

"I didn't let him see them!"

"Well, I guess I should be glad about that, huh?" sarcasm dripped off my words. "Get my kids down here… or do you want me to walk the halls to get them?"

"No. No. Let me have the secretary call for them."

Minutes later my beauties were in the office.

"Come on you guys. We need to go."

The four of us walked out of the school, got in the car, and drove to the ranch.

Chapter 36

"Okay guys, Momma needs you to help me pull together a few items as we're going to go to a motel tonight."

"How long are we going to go for?" Emma asked with glee.

"I'm not sure Lovie. But it's not safe here right now so Momma's movin' us into a safe house."

"Will we be coming back here?" doubt filled Ethan's voice.

"Yes son. I just need to get us in a safer place for a while … while your father is out here." I tempered my delivery in an attempt to not panic the kids.

My son nodded as he contributed a few shirts, socks, and a pair of jeans to the laundry basket – my makeshift suitcase.

"You know he was at school today," my son offered up.

"I did." *But I didn't know you knew.*

"I saw him…"

I stopped packing, sat on the edge of the bed, and gave him my full attention.

"… sittin' in Jimmy's car," Ethan continued.

I watched my son's face intently.

"What'd you do son? Did he come and try to talk to you?"

"I went over to the teacher on the yard. I pointed to Dad, Jimmy, and the Tracker and told her, 'He's not supposed to be here.'"

I smiled as I let the protective braveness of my son's action set in.

"You did good, real good Lovie." I stroked the line of his jaw. "Did that scare you a lot?"

I gazed into my boy's big blue eyes. They widened as he seemed to remember. He swallowed slowly. Then nodded. I pulled him close.

"Sorry." It was then that I shared my morning's events with him. "That's why Momma's takin' us to another safe house. Plus, the cops suggested it. And you know Momma's been listenin' to those who want to help me keep yah'll safe."

"Oh...kay Momma," there was relief in his voice.

We finished packing and headed for the car. I put the basket of clothing, jackets, and a bag of toiletries in the trunk as the kids got in and buckled up. Before heading down the driveway I checked to confirm my restraining order and my handgun were in my purse. Satisfied, I made my way out of Hart Flat in an effort to get my kids to the next safe spot.

"So, we'll need to grab some supper to take where we're going. Do you want burgers or tacos?"

I was hoping to lighten the mood with fast food.

"Burgers!" the girls sang out.

"Emma ... are you sure?"

Since she was about two, Emma had been bothered by spicy or acidic things due to geographic tongue. I still hadn't gotten over being protective and cautious of what she ate. Her head bobbed a few times. The boy sat in the front, with me, not saying anything.

"Son, are burgers okay?"

He shrugged his shoulders. I patted his leg.

Fifteen minutes later we pulled into the drive-through. Knowing it would be safest if we stayed in the car, together, I ordered burgers, fries, drinks, and one chocolate shake. Just in case the ketchup and mustard were too much for the ulcerations that might show up on Emma's tongue. It wasn't long before I handed my son the bag of yummies and then asked him to balance the drink tray on his lap.

"When do we get to eat Momma?" Bella inquired.

"In just a few minutes Bella. We aren't going very far tonight." We listened

CHAPTER 36

to the Dixie Chicks on the radio as I sang my own version of their song as I'd become accustomed to doing. "Without ... I am okay.... I found my way...."

It was then that my son snickered. I continued changing the words and making him smile until I pulled into the motel parking lot.

"You three stay here, let me get the key to the room."

"Which room Momma?" Emma asked.

"I don't know Emma, don't know just yet."

I checked the rear-view mirror, and then both side mirrors. I didn't see the green SUV.

I guess it's okay to get out, to leave them out here. I don't see any hint of him. The cop said he shouldn't be in town, but... why'd the officer tell me to get the kids to the safe house? I sat, frozen. I checked the mirrors again, then turned and surveyed the limited parking lot. *Go. Make it quick. That lady said she'd already made the reservation. She said I wouldn't have to give up too much information. The room's under her name. Go.*

I got out, turned, and, before shutting the door, I forced a smile.

"Lock the doors son."

Minutes later I was back at the car. The kids were sharing some fries. I motioned for my son to unlock the doors. He did with a smile.

"It seemed we lucked out. I parked in front of the right door. We're in unit two tonight," I forced cheer in my voice. I think it worked.

After getting the kids settled with their burgers, I retrieved the clothing and such. But not without surveying the area as the hairs on the back of my neck were standing on end.

Once back inside it was time for sleeping arrangements.

"We've gotta share beds and floor space you guys."

"I've got the floor mom. The girls can have that other bed."

"You sure son?"

He nodded.

"Okay, did you find the extra blankets and pillows they brought in for us?" Pillows were tossed around playfully. "Emma, how's that burger? Is it hurtin' your tongue?"

"Nope!"

A level of pride at being able to eat just like everyone else emanated from more than just her voice! She sat up straighter, bounced her knees as she sat cross-legged, and grabbed a few fries.

"Okay, then you guys can share the chocolate shake I got for you."

Cheers erupted.

We watched a rerun of a ranger in Texas before the heaviness of eyelids won out for the girls.

"Mom," my son walked up to the side of my bed. "Mom, I want the knife."

"Oh son. I've got this. I've got the gun under my pillow, here."

My attempt at reassuring him wasn't working, I could see as our eyes met.

"Mom. Please!"

At only ten, he was ready to stand up and protect his family.

"Okay son, but you know the agreement…."

"Yep. Stick it in and turn it," he said without wavering.

I watched him for a few heartbeats before pulling the knife out from under the far side of the pillow and handing it to him. I kissed him on the forehead before he returned to his bedroll.

Chapter 37

With no school for the next few days, I let the kids sleep in. The morning news show was on the TV, my new cell phone on the charger, and my craving for caffeine gained strength with each blinking of my eyelids. I unplugged the phone, flipped it open, and dialed Susan at the Safe House as I walked into the bathroom.

"… I need you to go to an address I'll give you. Do you have something to write on?" Susan asked.

"Yes ma'am, I do." I jotted down the address.

"Okay Momma," she refrained from using names over the open line, "you drive on out to that address. It will be a restaurant on the main street. It's not open at this hour, just wait in the parking lot. Call me again when you get there. I will come to you in a blue four-door and then you will be able to follow me to the safe house."

Within an hour the kids were ready, and we were heading down the highway, my handwritten directions leading the way.

"Where we goin' Momma?" Bella asked between bites of her egg and muffin.

"I'm not exactly sure love. We're just following the directions that nice lady gave me."

That seemed to satisfy my 5-year-old, as the questions stopped. Thank goodness. Because I didn't know where I was driving … but I guess that's the idea behind a Safe House.

"Oh look ... the grey restaurant, just like the nice lady said," I allowed a hint of cheer in my voice, even though it felt like butterflies had taken flight in my stomach, with so much unknown.

"What we doin' here?" my son asked.

"Is this the safe house?" Emma interjected.

"No. It's not the safe house. We're gonna park here and Momma's gonna call the lady that's offered to help us. She's gonna come to us and lead us there. It's the best way to keep everyone safe because we are not going to be the only family there needing protection."

I picked up my phone and dialed the last number called. During the fifteen-minute wait, I couldn't help but notice how smart it was – to set up a meeting in such a large wide-open parking lot ... one that has a clear view all the way around the building. Precaution, protection, safety. It would be hard for anyone watching to go unnoticed if they were following....

A lady in a blue sedan pulled up beside us.

"Hello... Kathleen?" a brunette said.

"Susan?"

The driver smiled.

"Follow me. We're going to move quickly now."

I turned the key in the ignition and followed her – out of the parking lot, right, left, left, right, right, right, left. Within minutes we were deep into this unknown cookie-cutter neighborhood.

Clever.

She stopped and waved for me to pull up beside her.

"Pull your car into that driveway." She pointed. "I'm going to park around back and be right with you."

Moments later she walked around the garage.

"Hello kids," there was a welcoming cheer in her voice, "my name is Susan." She waited a couple of ticks of her watch before continuing. She seemed to know to approach those filled with fear slowly. "Let's go inside." The kids sat still. "There's other kids inside who are looking forward to meeting you. Plus, I can show you the beds we've set up for you."

My wide-eyed children sat stiff in their seats. I took a deep breath, nodded,

CHAPTER 37

reached for the door handle and we all got out.

"Let me introduce you to the moms and kids. Then your mom and I are going to do a little paperwork," the kind tone of her voice soothed as she welcomed scared strangers into the unknown. She motioned to the room with bunk beds. "This is where you guys will get to sleep and mom too!"

She made introductions of us to the two other mothers and their kids.

"Do you ladies mind if the kids stay with you while Kathleen and I go to the other side to do the paperwork?" Susan asked as the two mothers smiled and shook their heads.

"Come on over here young lady," the taller mom said to Emma with open arms.

Emma bravely went to this approved stranger, surprising me with her resilience.

One of the young girls – I guessed her to be about seven – held up a doll, offering friendly play to Bella. My son stood, stiff-backed.

"I'll be right back. I think we're okay here," I encouraged him as I placed a hand on his shoulder.

"Would you like some Kool-Aid," the other mother warmly offered.

"Yes, please," Ethan responded.

The mom and I exchanged a smile.

"Come on. They're safe here. They'll be all right. It's just going to take a little bit for them to settle in," Susan encouraged.

We sat on either side of her desk. I began filling out the intake packet with names, addresses, etc. as we discussed our recent history.

"Well, I'm glad we can help provide you and your children a haven. I do want you to know that we accept men too."

My eyes widened. My pulse quickened. I gripped the arm of the chair.

"Oh no, they don't stay here. We have a different house for them to stay at… in the same housing development but not close to here. I just wanted you to know, in case we get a man in, I will be needing to split some of my time between both houses."

"Good." I slowly regained my composure. Relaxed a little. But full relaxation wouldn't be mine for a long time to come. "Where would the grocery store be? I ..."

"You don't need to worry about any of that. We want you ladies to stay here with your kids. We know how stressful coming here can be. We provide you with all of the food to cook for your children. If you jot down a list, with the other moms, I will be going to the store about noon, so you moms can enjoy making a meal together for your kids."

"Wow. Okay. This is totally unexpected."

"We know you guys are displaced, but this isn't your town, you don't need to get lost out in this new area.... That wouldn't be good for anyone. Plus, you are safer if you stay here the entire time. It's the best way we can help protect you."

I nodded in agreement.

"Now, remind me. Does your husband know the car you drive?" I shook my head. "Okay. You can leave your car in the driveway, then. Why don't you go get anything you might need from your car," she directed. "You can use that door," Susan pointed to a door behind me. "I'll wait for you. But, if I miss you, you can put your stuff in room number two."

Caution accented each step out of the office. I paused as I checked up and down the street. There was a palpable eeriness. I urged my hearing to identify sounds this ranch girl was not accustomed to. They weren't completely unfamiliar, but .... Track housing. Trusting strangers.

A light breeze pushed the California winter warmth at me. I swallowed the lump in my throat and walked to the car. While at the trunk, an unmuffled car drew closer and closer. I kept my head down and waited for it to come into my peripheral view.

"Darn it, Kathleen! It's not him," I chastised myself. "He didn't follow you. He wouldn't know where to come. He wouldn't know this neighborhood. Hell, you didn't even know about this area yourself."

The 1966 Chevy muscle car passed without incident. *Of course!*

"Hi," I said to the moms and kids in the living room, after dropping our laundry basket off in "our room". Emma and Bella ran up to me, encircling my waist with their arms. I hugged them instinctively. "Susan said yah'll might have started a list for shopping," I directed to the other mothers.

CHAPTER 37

"Yes ma'am, it's on the counter," Tameka informed.

The girls scampered off and my son looked up from the cartoons. The hesitant smile confirmed he was okay. As okay as he could be.

Us moms chatted about current planned menus and possible allergies.

"We were encouraged to make our kids' favorites. I am going to make egg rolls," Lona shared.

"Making ... egg rolls? Here?" I did not hide my astonishment.

"Yes. You haven't ever made them?" Lona asked like it was something I should already have learned in my 37 years.

"No."

"Would you like to help make them? We could even teach the kids too. It's a lot of fun!"

"Sure."

"We'll make them tomorrow... okay?"

A smile grew on my face at the welcome, the inclusion. It was then that there was a scuffle between the boys at the safe house. I stood to correct my son.

"Oh, we aren't allowed to paddle our kids while we're here," Lona warned.

My eyes narrowed.

"We can make them stand near the wall with their arms straight up or out like a T," she added.

I frowned.

"Okay son... up near the wall, face the wall. Arms up, straight. Maybe next time you won't snatch the clicker for the TV from anyone." He stood there, with periodic reminders of "arms up" for five minutes.

Over the next three days, my two oldest children spent time on the wall.

"I'm going to go call my folks. Let them know we're safe."

"You can step out on the patio if you'd like," Tameka offered.

I stepped out the sliding glass door into the sliver of a backyard defined by the six-foot high solid wood privacy fence. I pushed the dirt around with my foot as the phone rang through.

Two days passed before I got a call from Claudia.

"Gary and his foster son, you remember him?"

"Yes."

The image of the imposing thirty-something man came into my mind's eye.

"They went looking for Mike and that green car. They searched motels here in town and down in Mojave. They think they found that Tracker. It had Colorado plates ... right? They left a note under the windshield wiper for him. There's been no sign of him though. Looks like he's gone back to where he's come from."

"That's good," while I forced relief into my voice, it was not what I felt. My mind raced – *Where is he? Where is he hiding? Would he have given up? Did he actually go home, back to the ranch?*

"There's no threat anymore. You need to come back!" Claudia's insistent tone missed the persuasive and reassuring goal I think she intended.

"But... I need to check if there's any paperwork that needs to be done before I leave. I...."

"I need you here at the store! I have a lot of sewing students scheduled and no one else to work the front desk. Come on ... you're safe ... he's gone."

"Let me check."

"I need to know!"

I sighed.

"I will let you know later ... tonight."

"I need to know you will be here. It's safe," she insisted. "You guys can come back, and the kids can go to school. You don't have to stay away anymore."

Not wanting to put up with yet another person's decisions about my children and my safety, it was time to end the call.

"I need to go. The kids are playin' outside," irritation laced my words and with that, I closed the phone.

That night I wrote a thank you note, packed the kids' stuff, and prepared to head back.

"Ladies, thank you for being so kind, for sharing your stories, and time with the kids and me," I shared with the moms over coffee after we had put

CHAPTER 37

all of the kids down for the night.

"You know you can stay here longer," Tameka's compassion seemed genuine.

"Yes." I nodded. "I do, but I need to get back to work and we have an informal safe house to stay in." I took a deep breath. "Plus ... my friend ... says it's safe to return." I pouted. "And the kids need to get back in school. They've missed enough."

"You don't want to stay the weekend?"

"No Lona." I shrugged my shoulders, as a half-smirk half-frown came across my face. "Saturday is the busiest day of the week at the quilt store I work at," I sighed. "Plus, my friend has a bunch of students coming in ... so ... she needs help dealing with customers, cuttin' fabric, the cash register and all."

"Okay beauties, say good-bye to your new friends while I put our basket out in the trunk. I'll be back in."

Hugs and well wishes were shared all around – kids and moms alike.

"Come on, we need to get back to town before the store opens and it's a bit of a drive."

I dropped my thank you note off on the office desk before heading out to the car. As we left before breakfast, I treated the kids to a fast food meal, which enabled us to be back at the quilt store just before it opened. By 9:15 we pulled up to the back of the quilt store.

Later that afternoon my Mum and Dad stopped in the store.

"That was a long three days," Mom whispered in my ears as she hugged me.

"Can we take the kids to the ranch today? And have dinner later with you?" Dad asked.

Too many little and big smiling faces were looking at me for me to deny the request.

Chapter 38

The next morning, as the kids watched cartoons upstairs, Claudia, Gary, and I gathered in the room off of the kitchen where the computer was.

"Thanks for letting me check my emails," I said to Gary. "Oh, lookie lookie. An email from him." I began reading an email from Mike aloud.

"'...Thank you, for Tina, we had a long talk.' Guess he means my *new stepdaughter*," I made air quotes as I spoke, "She got her birthday wish, to speak to her daddy for the first time in twenty years." I sighed, smiled, and nodded to the computer screen as if anyone could see my satisfaction at doing something good for the girl. "Oh," I continued reading aloud, "and now he is saying I am lying."

"About what?" Gary said as Claudia came up to read over my shoulder.

"'... the lies you tell keep getting worse than the ones before... you call yourself a 'good mother' what kind of person are you, you want a divorce that's fine, you want to be with that DIKE that your business, but why do you try to wreck someone like that you supposedly loved for 15 yrs. Let alone my kids and you know this is true, and all this pretending to be sooooo scared you know it's a joke. If you were so afraid then why did you leave my children with strangers a take off to huston for a week really afraid yah and wheat you don't know about ins would fill a book.'"

CHAPTER 38

"Wow… he's really pissed," Claudia said.

"Yeah, sorry Claudia."

"Don't worry, he's just trying to get a rise out of you. But… what's that Houston comment all about?" Gary asked.

"It seems he's been using the neighbors to keep an eye on me since he left in late September including when you and I went to Quilt Market in mid-October, just after I filed the papers."

"Well, that's not good," Claudia quipped.

"Not good at all," Gary added as I took a gulp of coffee.

"Wow… he should really learn how to spell," Claudia said as she took a closer look at his email.

"Well, he didn't achieve getting his G.E.D. He only made it through the sixth grade, so it seems."

I joined my housemates in a laugh. It did ease the tension.

Chapter 39

"Thanks for driving back to this hearing with me, Dad."

His stern face, not hidden by his signature mutton chop mustache, did little to hide his bow-string taunt jaw muscles. He nodded.

"We should make Gallup in a couple of hours or so. We'll get supper and a room," Dad advised.

I wish I could afford to pay for this... fuel, food, the room. This is the shits, not having any money. Mike's keeping the rent, no doubt. And I'm trading the work at the quilt store for room and board.

"You want to drive? I'm getting a little stiff."

"Sure Dad. I'd be glad to help out."

He pulled to the side of the road. Once in the dirt, we both climbed down from the F250 dually before we stretched our legs by walking around the truck once, and then traded spots. An hour later he asked about the fuel level.

"We're about a quarter of, no, just under a quarter of a tank."

"Why don't you pull off at the next exit and we'll fill up before climbing that hill to Gallup."

"Good idea with this headwind and all," I agreed.

I eased my foot on the gas pedal, flicked the turn signal indicator, and steered down the off-ramp. I feathered the gas pedal and muscled the release of the clutch. It didn't take long to get the truck refueled and two

CHAPTER 39

black coffees. I climbed behind the wheel, and we headed east on Interstate 40. An hour later the sign for the Gallup exit fueled a bit of relief in me.

"Good timing with these flurries starting," I kibitzed as the mid-February weather was expected to be fickle at best.

Dad yawned in agreement.

Because we were both early risers, the next morning we hit the road as the sun came up. We traded off driving a few times on the second day. Dad pulled into Cañon City. He picked a motel after driving up the main street.

"I need a room with two beds. Two nights please."

The lady behind the counter started typing.

"Do you offer a senior discount?" Dad asked.

"Or a local's discount… like they do in Tehachapi?" I added with a bit of inquisitive cheer.

"Where do you live?" the clerk asked with a doubting tone in her voice.

I gave her my ranch address while showing her my Colorado driver's license. She gave us a discount and a frown.

"What time do we need to be at court in the morning?" Dad asked.

"We need to be in Judge Lawson's courtroom for a … ten o'clock," I confirmed after reviewing the restraining order.

We walked through the glass doors of the Fremont County Court House to find Mike sitting at a conference table to our right, behind reflective tinted glass that had given him a vantage point in which he watched us arrive.

What makes him think that – Johnny Cash all dressed in black – hat, shirt, pants, and boots plus the fake ass sad eyes and pouting – would change my mind? Effer!

I did my best to ignore this pitiful ploy, including muffling the snicker within me.

Dad and I made it to the front of the gallery seating in the courtroom. Mike walked in and sat on the other side of the aisle. He was not alone. A tall six-foot-something bald man was with him.

Could be his lawyer, maybe.

I sat, patiently, next to my dad. My hands in my lap, slumped shouldered, my head down to help me avoid any eye contact with Mike. My planned demure outfit – a simple nondescript modest dress and flat-heeled suede boots was the right choice.

I think the Judge will see I need the extension of the restraining order with that power play. That dressed all in black to intimidate me – both of them. At least I was hopeful my assumption was true.

Someone approached me as I waited for the judge. I saw men's black shoes and pant legs only inches from me.

"So…" the man started.

I kept my eyes focused on the floor.

"…where are the kids?"

My eyes followed up the man's form – his black loafers to his properly hemmed black slacks to his belt, vest, tie, white shirt, and black suit coat. Above his shoulders was his well-trimmed goatee, tan complexion, and shaved head. I couldn't help but notice he used his six-foot-four-ish height to loom over me.

"They're at a safe house," not knowing who he was I kept my answer simple, and in the appropriate soft tone, as if I were in a library.

He bent over a bit, sharing his words with me only.

"I'm on the board of the safe houses here in Colorado. I've checked," he did not hide his aggressiveness. "They aren't in any of the safe houses here in Colorado!" he nearly growled the last words.

Wait… he can't do that … can he? No one can let a guy who stands up for the effing abuser be on the board of any Safe Houses … that would be a conflict of interest! Dangerous! Good thing we are in a courtroom… because he's mad enough to have almost decked me.

"I said they were in a safe house!" like a chameleon my voice changed from the modest timid victim to the matter-of-fact, stern mother bear.

We locked eyes for a moment. He lost that staring match because I did not look away. He turned and walked back to the other side of the aisle.

You underestimated me you stupid, stupid man. Both of you are stupid. I am no longer anyone's victim. You've screwed with the wrong woman. Both of you bastards!

CHAPTER 39

I seethed in silence as I shared an eye-rolling with my father. He patted my leg.

Judge Lawson entered the room. Everyone stood. He gavelled the court to order, and his clerk called our case.

"Mrs. Walton. Please," he motioned me toward the plaintiff's table.

Mike and the bald asshole waited to be permitted to the respondent's table.

"We are here," the judge continued, "for the matter of a restraining order." He rustled the pages in the file in front of him, that I hoped contained the couple of breaches of the restraining order I had requested be sent here. "Mrs. Walton," he made eye contact with me, "do you feel a need to have this temporary restraining order extended?"

"I would like to have it continued through the divorce, sir," I said in the appropriate soft tone and volume.

"Oh, there's a divorce. Okay, this temporary restraining order will stay in effect as it is now covered under the divorce. It will be transferred to the applicable section and file. Thank you, that will be all."

"But your honor…" the bald man spoke up. "We need to know …"

"I am not hearing anything more on this. It is not my jurisdiction any longer."

"But your honor, she…"

Judge Lawson looked up, his face red with irritation, "I am **not** hearing any more on this matter!" There was a definitiveness to his words, only to be punctuated with the lowering of the gavel with a resounding thud.

Doesn't look like the judge likes being forced to repeat himself!

The bailiff walked over and stopped between the two tables. He raised his arm and focused on Mike and the rude bald guy. The bailiff's stern eyes expressed an irritation that spoke volumes. Mike and his misspeaking mouthpiece exited the courtroom. I did not move.

Moments later the bailiff relaxed his facial expressions, "Ma'am."

"Thank you."

I turned to walk out, my father handed me my jacket and the officer followed us to the doors.

Upon making it through the courtroom doors I couldn't help but notice Mike, the bald guy, and some woman, were standing only a few feet from the door. I swallowed the fear that flared up within me. Dad and I headed for the exit.

The threesome turned toward us.

"Where are the kids?" the attorney demanded as he strode behind me closer than I liked.

I glared at him over my shoulder and saw Mike was only a stride behind Baldy, as my dad and I neared the entrance. Just then one of the bailiffs walked out into the hall. The men dressed in black dropped back.

Chapter 40

A few months passed and I searched for an apartment to move the kids and myself to. In our small town, there were slim pickin's. I made appointments for two different places but got pushback from the first manager when I asked to put the apartment in my dad's name. "Oh, I don't know if we can do that. You and the kids will be living here, and he won't be," the manager said.

"But I can't have any of this in my name. We're stalking victims. Are you sure it won't work?" I heard the crack in my own voice as I commented.

She shook her head.

"Well, thank you. I'm going to have to look for somewhere they understand and can help me keep my family safe."

I sat in my car for a few minutes – tears dripping, hands shaking.

This is not going well. Why did I think this would work?

The second apartment manager was much more understanding.

"I do understand. I'm glad I can help you. I'll give you this application. Have your dad fill it out. Make sure you get the utilities in his name too. Okay?" She sounded like she knew the safety protocols all too well. "My ex-husband was not a lot of fun either. Back when his abuse was going on we didn't have safe houses to go to." She smiled kindly. "It's good things have changed."

She led me over to look at the apartments which resembled single-family dwellings.

"These are apartments?"

"Yes. It seems that the developer decided that these two- to three-bedroom unattached dwellings were the right makeup of an apartment complex. It works out nice." She unlocked the door of the tan apartment. "This is a two-bedroom. Would it be big enough for you?"

I walked in, noted the small kitchen to my right, checked out the bathroom, then the two bedrooms.

"What's back here?" I asked when I saw a door heading somewhere.

"Oh, it goes out to the backyard." She opened the door and presented the ten-foot deep, thirty-foot wide backyard with the nice high wooden privacy fence. "And you'd have a single-car garage to conceal your vehicle in … or whatever."

"Can I have a dog here?"

"Yes. Yes, you can," the cheer in her voice was so welcoming.

Within a few weeks, we moved in. But not before I made an appointment to meet with a lady to see about the rescue dog, she was looking to re-home. "John wants to help you get some beds for the apartment," Dad explained. "We've checked out some prices and we could get the girls a bunk bed while you and Ethan would have single beds. I can get a new futon mattress for you and then you could have a couch during the day."

"Thanks Dad!"

A couple of weeks after moving in I picked up Brax, the Rottweiler, from a lady who had rescued him from the Animal Shelter in Mojave. The first night the dog stayed with us he laid down in the living room in front of the futon that I converted into my bed at night. I pet him and he settled down. But a couple of hours later, due to my habit of being a light sleeper, I couldn't help but hear him get up. I slid my hand up under my pillow, encircling the grip of my revolver. The moon was bright enough through the kitchen window to illuminate the room. With my heart pounding, I watched the dog go into the girls' room. Less than a minute later he came out and headed across the hall to my son's room. Shortly after that, he came back and laid down in front of my bed. I released my grip on my gun.

"You're a great addition to our family," I whispered.

CHAPTER 40

I reached down and stroked his black coat. He lifted his head, looked at me with his loving peanut brittle-colored eyes, yawned, and laid his head back down.

"Cable, my first Rotty, used to go do perimeter checks too. I bet she's looking down from heaven smiling that you're taking care of her family now," I spoke in a soft soothing tone.

I settled back on my bed, focused on the country music coming out of the radio, and waited for sleep to grace me. I got used to Brax's nightly inspections of *his* kids. One night I woke to a few things well laid out in front of the dog. He had neatly laid his torn-up squeaky toy, by one of the girl's dolls, one of the boy's socks, and one of my socks. I was concerned I would have to scold him, but I noticed only Brax's toy was ripped up and the other items were carefully placed side by side in an orderly fashion, just as he wanted them. He slept contently. I chuckled but knew I had made the right choice. While I continued to hear him, nightly, get up and walk from room to room, gradually my mind allowed me to fall back asleep quickly.

Chapter 41

The children loved to play out front. They had the neighbor kids to play with and this Momma loved the strip of grass between the driveways that ran down toward the street. The tree was a nice touch, too. I tied the end of Brax's leash around the trunk. The neighbor came out his open door.

"You don't mind if I tie him here, do you?"

"No," Mark said with a smile. "He'll make those partiers across the way think twice."

"Yeah, this way no one should approach any of our kids!" I heard the protective glee in my voice.

My smile grew when the 'partiers' walked out their door and looked over at the big dog sitting vigil. They seemed to lock eyes with Brax. Their loud boisterous behavior calmed as soon as they saw him.

A week or so later Bella and I noticed a sheriff's car stop in the middle of the street.

"Momma, I want to go say hi! That's …" Bella cheered as she strolled down the driveway.

She almost made it to the asphalt when the dog raised his head looking ready to pounce as the volume and sternness of Officer Tanner's voice got louder.

"We should let him do his job there first. Then when he's done, I'll let you go say 'hi' to him." She glared back impatiently. "I promise."

CHAPTER 41

Bella trotted back up and sat beside her dog on the grass. A short time later Tanner walked to his car. I stood. So did the dog.

"Stay," I instructed Brax. "Hey there."

A smile graced his face.

"This little girl wants to say hello to you," I informed him with a hint of cheer, "if you have time."

"It's all good." The man crouched, eager to greet the 5-year-old he'd played a part in protecting. "How are you Bella?"

"I'm okay! We live here now!" She pointed to our dwelling.

"And do you like it?" he asked her, but looked up at me, an unease filled his eyes.

"Yes! We've got a dog!" her enthusiasm was contagious.

"I see that. He looks like he's a good boy."

"Can I give you a hug?" the little one asked merrily.

My cheeks flushed red as he glanced up at me for approval. I smiled and brought my shoulders up ever so slightly.

I guess he just got an unexpected request.

"Well ... I'd be honored to get one of your hugs," he said as he shared a hug with the little blonde.

Satisfied, Bella went back up to play by her dog.

"So, when did you move here?" he stood to his full height, his voice and face awash with concern.

"We've been here about three months."

"I didn't know."

"Well," I smiled half sheepishly and half filled with pride, "I guess we've been successful at being hidden in plain sight."

"I guess you have. But it's not the best area for you and your kids," he frowned and glanced over his shoulder at the apartment he'd just left. "I've had complaints of drug activity over there."

I mirrored his frown.

"I know. I've seen.... But it really was the only place in town accepting newbies and ... I've had to put it all under my dad's name. Some folks weren't willing to help us like that. So, I put us here, mid-block."

"Okay. Well, now that I know you're here I'll come by a lot more often. You hear from him lately?"

"No. Not since the times you came in the quilt store to take the reports. By the way, thanks for sending those reports to Colorado. I know they're helping."

"I'm glad. I'd better get going. Let me know if you need anything. Don't hesitate to call." He bobbed his head toward the druggies as he got behind the wheel.

"You betcha. It'd be the least I can do since you've helped me, us, so much. See you later Tanner."

After he pulled away, I rejoined my little one.

It's been so long since there's been so much tranquility in our home.

I beamed inside. But more entertainment was to come. I sat in the lawn chair, saw a set of eyes peering out behind the drapes across the way.

Yes, yah'll are curious now, aren't you. Who do you have livin' across the street from you? I sat up straight and breathed a sigh of relief. *I've done well if Tanner didn't know we were here. I know he's been lookin' after me like a little sister.* I allowed a smile to grow. *Mike doesn't know yet either. Yet.*

Chapter 42

The next morning the phone rang. Not many people had my phone number, so panic did not set in. Plus, I'd been recognizing John's voice, not to mention his number (thanks to caller I.D.), for a decade.

"Hello. Do you know who this is?" There was a playful cheer in John's usual greeting.

"Yeppers. John."

I poured the last coffee from the pot.

"You want to have dinner on Thursday or Friday? My friend, Ben, and I'll be coming back down through there, to get the gooseneck trailer."

"Um ... sure. Let me check with my folks. I'm working both of those nights, but I don't have to work late on Thursday." *A date?*

"How are the beds working out for you and the kids? I hope they're not too uncomfortable."

"No, John. The beds are great. I'm grateful for what you've helped give us."

"Well, you and the kids needed it," humbleness and sincerity laced his words.

"Yeah. You're always treatin' us like we're family."

I smiled as I noticed nothing had changed in the decade we'd known each other.

Sometimes I am amazed at how well we've gotten along. How one of our horse training clients moved to a consistent friend, even though it's been about nine years since we had his gelding in training. It was a friendship that had grown. We'd been over to his ranch for supper. Making supper together. He offered to drive the baby around the block... as if he and I were the couple and Cody was the guest. A light chuckle escaped my throat. And getting to know his teenage daughter. I shook my head, a bit dismayed, but glad for the long-time friendship and now someone who wanted to see me. At least I'm not completely unworthy.

"Okay, see you later this week," John said with cheer.

It was time to head over to the quilt store. With the kids off at school, I pulled out of the drive and stopped at the mailboxes. I was expecting the phone bill but got more. My hands trembled immediately at seeing *his* handwriting.

How the hell did he find us?

Dread washed over me, from my head down to my shaking knees. A queasiness settled in my stomach. My arms felt weak. I looked over one shoulder then the next, afraid to move.

Is he here... now... watching me? How? Maybe it was too easy puttin' everything in Dad's name. Probably. I chastised myself. But thanks to Mike I've no credit or bad credit at best.... I couldn't have done it without Dad and Mum's help. But now what? Oh, there's a letter from the Victims Assistance program. Humm. I wonder what this is.

I walked back around the car and sat behind the steering wheel. The trembling continued. I set *his* envelope and the phone bill on the passenger seat. Unsteady fingers opened the flap on the county envelope. I unfolded it to find a letter:

The children have been approved for a two-thousand-dollar stipend to help with expenses due to the stalking. Enclosed please find the check. We hope it helps with the expenses the stalking has caused.

I wasn't sure when Veronica asked me to fill out the paperwork that there was a source for this kind of assistance.

And... since I'm gonna have to move again. Damn. This sure has come at the right time. It's gonna help me pay for rent and... moving.

CHAPTER 42

I dialed 9-1-1.

"I'd like to report a breach of restraining order. ... Yes... I'm okay. I just need to have an officer come to my job, take a report, and get it on record. Thank you." I gave the operator the address to the quilt store. Deputy Tanner showed up and took the unopened letter and a report.

"When are you going to the divorce hearing?"

"A couple more months, if he doesn't find a way to postpone it again."

"Well, I will send this over to Colorado and maybe it will help."

"Here's to hopin'. Thanks Tanner."

"Keep your eyes peeled. Now that he knows your address again. Okay?"

"Yes sir. I sure will."

Mike was making it easy to show his disregard for the law. Disregard many would not take lightly.

A few weeks later, after John, his friend Ben, and I had gone out for supper, the phone calls came more often. John came down again and he took the kids and I out on a shopping spree. He purchased things I was going to struggle to afford – inline skates that made it so Ethan could join the local hockey league, and clothing all around. It was difficult for me to accept his gifts, but it wasn't the first time John had showered the kids with gifts. He had sent money down just before our last Christmas on the ranch, weeks before the house burnt down. It took some convincing on John's part, but I acquiesced. I knew, that while the seamstress jobs I'd picked up could help me get off of state aid and food stamps, month-to-month expenses were tight. I was still hoping to pick up a horse or two in training.

"Why don't you move up to my ranch? Get out of there. He won't know you guys are up here," John offered. "The kids would love it. I have a couple of horses. You could tune up the old Appy. Jamie's pony is still here. You love it up here. You know that. You always have. Plus, your Psycho dog is still here. And you seem okay with us dating."

When I didn't jump at the offer with a yes he changed up the subject.

"Why'd you name him Psycho again?" he asked. I could almost see him shaking his head over the phone.

"Well, out of the puppies our Cable dog had, only a couple of days after

Ethan was born, the pup we gave you must have felt pushed out of the puppy bowl, so he went off catching and eating grasshoppers. Psycho just seemed to fit him best, at the time."

"And you know he loves you more than he loves me," a bit of disappointment filled John's voice.

"Well, we did keep the pup for five months. He was my pup first," I playfully quipped.

"I still can't believe that time you came to the ranch and Psycho stopped walking with me and stopped listening to me. He would only walk beside you!" John almost laughed the last few words out. "But you should see your boy now. I watched him head out to pasture and take a coyote by the neck, snap it, and leave it laying there in pasture. He's definitely a big boy!"

"Yeah, that Rottweiler Bouvier cross was a positive breeding."

"Getting back to you and the kids moving up here. I am coming down, to give Jaime a car, in a few weeks. Why don't you jump in the rental car and come up here, take a look around, and see if you'd like to move up here," he suggested.

"Give me a few days… let me think about it and …."

I do love that ranch. Almost four hundred acres. Houses are not right on the highway, which will allow us a protective cushion. Only one way onto the ranch really, which I could keep an eye on. The one road in front of the ranch, that runs that full length, but what's up to the East or is it North? I don't remember ever going up that way. Elk, deer, moose, wild turkey, horses, and … and Psycho!

After a chat with my folks a few mornings later, about the letter, Mike knowing where we were, and the safety of their youngest and grandkids, we decided the Idaho ranch was an option.

"Plus, you don't know if he'll continue postponing the darn divorce," my mother said with a frown. "If he's allowed to move on with his life, so are you honey."

"I know. You're right," I said looking out the window, over the pond at the ranch I used to share with my children's father.

It used to be so peaceful here.

CHAPTER 42

I looked to my right. The oak tree the bald eagle had taken to repeatedly perch in came into view. He was not in "his" tree. Not today.

"Does the eagle still come?"

"Yes, he was here yesterday as a matter of fact," my mum shared with a smile I could hear in her voice without turning around.

And off to my left, I could see the top branches of the tree, at the edge of the ranch, where that breeding pair of hawks used to sit together, side by side. I moaned lightly. The Rascal Flats *I'm Movin' On* started "playing" in my head. I sighed.

This is no longer my home either. Another place I feel I don't belong. Damn.

"We can keep the beds here, we'll put 'em here," my dad broke the silence. "… in the spare room you stayed in before you had Emma. We'll keep the kids' mare. She's not eating much. And, this way, you'd have a chance at sleeping through the nights," my dad offered up.

How'd he know I'm still not sleeping through the night?

"But what about Brax?" the longing in my voice stung my ears. "John says, Psycho has had the ranch to himself … and with him being 10 years old, just like Ethan… the boy was born just days before the pups were born…." I reminisced. "It wouldn't be a good idea to bring Brax up there." I vacillated with my dilemma. "You know I wouldn't want to have the dogs fight. Cable's pup and Brax … I wouldn't want either of them to get hurt. What do I do with the dog?"

"We'll cross that bridge when we get to it," Dad reassured.

"You can bring Brax here. He can stay with the kids," my mom added.

"Okay. Whatcha gonna do about the search and rescue barbecue?" I asked, still not sure I was going to make the test trip to Idaho.

"We'll take the kids with us. It's always a kid and family-friendly event," Mom said. "The kids will be fine. Go. See if it's something you will feel safe doing – moving you guys up there. It could be a good spot. Plus, you and John have known each other for over a decade. It's a safe spot."

I looked back at my mother, blinked my eyes a few times in an attempt to adjust to the light change, swallowed, and forced my tight throat to move. Safe. *I need to get us safe.*

And we have loved each other as friends for a long time. Humm.

Chapter 43

While the kids and the dog spent the 4th of July weekend with my folks, John and I drove up to Interstate 90. I had been grinning since we'd pulled into Coeur d'Alene. While it had been about nine years since I'd been up in that area, my mind recognized many parcels. I took note of some of the changes.

The lake at Coeur d'Alene was beautiful with all of that clean dark blue water! I had forgotten how peaceful it made me feel just looking out at something so spectacular. I couldn't help but notice the many hues of the evergreen trees that loomed not far from the banks. And no smog. Still no smog. It nearly took my breath away, even now. The high rise at the resort came into view along with the boats at the dock. A few boats, out on the lake, came into view.

"There'll be more boats out tomorrow. They'll be having a fireworks event then," John informed me as I continued to look out the windows of the car.

Minutes later the familiar barn-red of the Wolf Lodge Inn Restaurant came into view on the north side of the highway. Although I'd never been there, it served to let me know we weren't far from Kingston. The Fourth of July Pass was next. I looked forward to seeing it again – the steepness of the decline, pine trees, and water coming out of cracks in the bedrock that always called to me. Winter water that glistened in the sunlight and often froze in icicle-like formations were not around today with the warm July air, although my mind saw them still. Today, the shimmering liquid played to gravity's demand as it fell to the manmade creeks on the outsides of the four lanes. This served as another landmark for me – let alone for many other travelers over the decades since the Fourth of July Pass was built beginning in 1859.

Once down off the pass the marshy wetlands of Cataldo came into view. I spotted a few Sandhill Cranes amongst the cattails and reeds. The reported oldest building in Idaho – the Cataldo Mission – still stood as the sentry. Its beautiful white porch pillars and the cross welcomed me, just as it had welcomed others, in droves, since the 1850s.

"It's still so pretty up here," I finally broke my awed silence.

Once we exited and crossed the road we followed the asphalt along the river. The two-story historic log-walled Snake Pit Restaurant came into view. I smiled wider.

"Do you remember this place?" John asked.

"You betcha. You're just up around the curve of the road... right?"

"Yes. Only about a mile or so." Although he slowed the car to the posted thirty-five miles per hour, the edge of his property came into view within minutes. "If you'll remember, my ranch comes all the way down here to the bridge and runs all along the road here."

I hadn't remembered that his land came down this far. But the creek and tall cedar trees welcomed me nonetheless. Within a quarter mile, we came to the driveway. John turned in and Psycho got up from his shady vantage point in front of the barn. He met us where the barn's turnoff connected with the driveway. I rolled down the window.

"Hello Psycho."

His ears perked at hearing my voice.

"Hey there boy," John greeted.

At the sound of his human's voice, the dog fell in, beside the car, and trotted up the driveway with us to the first house. He waited for us to exit the car. Going to John first and then me. I stretched my hand out for his inspection. He allowed his nose to touch my palm.

"Hi boy," I said, which caused him to attempt to wag his tail, the tail I had docked within weeks of his birth. It caused a wiggling of his back and

CHAPTER 43

hindquarters. I ran my hand over his head and shoulders. "It's good to see you too boy."

"Let her come in the house."

The comment was directed at the dog who looked up at his owner. Well, at least the man who'd been feeding and caring for him over the last nine years.

"Guess he hasn't forgotten you either," John said as the garage door rolled opened. "We'll go up through here. Let me grab your bag."

"Thanks. Okay Psycho ... I'll be back out, boy," I patted the black and tan dog at the shoulders taking note of his coat.

Hum, the blending of the Rotty and Bouvier gave him a pretty thick shorter coarse top coat – interesting. I bet that helps with the winters.

His mother had had seven pups in that last litter. Not expecting the litter mate, his brother, to get hit by a truck at about a year old, we'd sold or given away all of the other pups. This "pup" was the only one I got to see in his later years.

"Had you ever been in this house?" John asked as we ascended the steps.

"No. I don't think I had. Just in the blue house."

"Well then, welcome to the house," his husky voice was more than hospitable. "It has two bedrooms here on the left." He hesitated at the first door. "I use it as my office." He stepped forward. "This is the extra bedroom and here...." He took our bags into the master bedroom setting mine on the lowboy dresser. "It's only got one bathroom, but you can access it from either the master or the hall. You can put your clothing in this top drawer if you'd like." He motioned to the right.

He continued the tour of the master, bathroom included. I felt school girlish as we stood in his, no wait ... our room.

"Would you like to go get dinner and look at the other house tomorrow?"

"I don't need to eat just yet, but I will let you set the schedule," I remained guest-like.

"Well, then let's go down and check on the horses and you can meet Chico."

"Okay, but I'm gonna use the loo first."

John waited in the kitchen. He smiled as I approached.

"Walking or taking the car?" I inquired.

"Truck, we can take the truck. I like that one better." He smiled. "I wasn't planning on bringing that car home." He frowned. "I just hate that my daughter had those stickers all over that car down there. Did you see that?"

I nodded my affirmation.

"If that's the way she treats things I give her, then she doesn't …." He shook his head. "I just can't see giving her another car to act like a teenager about and childishly mess it up like that," he continued expressing his disapproval.

"I get it. I was a little surprised. It did look like a high schooler's vehicle."

"Well, let's go meet Chico."

We headed back down the stairs and out to the truck. The dog flanked the truck down the drive. We popped out and John gave me a tour of the barn. He showed me the tried-and-true fold-down rectangle feed doors that showed the age and the efficiency of the barn's design.

John walked over to the large rolling door, unlatched it, and slid it sideways. He tucked his tongue, just right, behind his teeth and whistled. A Leopard Appaloosa and a Shetland pony came to the door. He patted his steed on the neck. The pony inspected my outstretched hand before Chico could.

"He's broke to ride but he might need some tuning up. I haven't ridden him in a long time. He's not trained like you guys trained Kohas."

We shared a smile as we both remembered his dark dapple-grey Arabian gelding.

"He was an easy horse to work with," I complimented. "Sure miss gettin' the chance to ride his mum."

"Yeah. That damn dirty needle that infected her hip and damaged those muscles really messed her up."

"Whatever happened with that?"

"Well, that letter and information you guys provided helped that lawyer sue the shit out of the vet. She ended up breaking her leg out in pasture."

My smile fell to a frown, as the loss of a beautiful well-bred mare depressed me.

CHAPTER 43

"She gave you a sweet colt. One that I remember watchin' his knee darn near break level with his shoulder as he easily came up through the pasture." My mind filled with the first time I saw the graceful way the gelding moved. "What'd you end up doing with him?"

"Sold him. Turned a pretty penny, too."

"I bet."

"Okay. Let's go to dinner. Snake Pit okay?"

"Sure. It's been forever since I've been there!"

He opened the passenger door and I slid in. A few minutes later we pulled up in front of the historic building. He opened both the car and the restaurant's doors for me, reminding me that being a gentleman never goes out of style.

"Let's sit at the bar. Joe will be with us in a minute," John suggested.

"Hey there John. Hope you haven't been waiting long!" Joe said apologetically. "And you must be Kathleen."

He offered his hand. We shook.

"Yes," I smiled. *Wow... he told his friends I was coming. Oh shoot, did I just blush?*

"I'm Joe. My wife, Mary, and I own this place. Have you ever been here before?"

"Yes, I believe so. But not for about nine years."

"Well, it hasn't changed much," humble pride accented his words. "Why don't you walk around? Take a look. You are the only ones here right now."

I navigated between tables and chairs. My eyes darted from one trophy-style Elk head-and-neck mount to a couple of different Deer head-and-neck mounts hung on the walls. It was a quirky place with all of the mining hardhats that hung on the log crossbeams, old-time decorated bar trays depicting women drinking, and the old tree knot lamps on the mantle of the double-sided fireplace. It looked to be built out of local rock. The nostalgia helped with the charm of the place.

"Have these Elk and Deer come from around here?" I inquired.

"Yes, but many of them were here when we purchased this place," Joe offered up. "This was an old whore house. The gals would hang out over the railing upstairs and service the local miners, so it seems. I've been told it was a pretty busy place in her day. Now it's where we live."

"It's a bit cold up here for snakes… and I'm sure I'm not the first one to ask, but why is it called the Snake Pit?"

"I think it refers to the 'ladies' of the brothel," Joe added. "I don't think the fine upstanding women from around here, nor the Eastern Catholics from the Cataldo Mission, liked the gals being here. Especially when the red light over those steps, outside, was on."

We all grinned at that.

After a few drinks, a homestyle dinner, and a great conversation, John drove us back to the ranch. I put my clothing in the drawer cleared for me. I pulled my satin nightgown and toothbrush out. Setting the nightie on the bed, before going into the bathroom.

"Do you mind if I jump in the shower?" I asked.

John looked up and smiled.

"I promise, I'll make it real quick in case you want one too."

"No. Make yourself at home," he sounded pleased.

Minutes later John took his turn in the shower, coming out only wrapped in a towel. He was more interesting than the book I was reading. It was nice to be in his arms, in his bed, making it ours.

Chapter 44

I woke early, as usual. Before I opened my eyes, I took notice of a light snoring. He sounded so content.
It might take a little while to get used to that. I smirked.
The lack of draperies on the large window above the bed bathed the room in a warm light. Instead of tossing and turning, I slipped out of bed. I was grateful for the thick carpet that muffled my careful footsteps. Once in the kitchen coffee grounds were not easy to find and I was afraid of the old complaining hinges would wake John. I walked to the living room windows. I gazed out at the pasture.

It's still so peaceful out here. My breathing was deep and relaxed. *Only one way into the ranch. You can see people coming up the highway ... for almost a mile. Its quarter-mile driveway... that will be helpful.*

I took a cleansing breath even as the morning's near silence was broken by John as he cleared his throat and the bed creaked. Moments later he came down the hall.

"Good morning," I said with a smile.

He responded in like kind.

"I hope I didn't wake you. I'm... just an early riser."

He wrapped his arms around my waist. Pulled me to him.

"No. You didn't wake me."

Our lips met.

"I would have made coffee, but I don't know where things are yet."

"Let me show you."

He took me by the hand and led me to the kitchen.

"While this is the pantry…" he pointed to the closed door, "I have the grounds in this."

He opened the cabinet to the left of the sink. The hinges creaked loudly in the mountain silence.

Glad I didn't go looking for it before he woke up.

He made a pot of coffee as I leaned against the peninsula. As the beautiful black liquid dripped into the carafe, I opened the cabinets to the right.

"The cups are right here," he shared as he reached for the cup tree next to the maker.

"Oh!"

Minutes later he poured the cups near full and handed me one.

"Thank you."

We walked back to the front room and sat on the couch.

"I figure we will go in for breakfast, meet up with Ben and Andee, they wanted to say hi to you, and then we'll go over to the blue house."

"Okay. Sounds great. Remind me… Andee is…?"

"Ben's wife."

After a sip, I smiled.

"Ben's wife, yes. Andee. Okay."

~~~~****~~~~

We met at the Snake Pit for breakfast.

Wow, they're so welcoming. So cheerful. So, kind. It's been so long since someone seemed genuinely eager to meet me.

"How long have they been married?" I asked as we drove back to the ranch.

"Oh a few years. Their age difference never seems to be an issue."

"Well, that's always a good thing." I chuckled knowing John was at least 20 years my senior.

"I had a renter here for a while," John said as he pulled up to the blue

CHAPTER 44

house. "They just moved out. It was a lady I know and her teenage kid." He stuck the key in the lock. "I hope she left it clean. She's usually a pretty clean lady."

We entered and John became my tour guide again.

"Down here, I figure you can set up your sewing area and a place for the kids to play."

I nodded.

"This is where the washer and dryer are."

"That's a deep orange."

"Yeah, the house was the highlight of the seventies, when they built it."

We turned and climbed the stairs.

"We have this bathroom for the kids to use," he continued the tour. "I figure the girls can share this room and the boy can have this one." He hesitated momentarily…. "And this will be our bedroom. We have our own bathroom here too."

The dark red carpet was not as dated as the light pink tub and tile. I smiled my approval before he led the way back to the TV room.

"See we have this nice wood stove here."

"Do you heat with just the fireplaces and wood stove?"

"Mostly."

We walked through a second opening through the formal dining room, past the large table and chair set..

"And this is the kitchen."

The burnt orange Formica with golden tile accents confirmed the date of the house.

"I was told this kitchen was featured in a magazine back in '72. It was the state of the art back in those days," pride filled his words.

"I bet it was."

"We have a small pantry, and this door leads to the back steps and where we had the pool before. But we weren't using it, so I had it filled in with dirt a long time ago. I have a small loan payment of $300 a month. Because I pay cash for everything, I couldn't get credit, so I took the loan out to build credit," he smiled.

Why does he pay cash for everything?

"That and the power bills are all I have. Do you think you can run a household off of three thousand a month?"

I tried not to let my jaw drop.

Three thousand a month! Damn, I've been runnin' one off of five hundred! I swallowed the lump in my throat. "Yes. Yes, I've been running off a lot less!"

"Okay, so let's move you and the kids up here. You'll be safe and they will love it here as much as you do," he encouraged.

I smiled, nodded, and accepted.

"Here, put this in your wallet."

He handed me a credit card with my first name and his last name on it. You can use this when you need it.

He took me to the airport in Spokane the next morning so I could pack things up at the apartment.

"I'll drive the truck down next week and we'll come on back up. Is that okay?" he said before kissing me.

"Yes. I don't have much to pack up."

"Great. The kids will still have time to have some fun before school starts."

Chapter 45

Getting back to my children took a bit of planning. The plane landed in Burbank and my sister, Sheryl, picked me up.

"Thanks for comin' to get me."

"No problem. Mom's gonna meet us at my house and drive you the rest of the way."

Small talk was made, and I brought Sheryl up to speed on the motivations for me to move. She was filled in by the time we met up with our mom. As I changed cars, I felt like a hushed package being shuffled from one pickup to the next.

But in an hour and a half, I'd be back with my beauties — I focused.

Kisses and hugs were shared between my beauties and me. The dog came up for his hellos too. We didn't spend much time with my parents. We got in my car and I took the kids and dog back to our apartment.

"Mommy, are we moving?" Emma's enthusiasm was contagious.

"Well," I glanced at my kids huddled around the dog in our apartment living room, "would you like to live back on a ranch? Or should we stay in this apartment?"

The girls got up and started jumping around the room, squeals accented their movements.

"John told Grandpa he's got horses for us to ride," Emma shared with a cheer as I realized my parents seemed to have been preparing the kids this weekend.

"Yes, I saw them this weekend. He has a spotted one, an Appaloosa, and a pony," I explained.

"A pony ... like Lady?" Ethan showed some interest.

"Well, it's brown instead of chestnut, but yes like your Pony Lady.

His interest was piqued. We shared a smile. I continued to try to get the kids excited on this next phase of our ever-changing journey.

"And you girls will share a room. Ethan, you can have your own."

"Where will you stay?" Bella asked.

Semi-prepared for the question, I tried not to hesitate.

"Across the hall in the room with John." I waited unsure what they would say.

"Okay!" The simple answer sufficed my youngest.

With no other questions, the kids quieted down and went out to play.

The next morning, I informed my landlady about the impending move for safety reasons. As expected, she was supportive, after I told her about the letter. The packing – repacking actually – was easy.

"We'll put the bunk bed in the spare room here on the ranch," my mom said with a smile. "You know... in case we have others come down for visits." Her smirk was entertaining, especially because so many think Tehachapi *is so far away.*

"It'll be good to have my bed couch for downstairs at the ranch in Idaho." I beamed. "Maybe yah'll can come up for Thanksgiving or..."

"Yeah, or maybe for hunting," the glee in my father's voice was childlike. "John and I've already been talkin' about it."

"Okay, we're all loaded up. Ready to go?" John said.

"Let me do one last walk-through from front to back and I'll be out," I responded. "Yah'll say your goodbyes to grandma and grandpa."

My walkthrough yielded nothing. I stepped from the kitchen into the garage. It was as empty as the day before we moved in. I set the keys on the kitchen counter and turned the lock on the door before shutting it for the last time.

"Okay, up top Lovies." I opened the passenger side doors of the double cab of John's pick-up truck. "Get your hugs first kids."

Hugs were shared, including with Brax before the kids climbed up in the back seat.

"Travel safe," my dad's voice was instructional, yet... as he wrapped his arms around me, he reassured me, "We'll meet up for the divorce hearing. You won't be going alone."

"Thanks Dad."

Mom and I embraced. While it felt like there was some frailness to her light five-foot six-inch frame beneath my arms, I knew that her strength lay in helping her daughter get her grandkids safe.

"I'm sure glad you fell in love with Brax too Mom. Thanks for takin' him. He'll protect you too."

I reached down and embraced our four-legged protector.

"Thanks boy."

He sat beside my mom seeming to understand and accept the handoff, better than me. I sighed before forcing myself to focus on our safety and some happier times.

Chapter 46

The day-and-a-half drive came and went as an adventure the kids and I had become accustomed to finding in each move.

"Well, here we are," John said as he pulled in the drive.

"This is a pretty place," Emma enthusiastically chimed in. "I don't think I've ever seen such a pretty ranch."

"Well, only Ethan has been here before, so it's all going to be new," I assured her.

"You won't remember this place much though Ethan you were just a babe in arms when your mom and dad brought you here with them for dinner one night," John shared as he pulled up the drive to the first house.

"Who's that?" Bella asked.

"It's the dog your mom and dad gave me," John answered.

"That's Psycho! Remember me tellin' you about 'im?" I chimed in. "It's the dog that was born the same week as your brother."

"Let's get you guys settled into the house and we'll go down to meet the horses after a while," John announced as he put the truck in park. "And don't worry, he doesn't bite ... unless he's real hungry," the snicker that accented his words was lost on my son.

Ethan having been bitten by a dog years before, hesitated as I opened the back door.

"Son, it's okay. He already knows you," I waited for the boy's eyes to meet mine. "He's a brother to your Toby dog you've heard so much about. And,

CHAPTER 46

they're both sons of your Cable dog," I hoped my cheerfulness would ease his worries as I reached down to pet the big dog. "Hey there boy." The dog turned his head and sniffed the boy's shoe. "See, he likes you ... just like when you were little."

My son accepted the gentle welcome of the dog and got out of the truck.

Once in the house John showed the kids around and explained we would move to the big house in a day or two.

"You guys hungry?" John said.

"Yeah," emanated musically from the kids.

"Well, let's jump in the truck, feed the horses, and then go on down to get a bite."

Eagerly the kids headed out the front door and down the steps. We pulled up the rear. The kids patiently waited to get in the truck.

"You want to ride in the back of the truck?" John asked with a healthy grin.

Wide-eyed the kids looked at me. I smiled and nodded.

The tailgate was lowered, the kids were lifted up, taking seats on the wheel wells. Which garnered an approving smile from John.

"What about Psycho?" Bella asked.

"He'll follow us down all on his own," he informed her.

Once at the barn, John whistled for his horses to come in out of the pasture and then opened the back barn door.

Emma and Bella hung tight to John while I stood with my hands on Ethan's shoulders.

"See the pony?" I said in a hushed voice.

He nodded. I wrapped my arms around him, and we shared a deep cleansing breath.

"You don't have to get near them right now. We'll come down this week and meet them, okay?"

I felt him relax as he leaned back against me.

"Okay, let's go get some dinner," John cheered on.

"Where we goin'?" Emma asked as the back passenger doors were opened.

"This fun place called the Snake Pit."

"Do they have real snakes there?" The excitement in my daughter's voice was undeniable.

I grinned. "Buckle up. It's a bit of a ways up the road."

"Okay," was the unanimous response.

"They might have some snakes there... we'll have to wait and see," John informed.

I rolled my eyes and pursed my lips but couldn't help notice the three smiling faces in the back seat.

John chose a table near the big fireplace and proudly introduced the kids to Mary and Joe.

"It's nice to meet you, we've been looking forward to it for a while now," Mary welcomed.

"Do you have snakes here?" Emma asked.

"Nope, they aren't on the menu anymore," a smirk graced Joe's grandfatherly face.

"Okay," Emma sounded disappointed, as if she had been planning to order snake, right off the menu.

I know she would have ... if they offered it. After all, my 8-year-old was fearless more often than not.

Before 8:30, the tired kids bedded down in the one guest bed.

"We'll start moving over into the blue house tomorrow. Sleep well," John said as he left me to tuck them in.

"I'm just across the hall. The bathroom is across the hall too."

My kids' heavy eyelids warmed my heart.

"Anyone need to go to the loo before I turn the light out? Bella?" A trio of shaking heads gave me my answer. "Okay." I kissed them goodnight. Bella wrapped her arms around my neck, tightly. "I love you too," I responded to her silent comment. She released her loving grip. "I'll see you in the morning." I paused at the door, my fingers on the light switch. Three beauties, all content, settling in shouldn't be too bad for them. "I love you guys. Night."

I heard yawning — assured snoring and smooth shallow breathing would

CHAPTER 46

follow.

I pushed the switch down. The lack of streetlights brought a comforting darkness to the room. The hush of ranch noises, or the lack thereof, became the soothing lullaby my babies were accustomed to.

Chapter 47

I woke before everyone in the house and made coffee. I will never know if the soft drip, drip, drip, or the comforting nutty smell of the coffee woke them. Nonetheless, the footfalls of my beauties announced them.

"Good morning," I said in a mellow whisper, hoping it would encourage them to use their low-volume voices.

It worked. Hugs were shared instead of excited loudness.

"Would you guys like some coco?" Nods were my answer. "Okay." I set off to get that done. "You guys can sit on the stools on the other side of the counter, there." The cocos were ready. I poured myself a cup of coffee. "We'll get dressed, after a bit, and you guys can come down with me and we can feed the horses ... if you'd like."

Again, nods.

After meeting the horses and playing with the cat we noticed John was pulling up at the barn.

"Hello," his deep voice beckoned.

The girls ran to him as he came into the barn. He sported a wide smile.

"Hope you don't mind." I shrugged. "We fed the horses after I introduced them again, to the kids... didn't want to wake you."

"Did Chico let you pet him?" John asked.

"He did!" the girls excitedly answered together.

John glanced over at the boy, raised his eyebrows, and waited for a response.

CHAPTER 47

"Ethan was working on makin' friends with the pony," I filled the silence. "The pony and Chico may take a few days to make friends with, don't you worry," John encouraged. "How about we go get breakfast, move into the blue house, and then go grocery shopping to get food for us all?"

The kids looked back and forth between John and me. I smiled letting them know the plan was acceptable. We got in the truck and headed to the Snake Pit.

Before the day was over, we had deposited boxes in the lower-level room, broke down the beds, and set them up in the blue house. Grocery shopping was done in Pinehurst.

Chapter 48

"We forgot to go by the school yesterday. Can you show me where it is today?" I asked John.

"Sure. They'll be going to the one in Pinehurst, just like Jamie did." A proud smile came upon his face each time he spoke about his daughter. "I'll drive you by there today and show you guys, it's over near the store."

The kids were eating cereal at the kitchen peninsula when John brought up rafting.

"So... I have this raft in the shop. Would you guys like to go rafting on the river right across the road from the house tomorrow?"

Wide-eyes, smiles, and mumbled 'yeses' could be heard over the spoons and crunching.

"Can we?" Ethan asked.

He looked from John to me and back. Glee filled the boy's eyes.

I raised my eyebrows, smiled, and nodded.

"We'll go look later this afternoon. Your mom has some things she needs to check out in town, like your school and the store. Then we can have some fun. We may have to inflate the boat before we use it."

Smiles were shared all around.

The small-town school was off the main drag of Pinehurst. The grocery store was a couple of blocks from the school. The quaint mountain town breathed a welcome into my lungs. We stocked up on a limited amount of

CHAPTER 48

soda, ice, and munchies for the rafting as well as fixings for meals for the next couple of days, including steaks for John to barbecue. He had grabbed a six-pack of long necks and a bottle of wine.

As the afternoon rolled around, we found ourselves in the large steel-sided shop past the barn. The kids surveyed all of the equipment – the tractor, riding lawn mower, tools, and recreational toys. They were different toys than we had on the ranch in Colorado. We had been focused on purchasing tools related to providing a living for the family with limited recreational toys.

"See, I've got this raft and these oars," the cheer in John's voice fostered excitement in the children. "We'll inflate it with the compressor, put it in the truck and you and your mom can float down the river tomorrow."

"Do you still have the snowmobiles?" I queried as I noticed my older girl spying the skis and poles hung on the wall.

A frown appeared on John's face.

"No. We just never got enough snow to use them. It really doesn't snow that much here."

"Let's go up and get ready for supper," John suggested.

"Don't we need to feed the horses?" Emma asked.

"No. They have enough feed in the pasture." John smiled at the girl's attention to detail.

I beamed, glad to see the responsibility of my children shine through. John put the brushes back in the barn and we headed up to the house. He wanted to treat us to barbecue steaks and we were not going to say no.

At the end of the night, I tucked the kids in with little effort or complaints, they settled in and fell asleep quickly.

The next morning, we fed the horses before ourselves and did some chores around the house before it was river time.

"Go get your suits on. I'll grab some towels to put in the truck, for when we get out," I instructed the kids. I donned shorts and a tank top before accepting the small ice chest from John.

Soon we were all down in the shop. The air compressor hummed, and John asked Ethan to help him air up the boat. My eyes widened.

How will he know if there's enough air in it?

Until he put his foot on the side of the raft and stepped down, I couldn't tell there wasn't enough air in it. Minutes later he pushed on the rounded side again. It had more resistance. It bounced back instead of collapsing under the weight of his foot.

"Okay, let's put it up in the back of the truck. Bella, will you hold the oars please?" John asked, not leaving out the littlest one.

He looked at me. Following his lead. I grabbed the rope that encircled the boat.

"One, two, three." We lifted in unison and my son stepped up steadying the rear of the boat as we put it in the back of the truck.

"Thanks Lovie."

He beamed with pride. So did John.

"Before we go, we need to get you guys in these life vests," John said as he walked to the metal shelving unit. "Come on over here. Let's try these on you." He motioned to the children. "Keep those buckled up the entire time, okay...."

The kids all nodded.

"You want one?" he asked me.

I shook my head. And with that we all got in the cab of the truck. John drove over the bridge up North of the ranch. Then he turned right, along the other side of the North Fork of the Coeur d'Alene River. He seemed to enjoy telling us all about the area as he played tour guide describing this and that.

"This is a campground that sometimes gets flooded out, in the Spring, but is a nice place and seems busy a lot," he explained.

"This is above the ranch, right?" I asked.

"Yes. You can't see any of this from the ranch." He pulled over to the side of the road. "This looks like a good place to get you guys into the water."

Oh... is he not rafting with us? Butterflies seemed to take flight in my stomach. I did my best not to let my surprise show on my face.

"Okay, remember where I showed you that the river comes along that piece of my property on the other side of the road?'

CHAPTER 48

"Where the ponds are?" I responded.

"Yes."

I nodded.

"I'll be there waiting for you guys. It'll take you a couple of hours to float down there. But I will be there to bring you guys back to the ranch."

We disembarked the truck and walked down the path to the river. We adults held on to the raft while the kids got in. The oars and the ice chest were next. I got in last while John steadied the inflatable.

He let go.

I started stroking the water with the paddle. The current took more control of the boat than I had hoped for. Patient concern covered Ethan's face. I couldn't get the raft to move the way I wanted it to ... away from the bank.

"Have you ever done this before?" he decided to ask.

"Nope."

Focused on getting me and the raft to speak the same language ... I did not look up. Adrenaline pushed the excitement laced with determination, and a bit of panic through my veins. The current was swirling in a small alcove. I paddled harder and learned to paddle my children to safety. Admittedly, I was glad the water was only four feet deep.

"I can get out and push the raft if I have to," I told myself more than him.

"Really?"

"Yeah. No." I increased my strokes and started the boat to move away from the dirt wall. "I've got it though. No worries." Okay... I was a little worried. But just then my son put an oar into the water on the other side of the six-man boat. "That's it, son. We've got this." Without looking up at the nervous man I said, "See. We've got this. See you in a couple of hours."

Ethan and I managed to get the grey vessel out into the near middle of the four-foot-deep clear water.

"See..." a trace of trepidation still tinged my voice. "We've got this, you guys."

My anxiety subsided as my boy and I managed to steer the raft. The giggles heard over the next couple of hours were not just from my beauties as we were not the only ones floating down the North Fork of the Coeur d'Alene River. A couple of hours later I spotted John. He was on the left bank motioning for me to head his way.

"Thank you for that!" Ethan was the first to express his appreciation.

It's wonderful to see the kids relax, have fun, and not be afraid... I think I made a good move God. Thank you for your guidance and ... for putting this man back in our lives more fully.

Chapter 49

Dad and I got into Colorado Springs Airport within thirty minutes of each other.

"You already get the rental?" I asked as we waited for my bag to come around the carousel.

He jingled the keys. Within minutes we both had coffees and were headed out of the parking garage.

"Is the one-fifteen the easiest way to get there?" He sought clarification as he drove.

"Yeppers."

Forty-five minutes later we were in our hotel room.

"Hey, we've got about twenty minutes before we need to be at the attorney's," I reported once in the room.

"Okay, I'm gonna put my feet up for a few," Dad said as he plopped on the closest bed.

We made it to the lawyer's office, papers in hand, just in time.

"She'll be right with you," her secretary said.

Within minutes a lady with long blonde hair emerged from behind the inner office door.

"Kathleen?"

"Yes ma'am." I stood.

"Come on in," she welcomed. "Please sit." She motioned to the two chairs opposite her desk. "It's nice to finally meet you. Did you…"

"Yes ma'am. Here you go." I handed her my folder.

She reviewed it in silence.

"You did all of this by yourself?" cheerful surprise filled her voice.

"Yes ma'am."

My cheeks flushed and my dad smiled with pride.

"Well, because you did all of this you've saved yourself five hundred. So, it'll be only a thousand."

"Do you mind if I write you a check?" Dad chimed in.

"This is my dad, Dory Kline."

I motioned.

The attorney smiled. Looked back and forth between father and daughter.

"A check, yes sir, that would be fine. Are you planning on going to the property and making sure all is how it should be?"

Dad and I exchanged glances.

"I guess we could do it right after this," I answered.

"Can you call someone and make sure he's not there?" she queried.

"Yes," I said. "I can call the ranch number. The Realtor is waiting for a call too."

"Call for a civil standby also, please!" she stressed as she perused at the court documents. "Let's call now… can you?" she insisted.

"Yes."

She offered her office phone for the call.

"Hello."

"Suzanne?"

"Hey there Kathleen," the cheer she shared now and over the last seven years of our friendship made me feel loved.

"You livin' back out at the ranch or did I call the wrong number?"

"Yeah, I'm back out here, keeping an eye on things."

"Well, at least I know things are being looked after then." I smiled. "Do you mind if my dad and I come out? I need to have Randy come to evaluate the ranch. He might want to purchase or sell the property for me."

"Um…."

"The divorce hearing is tomorrow, and the attorney needs my valuations."

"No. Come on out. It's all clear."

CHAPTER 49

"Okay dear. We'll be out about two."

As I handed the lawyer the receiver she smiled. She put up a hand.

"Why don't you call this Randy to confirm he can meet you."

I dialed his number and got confirmation for 2:00 p.m.

It was then that she accepted the handset back and dialed the Sheriff's Department.

"My client needs a civil standby. Can you have someone meet her and her father at 2:00 p.m.?" She gave dispatch the address.

"Oh yes! I'll get someone else out there to meet her," I could hear the cheerful and friendly voice on the other end of the phone.

Must be someone who's picked up the line and helped me before. I smiled as a bit of home-grown relief grew within me. *It is nice to be home ... kind of.*

"I want you to call me after you two leave. Let me know that what you see is what he's agreed to take... only."

"Yes ma'am."

"Then I'll see you at the courthouse tomorrow at 9:45."

We ended the visit but not before I gave her my cell number and a nice handshake. Dad and I walked out.

"Well, it sounds like you picked a good attorney," he said dryly.

A half smile grew on my face.

"Yeah. Let's just drive out to the ranch. I don't want to be late," I requested, knowing this was no time to be on Dad's casual time schedule.

"Okay," he said as he checked his hip for his service piece.

Once in the gates, my head was on a swivel. Dad parked beside the single-wide rental. My smile grew with each step of my dog who walked up to the unfamiliar truck.

"Hey there boy," I said through the unrolled window.

Coojoe wagged his stubby tail so enthusiastically the full-body quake interrupted his walking. I got out of the truck, crouched, and wrapped my arms around him.

"Hey buddy," I said as he placed his head in the crook of my neck.

"Hey girl!"

"Hello Suzanne," I stood to embrace my friend and previous employee.

"It's good to see you." Her embrace was filled with love. "Do you remember my dad?"

"I do. Hi Mr. Kline!" her bubbly cheer lightened my mood, as had been the case over the years.

Minutes later a truck and cruiser pulled up. The real estate agent and an officer got out of their respective vehicles. Introductions and explanations were made before we headed to the barn. The five of us, counting my dog, headed for the barn. Suzanne went back into the mobile home.

Randy and I led the way as the cop and my father followed behind me. My heart warmed and fear subsided after I climbed through the two-wire fence as my dog resumed his position to my left. He kept step with me.

"So this is a ten-stall barn, but this…" I pointed to my left toward the metal shed, "we used for hay storage and a mare and foal run."

It was then Coojoe, without missing a step, turned his head toward the first section of the shed row. His protective warning was not ignored. Glad for my peripheral vision, I saw Mike cowering in the doorless second stall that we used as a tack room. My pulse quickened. My jaw tightened. Anger surged through me.

"He's in the stall right there," I said over my shoulder to the officer as I motioned toward my soon-to-be ex.

Effer… you can't effing hide! Not when my dog rats you out. I snickered. *You may be feeding him but I'm still his human.*

"Got it ma'am," the officer said as he walked over and spoke with Mike.

Determined to not let him get the best of me, I continued. A deep breath helped me focus.

"Now," I continued explaining the pluses about the ranch. We neared the end of the stalls, "these rafters are for sale.…"

"Are they?" Randy's interest was piqued. "What's the span?"

"Thirty feet. They were ordered to span this." I pointed toward the hole Mike had carved out of the knoll with the tractor he just *had to have.*

Just another pipe dream. He was never going to build a home for us. Bile bubbled up into my throat. *Just another unfinished project. Another time he didn't follow through. What a waste of money. A waste of hope. Another lie.*

CHAPTER 49

"Are they still usable?" Randy noticed the darker shades of the top rafter.

"Yes. They're still banded ... you might need to replace the top one, but they've only sat out a couple of winters."

"How much you want for them. And yes, I could use them."

"Well, I paid three grand ... so...."

"How about fifteen hundred?"

"How about two?" I countered.

"Seventeen."

Knowing I had the receipt to prove the original cost and I needed the funds I didn't vacillate for long.

"I'll get you a check before we leave today," he said able to sweeten the offer.

"Great," I said trying to not sound too eager. "They're yours."

We walked around the end of the tenth stall.

"Do all of these panels come with it too?"

"Yes sir! I intended more but it seems he's loaded some on the trailer." My mare, Cee Cee, raised her head at the sound of my voice. I climbed up and over the rails. "And so does the tire round pen over there." I pointed to the far side of the arena.

Within a few strides, by both the mare and me, I rubbed my hand across her smooth chestnut coat before I wrapped my arms around her neck. She blew air out of her nostrils and lowered her head, relaxed.

Randy continued asking questions as the other two mares came closer.

"Hey girls," I greeted them as I pet the mares I had bred for and foaled out.

Cee Cee pushed her way back beside me. I resumed focusing my attention on her.

"It's eighty acres, fenced on three sides, its own well, a ten-stall barn, arena, round pen, a double-wide, and a single-wide ... right?" Randy confirmed.

"Yes sir. And we're the only ones out here on the two thousand-ish acres," I informed the Realtor of the additional benefits to this property.

I noticed the officer walk up and stood beside my father at the end of the arena. We made eye contact.

"It's okay," he mouthed.

I smiled as I hoped it all was.

"Okay girl. I gotta go."

My mare picked up her left front hoof placing it down on top of my foot. I pushed her shoulder lightly… but nothing. I repeated with more force. She refused to budge. I shoved her shoulder as I scraped my foot out from under her weight. I heard snickering from just outside the arena.

"I guess she doesn't want me to leave," I said shaking my head.

"I guess not!" Randy said enjoying the exchange.

I limped over to the panel before climbing out over it. The chestnut mare lowered her head, seeming to pout. She mirrored what I felt in my heart as I left her behind. As the five of us walked back to the vehicles the officer stayed close to me, ensuring my safety. Mike remained out of sight.

"I'm just going to say goodbye to my ranch hand," I said over my shoulder, as I hesitated before we got to the vehicles.

The three men stopped and waited outside the single-wide, Coojoe continued escorting me.

"You'll keep an eye on my Coojoe…" I crouched and lovingly stroked his head as he leaned into my leg. "…won't you?" my voice quivered.

"Of course," I heard the genuineness in Suzanne's voice.

Tears welled in my eyes as much for leaving Coojoe behind as Suzanne and my home, again, as I readied to go back into hiding after the hearing tomorrow. Hugs were shared between my long-time friend and me. I turned and faltered in my steps as I looked around my old dwelling once more.

"See you…." I said, instead of good-bye.

She kept the dog inside with her.

"Thank you," I said to the deputy after exiting the house. "I am so glad you were here. I …."

"Yes ma'am. I am glad I was here too. But he's not going to bother you anymore today."

I smiled uncomfortably.

"I'll follow you out."

"Thank you."

CHAPTER 49

Randy handed me a check.

"I'll wait to cash this until I am sure I'm granted all of this by the judge. Okay?"

"Oh, yes. You said your hearing is tomorrow... right?"

"Yes."

"Okay. You'll let me know when I can pick them up?"

"Yes. Thanks for coming out and ... for helping me with this."

"I'll send you the listing papers and all, later."

With that my father drove me off the ranch, for the last time.

The next morning the attorney called me at 8:30.

"We've had a change of plans. Can you meet me here instead of the courthouse?"

"Sure."

Chapter 50

Instead of sitting outside a courtroom, my father and I now sat on the off-side of my attorney's desk, again. Stomach acid bubbled up in my throat as we waited for the unknown.

"It seems your husband had a heart attack yesterday," she informed. "We are waiting for a call from his attorney now, but I don't think we'll be going to court today."

"What?" Disbelief washed over me. "He was fine yesterday." I scowled. *That is awfully convenient.* I silently screamed as my jaw muscles tightened. *We're never gonna get this divorce completed!*

"Pretty convenient though, don't you think?" she kibitzed while searching my face for a reaction.

She sounded like she doubted the validity of this claim, too. Hmm.

"Guess he didn't like the cop stoppin' and talkin' with him yesterday," a sarcastic snicker escaped my lips. "Tellin' him to stay away from me... I bet... but..."

Fact or stall tactic? The debate raged inside of me. *He had a stent put in his heart, years ago. But....*

The lawyer cocked her head and raised an eyebrow just as her desk phone rang. She raised an index finger to her lips looking at me square in the eyes and depressed the speaker phone option with the other.

I nodded, agreed to remain quiet, then looked to my right. My father barely moved his head off center as he acknowledged understanding in silence.

CHAPTER 50

"Yes, hello Mr. Cohen. Have you located your client?" She waited for opposing counsel to enlighten her.

"My client is in the hospital at St. Thomas More in Cañon City," Mr. Cohen reported with a somber tone.

"Well, would you like me to meet you there and we run the papers up to him, it's only a few blocks away? We could get this settled today...."

We all anticipated the response. But just as quickly as my hopes were raised, that this could be concluded, Mike's lawyer responded.

"Oh goodness, no! I don't want to cause him another heart attack," Mr. Cohen couldn't hide his concerns.

"Well," a chuckle escaped her lips, "at least he'd be in the right spot if he did!"

I stifled my laugh.

"No. No. No... we're going to have to reschedule. My client said the results from his blood gases are not back yet."

I could almost see opposing counsel shaking his head.

"Okay, if you insist. I will agree to set a new date. Will you contact the court and then let me know what date they have chosen? But let's not drag this out, the kids need to be put in school soon."

I smiled at her clever and rightful leveraging.

"Well, it would be best if my client knew where the kids were? She's only got a P.O. Box listed."

I proudly jutted my chin toward the man's voice and shimmied my shoulders in defiance.

"It's a tight fit Mr. Cohen, but with your client's history ... I'd've kept even that address from him if I could have."

"Hum." He held the open line in case more was to be revealed. When he got nothing, he said, "I will call the courts now."

"Thank you. I look forward to hearing back from you and the court soon." She reached out and disconnected the call. "Well... you heard it. I wonder how we can verify this?" she inquired.

"I can call the hospital," I offered.

Doubt filled her eyes.

"After all... I am his wife... still... as of today." I scrunched my nose and shrugged my shoulders.

"Good idea. You think it'll work?" my attorney asked.

"Um... well, let's try."

"Do you know the number?"

"No, but if you've got the yellow pages...."

"Oh, yes."

She turned in her chair and swiveled back toward me with the all too familiar small-town directory in her outstretched hand.

I flipped to the yellow pages. She sat, fingers hovering over the number pad on her phone.

"Two, eight, five," as I spoke, she depressed the numbers, "two thousand." She handed me the receiver. "Cardiac nurse's station please?" I managed a kind tone.

"Yes, this is Sister Sophia."

It was the same sweet nurse that had tended to me a few years ago when my acid reflux mimicked a heart incident and the one that had been assigned to Cody his first time on that ward.

"Yes... hello Sister. This is Mrs. Cody Walton. I heard my husband was in hospital and our children are quite worried about their father. We are not in Cañon City at this time so I was wondering if you could give me an update... so I can tell the children?"

"Oh, yes. He is here. I am his nurse assigned to him at this time."

"It's good he has you looking after him again. Did he...?"

"No Mrs. Walton. He did not have a heart attack. The tests did come back ... he has ..." she chose her words carefully, "... intestinal distress."

I remained wife-like.

"Oh, thank you Sister. This will ease the children's worries. I'll let them know."

"Yes ma'am. Tell them not to worry. He will be just fine. He should be released later today."

"Thank you, Sister." I handed the receiver to the attorney, who was grinning. "Well, it seems he did not have a heart attack as he thought. He

CHAPTER 50

has," I employed air quotes, "he has 'intestinal distress'."

"Just what I thought. He faked it," she jotted down notes on her pad. "I still can't believe you were able to get that information," she said wide-eyed.

"Maybe she remembers he has a wife and kids from his first time in there," I said with a gleeful smirk as I sat back in the chair. "It is a ... small town still."

"And then there is you...."

"What?" I played up the surprise.

"... Intestinal distress.... So the nun confirmed he's full of shit!" The lawyer across from me stirred the lightness of the mood in the room.

"It seems so," Dad finally spoke up with a lighthearted agreement.

I could not hold it back any longer. Laughter erupted.

The three of us enjoyed a collective laugh before we rehashed the happenings at the ranch.

"Okay," she said as she finished up her notes.

"When do you think the next hearing will be?" I asked, my mind flitting to anticipated expenses I didn't have the funds to cover.

"No." She raised a hand and slowly swatted at an invisible fly. "Don't worry. I am not going to make you come back down for the next hearing. We can't count on him ***not*** doing this again." Her expression drew stern. "I'm not letting him drag you around anymore than he already has. And I will tell the judge just that. He's not the first husband to play these games," she grimaced while shaking her head.

"Ah, okay. Are you sure?"

"Sadly," she nodded, "he won't be the last. The judge has seen this before too." She attempted to reassure me. Without looking up she continued, "I want you to get on state aid up there. They will keep your address from him too," she instructed.

I slumped in my chair.

"I hate this," I said half under my breath as I focused on my lap.

"Please don't," compassion filled her voice. "It's not your fault. He's the one making you not able to get a job or keep it for that matter. How can you... when he's forcing you to move all of the time just to keep you and the kids safe? Plus, it will help the judge see the need for child support."

"You going to share all of that with the judge?" Dad asked.

"Yes, Mr. Kline."

"Okay…. I guess," I acquiesced, sat up – slumped shouldered, took a deep breath, and accepted what I needed to do to provide for the kids.

She stood signifying our meeting was done for today. My father and I mimicked her silent communication.

"Are you guys heading back today?"

"No. Thought we might be in court all day. We head out tomorrow," I informed.

"Okay. Enjoy your evening you two. I'll be in touch."

With that she closed the door behind us.

Chapter 51

After buckling myself in, I checked my ticket. One-hour layover in Salt Lake City…

A couple of hours later my connecting flight landed in Spokane, Washington. I disembarked from the plane, collected my suitcase, and rejoined my family – John and the kids were there to pick me up.

"I got to see Coojoe, Suzanne, It's the One, Cee Cee, and Rosie…" I recapped the positive highlights of my trip to the kids, remembering to be upbeat.

As we drove in the driveway, I felt an ease wash over me even though my divorce still hung in the balance. I let out a cleansing breath. Before I left I felt like a refugee, now, as we reached the top of the driveway I felt … *home*.

Chapter 52

I walked up to the blue doors of the school. I surveyed the access points to the building – two so far. I took note of the fenced playground. Acid bubbled in my stomach. An unstoppable cramp altered my gate. My jaw muscles tightened. Clammy palms required a more secure grip with my fingers on the metal door handle than anticipated. I opened it. Took a deep breath, held it for a count of four … blew it out as I entered.

Here we go again! I wonder how much convincing it's going to take to make another stranger understand this out-of-state restraining order is valid, valid in this state too? They don't know me from Eve. I'm a stranger to them.

I fought to hold down the acidic burp. I failed.

I need to make them understand … he's not to be trusted.

I swallowed a lump in my throat.

But what if they don't believe me? What if they don't take this at face value? Respect it? What if he comes here and sweet-talks them … too?

Standing at the counter I shifted my weight from foot to foot as I waited for the secretary to get off the phone.

"I need yah'll to take serious this protection order," I said sternly to the stranger in the office at the Pinehurst Elementary School.

Maybe that was a bit strong. She hasn't even said 'no' yet. I chastised myself. *You need them. They won't help you if they don't like you.*

"Oh, please don't worry." The school secretary looked up from the kids' file. Compassion filled her eyes but did not overshadow her confidence.

CHAPTER 52

"Your's is not the only protection order we have on file," she exuded trust. "We take these things seriously around here."

"Worry... ma'am that's all I do."

I shared the abridged version of our last year.

"I understand your apprehension," the softness of her voice calmed the panic in me.

"He's still in Colorado but... I've come to not trust him at all."

"I understand. We will do our best to help you protect your children. Have you been to the Shoshone Family Center in Kellogg?"

"No. I haven't."

Her face was awash with kindness – soft eyes, a gentle smile, and empathy.

"It's not hard to find ... when you're ready."

She gave me the start dates, teacher's names, and classroom numbers.

"No one, and I do mean no one is allowed to pick up any of my children except myself and the man who's ranch we are stayin' on." I tapped the pages of the file. "I listed only us."

She smiled. Her chin moved up and down ever so slightly as she checked the appropriate page.

The next day the kids and I went to the social service office in Kellogg. I grabbed their packet and filled it out. I'd gotten used to carrying my important information with me, both physically and mentally.

"Due to your emergency need, I'd like to have you meet with a case worker right away," the brunette said, a bit wide-eyed. I shrugged my shoulders, showed no resistance. "Okay. I'll be right back."

Minutes passed before the brunette came back to the receptionist's desk. We made eye contact. She smiled and motioned for me to come up to her.

"I'll be right back. I'm gonna be over here, Lovies."

The kids didn't even look up. It was refreshing to see them focused and not concerned. I wished it was the same for me. I crossed the lobby.

"Samantha will be right out to see you," the receptionist whispered.

I nodded and rejoined the children.

A short time later a medium-built blonde-haired woman came out into the lobby through a side door. She glanced around to find only the four of us in the waiting area.

"Hello," she said with an outstretched hand.

I stood and accepted her greeting, taking hold of her hand.

"Can you and the kids come with me into this cubical?"

"Yes ma'am. Hey you three, let's go in this office with this nice lady."

"Can I bring this book?" Emma requested.

"You sure can!" the blonde responded.

Emma smiled as she and her siblings got up to follow us.

"I'm Samantha," she introduced herself. "We're going to go in here while mom and I talk... okay?"

She led us to the doorless office. She stepped behind the desk. I chose the chair closest to the corner. Ethan sat in the other chair while the girls sat on the floor.

"I see you have an existing restraining order," she assessed.

We reviewed the happenings of the last seven or eight months. She made notes in our new file. Just like the others had.

I wonder how many more times I'm gonna have to tell this story? I sighed as my insecurities multiplied.

"I'm glad you've marked the box to have your address kept private. Do you have your restraining order with you, so I can make a copy?"

I nodded and pulled it out of my hard plastic briefcase and handed it to her.

"And no utility bills?"

"No. We are blessed to be staying with a family friend. And I won't be putting *anything* in my name. Nothing!" My eyes widened as my tone became defensive.

She put her hands up, palms facing me.

"No. No. Don't worry, I'm just confirming. Guess I should have said that first," she was apologetic.

I sat back in the chair, stiff backed, took a deep breath, and worked to see the help she was offering.

As she left the room, I fidgeted with my briefcase and struggled with my fears and frustrations.

CHAPTER 52

I hate having to ask everyone for help. This is getting old already. Can't he just leave us to live… a calm quiet life. Why, I fought back the tears, *do I have to keep coming to others to help me keep my darn kids safe? WHY! I hate this. Everyone who claims to be able to help me wants nothing but information from me. Information I don't trust them with!*

My pulse quickened.

Don't let the kids see you get upset. Don't let this upset you. You need these folks' help. You're doin' what you need to do. You wouldn't need to do this if… he…. Lord, I just hope he leaves us alone.

I quelled the scream that desired birth. Looking down, more to hide my eyes from my children, I smiled as I caressed the opaque plastic briefcase and traced the white petals of one of the half-dollar-sized daisies.

"Here's your original," Samantha said as she reentered the cubical. "I would like you to go to the Family DV Center. The lady, the director, Sylvia is waiting to see you and the kids."

My eyes widened as insecurities about being somewhere new again, the unknown of a new town, surged through me. My heart pushed my blood harder, faster.

Samantha slid a piece of paper with the address and directions across the desk.

"Do you know where this street is?" her tone was soft, encouraging, and supportive.

I shook my head. She slid the paper close to the end of the desk.

Exhausted from fighting so many battles, with much hesitation and halted movements, I reached up and accepted her offering.

Chapter 53

Samantha's directions were easy to follow. They led me to a parking lot with a handful of businesses in the strip mall. It was eerily devoid of cars. Stifling the dread that filled me I checked my surroundings. My grip on the gear shift tightened as I put the car in park. The skin over my knuckles went from tan to white. I took a couple of deep breaths and exhaled each one. I worked to slow my rapid heartbeat.

He doesn't know where you are yet. He wouldn't come this far... would he? I repeated to myself.

"Okay kids let's go in and meet this nice lady," I forced a cheer into my voice.

Looking over at my son, his bright blue eyes calmed me. The playful giggles of the girls telegraphed they were not worried. Braveness was called for, and letting someone new know things about us was needed. Before moving, I scanned the parking lot. I saw no one who resembled my soon-to-be ex.

"Okay yah'll...."

I opened my car door. The threesome followed my lead. My head swiveled as I surveyed my new surroundings. I pulled open the glass door to the Domestic Violence office, letting the kids enter first.

"Good morning." A lady in her fifties greeted us.

"Um. Sylvia?"

I couldn't help but notice the silence in the room. It was a room devoid of sound, one that made my ears work harder as I listened for something, anything. It was too quiet in there. *Why she didn't have music on?* Maybe she turned it off as we walked in. I couldn't work in this much silence. My mind would be searching for sounds! Like it is now.

"Yes. Kathleen?"

"Yes ma'am," my voice was soft and weak, as were my leg and arm muscles.

"And who are these little ones?" she asked as she advanced.

After I introduced the children, Sylvia was gracious with them.

"May I give you guys something?" Sylvia looked at me for permission. I nodded. She handed the kids a blue cloth bag each. "These bags have been put together for children just like you."

I shrugged my shoulders, forced a smile, and nodded permission for them to accept. They deserved presents – presents I hadn't been able to give. Plus, something special never hurts.

"Would you guys like to watch a movie or play over here…" Sylvia pointed, "…for a while?"

For a while! Bile rose up into my throat.

She led the kids over to the play area, turned on the T.V. and *The Little Mermaid* started. While it was nice to witness my children responding well to yet another stranger, it made my pulse quicken and my hands sweat.

These kids… I am amazed at them. They are adjusting… to the moves…. This fourth move. And to the new people… oh so well.

"Please… sit," Sylvia motioned to the chairs at the round, adult-height table on the other side of the room.

I evaluated the distance between the table and the children … the table and the door.

It's only two strides between the table and the kids. It's only two strides!

Sylvia patiently waited for me to decide if I was going to accept her invitation to sit.

I took a step forward, pulled out the chair, and turned it so my back was not facing the entrance. Before sitting I checked on the kids, again. They seemed content. I sat. Sylvia sat.

She asked a few informal questions in a non-threatening manner, but…

my shoulders remained tense, and my back stiff.

"How long have you been here?"

"Since the end of July."

"Have you ever been here, in this area before?" She was dancing around why I had brought the family to Idaho from California.

"Yes," I guardedly answered.

"Oh," she smiled. Making small talk as she gathered tidbits of information.

"Is *he* here in the state?" She kept her volume low to keep the conversation between the two of us.

"Not that I know of," my protective resistance was palpable.

"Have you had your order recognized here in the county, in this state?" Sylvia got around to asking.

My brows knitted.

"No ma'am."

"I'll get some paperwork and directions for you. You'll have to file the request up at Wallace." She responded to my confused expression. "You're just going to be asking the court and the judge to recognize your restraining order. That way they can enforce it and help protect you and the kids."

"Oh. Okay."

I fidgeted in my seat, turned my head, and checked in on the kids – glad my nervousness was not overflowing into the children.

"Have you filed for a concealed carry permit?"

"No." *Oh my god, how does she know that I carry a gun with me?* "Not yet, to tell you the truth, I don't know how to."

I focused on my cuticles.

"How about I make an appointment with the Sheriff for you, after you file, to have these recognized?"

Surprise flashed in my eyes.

Wow....

"Okay." She smiled. "Would you be able to meet me up at Wallace, at the courthouse tomorrow, say ... 10:15?"

"I guess so."

"Have you been to Wallace? Know how to get there?"

CHAPTER 53

I nodded.

"Okay. We'll meet up tomorrow." She directed her attention to the kids. "Hey kids, why don't you bring your new bags over and show us what you got?"

The kids came, blue bags in hand.

Emma and Bella put their bags on the table.

"OOHH," Emma said as she pulled out a purple and white crocheted lap robe.

A smile grew on her face and delight filled her eyes, purple was one of her favorite colors.

"What else you got in there?" I asked.

"Um, a stuffed bunny..."

"My blanket is ... pink, yellow, and white! And I have a stuffed animal too," Bella cheerfully shared.

"Son?"

"Mine is blue. And there's some pencils."

"And a coloring book and crayons!" the youngest squealed.

"And a book!" Emma added as she flipped through the pages. "And a brush for my hair and a toothbrush too!"

"Look Momma," Bella pulled a smaller plastic pink brush out and began running the black plastic bristles through her hair.

"Where?" I stammered toward Sylvia.

"These are the *My Stuff* bags from the Dr. Laura Schlessinger Foundation. Do you know who she is?"

"Yes ma'am. I sure do." I chuckled. "My dad and I often found ourselves listening to her shows even when we weren't together." Some of the conversations her radio shows sparked between us .... My smile grew.

"These bags were donated from Dr. Laura Schlessinger's foundation. This is your 'My Stuff' bag. They were put together just especially for you," Sylvia's cheer increased everyone's enjoyment of the unexpected gifts.

The kids stuffed their new goodies back in the blue bags and we prepared to leave.

"See you tomorrow at a quarter after ten?" Sylvia confirmed.

I nodded as the knot in my stomach loosened. We left without most of the doom I came in with.

Chapter 54

After meeting with Sylvia at the courthouse we walked over to the police department. The appointment with the Sheriff went well. Less than a half hour later I pulled into the driveway. I noticed John's truck was parked in front of the shop, I pulled in and parked beside it.

It didn't take long for me to find my beauties. All I had to do was follow the small engine noise. I walked toward the pasture to find Ethan and Emma on the riding lawn mower.

"You didn't tell me the two older ones could drive," John's voice telegraphed joy.

"Yeah," my cheeks reddened. "They've been driving since they were about two."

Pride emanated from my wide smile as I watched Ethan navigate the green and black beast as it ate up and spit out the pasture grass.

Emma saw me and waved.

"It took both of them to weigh down the seat to get it to run," John explained. "It's designed to stop running if there is a weight change and you fall off of it."

"I had no idea they worked that way."

"They aren't going to get hurt. It's safe."

"Oh, I'm okay with it," I responded not taking my eyes off of them as Ethan made another turn of the steering wheel. "He looks like he's got this!" I looked around for my youngest. Not seeing her I inquired, "Where's Bella?"

"She's playing with the cat."

"Okay."

"She's sure taken to that cat!"

We both shared the unspoken relief that the kids were adjusting to this ranch, the new family structure, and the relaxing home life we were providing them.

"How'd it go?" he asked.

"I got the papers filed and met with the Sheriff."

"You did? I didn't know you were meeting with Matt," John's eyebrows raised as he spoke.

"Yeah. I wasn't expecting it but the gal from the center walked me over and introduced me."

"So... he accepted your CCW request?"

"Well ... I didn't even turn it in."

John's eyes narrowed.

"He just approved me to carry. Concealed or openly."

John grinned and nodded his approval.

Ethan turned the mower again, looked up, saw me, and smiled, as he straightened it out, staying focused on where he was driving.

"I told him he had to have straight lines." A mischievous smirk came across John's face. "He's doing a really good job!" a twinge of surprise laced his words.

"Yeah," this Momma smiled widely. *He sure looks like he's enjoying this... workin', being trusted, and learning new things!* "He's good at many things, huh!"

A couple of days later, I came down from the house and found Bella sitting on the seat behind Emma on the mower as they cut the grass in the larger unfenced pasture.

"I'm surprised they're heavy enough to trigger the sensor," I acknowledged, as John and I watched the girls.

CHAPTER 54

I glanced around and found Ethan with his dog. My mind flashed back to Cable, our old Momma dog, and Ethan some nine-plus years before. My firstborn was crawling around the single-wide living room as I did dishes in the kitchen at the nose of the trailer. The 12-year-old bitch lay in the opening between the two rooms.

As I watched Ethan and Psycho, I smiled remembering – Cable was hurting that day… she could have turned toward the source of her pain, our boy who was leaning on her back, and … she could have bitten him. But, unlike some dogs, she loved her boy more than anything and gave grace to the child.

I smiled, now, at my blessing of having had Cable-dog around the boy when he was so young. I smiled at Mike having picked a guard dog who seemed to know the difference between a naive child and an adult who should know better. She was protective and seems to have passed a lot of that onto her pups. And now Psycho seemed content as his mom used to – with his head in the boy's lap.

"Relax," John said in a soft tone, "they're settling in just fine."

"You might have to share your dog some more," a light chuckle escaped my throat.

"I noticed," John frowned and rolled his eyes.

John waved the girls in from their cutting chore.

"You don't let the horses loose out here… in this pasture do you?" I inquired. "It's unfenced…."

"No." John smiled. "But the girls wanted to help out and so I let them cut the grass out there. It gives them something to do. Okay, let's make sure the blades are up before you drive this over to the shop," John said over the engine noise as Emma got closer. He pulled on a lever. "Okay, drive this on over to the front of the shop."

After the machinery was parked inside we headed back up to the house for barbecued steaks, corn on the cob, and I made a salad. John and I were treated to giggles from the kids as they played and drew at the picnic table. We sat back and watched the sunset as we ate our supper.

Chapter 55

"The court granted your divorce," my attorney informed me over the phone.

I stretched the curly wall cord out and sat on the stool at the kitchen island.

"Good." I sat, filled with a mix of relief and uncertainty.

My muscles stiffened as I waited for the unknown to be unleashed. With this being my first experience with divorce I did not know what details of the agreement we had been trying to hammer out would be changed, if any.

"I'm sending you your copy. The opposing counsel pushed for your address, for visitations and all, and I told them you had work to go to in Idaho and that's why the kids were no longer in the state."

"He's gonna know where we are now." I shook my head at the thought – and dread that he would know *exactly* where we were – filled me. "We used to come to this ranch together. He'll know where we are, P.O. Box or not, when I provide him with the phone number." I swallowed a lump that had rapidly grown in my throat. He'd probably guessed it months ago when the mailing address was given to his lawyer. "So, the stalking wasn't brought up?" I clenched my teeth.

"Not exactly, but Judge Marshall knows all about it. She's got your entire file including the police reports from our Sheriff Deputies here, the Florence PD, and breaches the cops sent on over from California."

"Okay." I sighed. "So, she's not mad at me?"

CHAPTER 55

"No. I think she understands why you and the kids were not safe here." Relief filled me.

"The last thing I need to do is make the judge mad at me."

We both chuckled at that.

"He can start his phone visits now too. So you'll have to provide him with a phone number to call when he emails you."

"I don't think I'll have to *give* it to him. He probably knows it as he'll know where we're staying ... at John's now, who's been a family friend for a decade. And those phone calls ... are on Mondays?"

"They pushed for three calls a week, so I gave in for two – Mondays and Wednesday nights at 7 p.m."

"For how long?"

"The papers say, 'for a reasonable amount of time.'"

"But what does *that* mean?" I waited with bated breath as my mind reeled from the legal vagueness.

"It means as long as he doesn't get shitty he can talk to each kid. So stay close while they're on the phone and if he gets shitty then hang up the phone. Call that visit done." She emboldened me. "He *can* start his in-person visits, too. But I'm not sure when that might happen nor where he is at this time as he was not at the last hearing."

"But..."

"The judge agreed to them being supervised," my attorney assured me. "He has to make arrangements with you for the supervised visitations two weeks in advance and only contact you via email. The judge agreed to make your protection order permanent. Your ex can *only* contact you via email."

"Okay. Thank you."

I breathed a sigh of relief. *I hope he takes this seriously and stays away from me.*

"He requested, and I thought it reasonable, that you must tell him if the kids become majorly ill," she informed me of the additions to the decree.

"Well ... okay. I'm a little surprised at that," I sniped, knowing he'd shown no care about his older four children's well-being over our entire marriage, "but okay, I can do that."

"I didn't think it was out of the question. So, you don't have to email him for colds and the like, just big things like surgery, etc."

I nodded my understanding as if we were not over 1100 miles apart. She allowed a bit of silence to linger between us.

"Do you have any questions?"

"No. No. Thanks for all you've done for me ... and the kids."

"It was my pleasure. If you ever need something... let me know. Keep records and be well."

"Thank you ma'am."

~~~****~~~

A week later I had the official stamped divorce papers in my hands. I reviewed them with John. It was time for a visit with Sylvia.

"It's good to see you. Coffee?" Sylvia asked as I came in. I nodded. "Did you get the kids in school and all?" she asked as we sat.

"Yes." We caught up.

"I saw that the court accepted and acknowledged your orders of protection," she announced.

"Well, I have new ones." I pushed my divorce papers across the table. "Do I have to take these papers up too?"

A smile grew on her face.

"Yes. To the court. Was he ordered to pay child support?"

I pursed my lips and they contorted as I frowned.

"Yep. A whole fifty dollars a month." I shook my head knowing I couldn't buy squat for the kids with sixteen dollars and sixty-six cents each per kid per month. "If he'll pay even that."

"It doesn't matter if we think he'll pay it. It's more important that he's ordered to. I want you to take a copy to the welfare office and a copy to the school too – to show you have sole custody. And I'd like to make a copy for your file here if you don't mind."

Sylvia made a couple of extra copies for me to give out.

"Do you have time to go up to Wallace?" she asked.

CHAPTER 55

I checked my watch, "Yeah."

"Do you want me to go with you?"

"No," I beamed. "I think I can do this one." I sat up a bit taller.

"Okay. Let me know if I can help you. If he becomes an issue again… don't hesitate to call and report. Are you working yet? Do you need an extra copy for your boss?"

"No. I was allowed to enroll in a couple of classes as I didn't know where this divorce thing was going to stand."

"That is making good use of your time. It'll let you settle in."

She smiled encouraging approval.

"Settle in… that's a concept. Now what else will change?" I retorted.

Sylvia's smile reinforced the idea that all would be okay. I swallowed the lump in my throat and stopped making eye contact with her.

"He's not here is he?"

"No." I shook my head. "Don't think so. Not sure where he is. The lawyer said he wasn't at the last hearing. But he's got to move off the ranch as it was awarded to me." I visually searched the tabletop for answers as if it had them – there were none. "He gets to start his calls, which I am expecting any Monday now and… visitations." I looked up at Sylvia. "How does this supervisor thing work?"

"Oh good, you got the *supervised* visitations!" She didn't even try to hide her excitement. I heard the uptick in her voice. "He's got to provide one you approve of. If there's a cost, he has to pay for it. Remember… you don't need the supervision… he does, so he bears the cost."

I nodded.

"It's part of the cost of his visitations," she sternly reassured.

The tightness in my throat relaxed.

I left her office and headed up the freeway to the courthouse. The desk clerk was pleasant and took my divorce papers as I filled out the request for them to be recognized.

"The judge should see these this week," she said as she placed the papers in a file.

As I drove home I became filled with concern about how soon the phone calls and visits would start. I didn't have to wait long.

The following Monday the phone rang at 7 p.m. sharp. John and I shared a look.

I got up off the couch to answer it.

Only time will tell if Mike figured out where we are, especially since I still haven't gotten an email from him, asking for the phone number.

Nausea, akin to seasickness, hit me in the stomach and head. I had dreaded hearing my ex's voice again for a long time.

"Can I talk to the kids?" Mike asked.

We were cordial to each other.

"Hey Ethan, phone's for you!" I pushed cheer into my voice.

The boy came towards me awash in confusion. I hadn't told them about the impending phone calls – in case their dad didn't call. I didn't want to get their hopes up.

"It's your dad."

I smiled and extended my arm, handing the phone toward the boy. Skepticism, after all, it'd been over a year since they'd seen or spoken to him. The girls came to the kitchen too.

"You guys get to talk with your father twice a week now. Mondays and Wednesdays at seven."

I hit the speaker button on the phone so they could all hear him. The smiles grew as they heard his voice. Watching them made me glad the lawyer gave them two times a week to talk to him.

This stalking shit should be over now that the divorce is final. I found myself hoping.

Each child joined in the conversation and said 'hi' to their father. Small talk was had. Mike checked in with each child to make sure they were okay and in school.

"I've missed you guys," he said – it sounded genuine.

And then the conversation turned.

"Your mom's kept you from me ..." the kids' smiles turned to gaping mouths and wide eyes as they turned to look at me. Their disbelief was undeniable.

CHAPTER 55

That's where you crossed the line. Now you've spoken to them for a reasonable amount of time. *And your time is up.*

I matched their frowns as I hung up the phone.

"I'm glad you guys got to speak with your father," I tried to help them find the positive even if I struggled to maintain a genuine tone. "Remember, he's allowed to call on Wednesday nights too, so you can expect that."

I tried to end this on a positive note.

The calls came twice a week. Sometimes they were cut short and other times he focused on the kids.

The email came next. He wanted to see the kids.

Chapter 56

I wheeled the office chair over the no-loop carpet from my sewing table to the computer desk in the ground-floor den John had helped me adapt to fit my creative needs. The eight-foot-wide section of the room made my two working areas ideal, because they were close I could optimize my time by splitting my efforts between both the computer and the sewing. Especially since the lag of the dial-up Internet connection and my lack of patience were competing.

With the computer turned on, I rolled the chair over to the sewing table. A series of beeps followed by high-pitched notes told me the connection was in the works. I was able to work on my sewing projects while waiting for the computer to connect. I periodically rolled over to see if my email had loaded.

Hotmail finally opened up, Mike's email came in and dread filled me just at the sight of his email address in my Inbox.

Easypet:
I want to see the kids in 2 weeks

Shit! My heart raced. *He's gonna be here... in two weeks.* A queasiness punched me in the gut. *He knows where we are.* A lightheadedness followed. *Shit!* After looking over my shoulders and moving four times to get away from him ... now he's going to be back in striking distance. *It's been a year. He's just wanting to see the kids. It was bound to happen. You don't have to see him.* I coached myself to focus on the benefit to the kids as I mustered up

CHAPTER 56

enough strength to respond to his email.

Me:
Yes, you can come to visit the kids. They are looking forward to seeing you. But you have to have a supervisor and it has to be one I approve of.

I clicked "Send" before rolling back over to continue working on the sample quilt blocks for a client. Hours later another email came in.

Easypet:
I don't know anyone up there! How am I supposed to pick someone

"Well how the hell **am I** supposed to pick one?" I kibitzed as if he could hear me. *We haven't lived here very long. I don't know many people. I mean ... I go to church with a few but ... that doesn't mean I know any of them!*

I reconciled my worries. The reality was that I really wouldn't want Mike to pick a supervisor, a supervisor I didn't know. I really wanted someone I could trust. Someone I could trust who'd look after the best interests of the kids.

Me:
Okay, I will look to see if I can find one, but if there is a cost for this person to spend up to eight hours supervising your visit then you will need to pay it.

I kept my comments factual and steady, even though my stomach was in knots. With *Send* clicked I went back to my sewing projects, in hopes of changing my focus. But not for long.

I headed upstairs.

"Hey, John. Do you know anyone who could and would be willing to be a supervisor for these darn visits that Mike is starting to request?"

"Let me make a couple of calls," John said with confidence.

I went back down to my sewing room to help distract my mind from the unknown. I couldn't help but struggle with my thoughts.

*Great, now it's **my** responsibility to find someone to supervise **him**! Great! Just what I need. I didn't count on this. Why didn't I count on this? I should have thought ahead. I wish someone, like my lawyer had warned me.*

Sitting in front of the sewing machine, I laid my hand on some fabric. The smooth cotton pieces were from a fabric designer I met last October, at Quilt Market. She hired me to make quilt samples out of her material. Inspiration of quilters was the goal of showcasing the circa 1877 reproduction fabric in a quilt block popular in that era. A Log Cabin block just seemed to be right.

*Who would be willing to waste a Saturday, **for eight hours**, for someone they didn't even know? I sure hope John finds someone, after all, these kids really deserve to see their dad!*

The wall of windows the sewing station lined allowed me to gaze out over the pasture. I stared out the windows, took a deep breath, and hoped my tense muscles would relax. It wasn't working.

I positioned the cotton on the cutting mat, aligning the edge of the cloth with a vertical line on the mat. I placed the clear ruler on the pastel pink fabric. I stopped and gazed out the window as a bull moose walked up to the salt lick.

His visits were something I'd come to look forward to.

After a few minutes of watching my new pet – even if he didn't know he was mine – I noticed he was settling in for a nap by the stump in the clearing. I continued working on the Log Cabin quilt blocks. Once a calmness had been gained, I climbed the stairs. John joined me for a coffee before the kids got home from school.

"I've had some luck," John reported. "I've got a friend who is a retired LAPD officer. He said he is checking his schedule and will get back to us tomorrow."

"You found an ex-cop to be a supervisor? Up here?" My body relaxed a bit. A smile grew. "Thank you. Thank you so much, John." Relief filled every cell within me. "Mike won't like it – being watched by a cop, even if he's a retired cop, but too effing bad! It would make me feel comfortable. I hope the retired officer says yes!" I breathed a bit easier.

The next day I was able to send off an email. A few emails went back and

CHAPTER 56

forth with my last one confirming:

Me:

Okay. The supervisor, Tom, will meet you in Wallace at that restaurant you mentioned. He will be there at 8 a.m., I will drop the kids off at the same time. You are not allowed to leave the county and I will pick up the kids no more than eight hours later – 4 p.m.

"Come on you three," two weeks later I used my motherly cheerleader voice. "Let's get in the car so you can go see your dad!"

Grins covered the children's faces, which made me smile. Even if their dad and I didn't get along, they should get to see him. They've missed him so. I knew this and wanted this *for* them. They bounced down the stairs and got in the car ahead of John and me. We drove the miles answering the kids' questions as best as we could.

"What are we going to get to do?" Emma asked with enthusiasm.

"I don't know," genuine cheer was easy for me when I saw the joy exuding from the kids. "All I know is he can't take you out of the county, but you don't have to stay at the place we drop you off at. You're going to have a great time you guys!" I encouraged. "Oh yeah, remember I told you there would be another man there… to just watch after you three, as the judge ordered, remember?" I turned back to see the kids as John drove. "Tom. Tom is his name. He will be there for the entire visit. Just in case you need anything."

While I worked hard to hide the nervousness I felt about this first visitation, I hoped my excitement for their visit, while authentic, outweighed my apprehension and lack of trust of a guy who'd lied to me for over a decade. He'd lost all trust previously granted. I struggled with the fact that lies come more easily for him than the truth. What if he was lying now too? Does he actually care for his kids, these kids? He'd shown the ability and willingness to not care about the children he had made. After all, I didn't even know he had four other children! He never mentioned the four other kids! What the eff? Who does that?

John pulled up in front of the pizza parlor, as agreed. Tom was already there waiting for us in front of the restaurant. We introduced the kids to Tom, and he escorted the kids in for their visit, but not before hugs were shared between the kids and me.

I got back in the car, my pulse beating strong in my belly, my jaw clenched. I forced a deep breath. John slid onto the driver's seat, reached over, and patted my thigh.

"It's gonna be okay," he reassured me.

Peering toward the building that engulfed my children, I noticed that I couldn't even see if Mike actually showed up. The tinting on the windows forced me to strain my eyes. Butterflies seemed to take flight in my stomach. The kids couldn't even be seen. My throat muscles tightened.

This has got to work, be the right thing. They really need their dad in their lives.

"Let's get something to eat," John suggested. "Then we'll go back to the ranch and stay close in case this doesn't go as well as we hope."

John pulled the car away from the curb.

"We'll only be a few minutes and miles away… right," my voice quivered as I tried to convince myself this was all going to work out. "And Tom will call us, right, if something goes awry."

John nodded.

If everything was going to be okay, why was my mind screaming *No*?

Chapter 57

Calls continued to come from their father on Monday and Wednesday as scheduled, but there was a change in the children. One I couldn't put my finger on, but attitudes were changing.

"Mom!" Emma hollered as she came in the house.

The hair on the back of my neck raised.

"Ethan's hit me!" she said with a serious tone.

"Are you okay?"

"It hurts," she said as she rubbed her arm.

"Let me see Lovie!"

I lifted her sleeve, kissed the red mark, and took my 8-year-old in my arms. Bella came in, out of breath.

"You okay?" I inquired. My youngest nodded. "What happened?" I addressed them both.

"We were all down in the pasture, by the barn. Ethan was chasing us with a stick and hitting me with it," Emma reported. "He wouldn't stop!"

My jaw muscles tightened, and anger flourished.

"Why don't you two go up and I get a movie ready for you to watch?"

My girls smiled.

I waited for Emma to let go of me before I released my embrace. We walked up the stairs. After choosing a movie the older one offered to put it in the VCR. I walked to the sliding door, opened it, stepped out on the balcony, lifted my fingers to my mouth, and whistled.

"Son!" I bellowed.

He stuck his head out from around the barn.

"Get up here!"

I waved him in and waited for him in my sewing room. I only had to wait a couple of minutes before the screen door announced Ethan's arrival.

"In here," I hoped my stern tone conveyed my anger at the situation.

My sullen boy stopped a few feet from me.

"What is going on with you?"

He said nothing.

"We don't hit! You are not allowed to hit your sisters! That's always been the rule!" My temper simmered – jaw muscles remained tight. My wide green eyes bore down on the 10-year-old. "What makes you think it's okay for you to hit your sisters?"

He shrugged his shoulders with downcast eyes. Silence filled the room.

"Well… then get your bum upstairs…" I raised my arm pointing in the direction of the door, "… to your room and think about it!"

He walked out of the room, not denying these actions.

I don't get it. This is a new behavior for him. What the hell!

It was time for coffee and to sit with the girls. Later that night I informed Ethan that he was grounded and restricted to his room for a week.

A couple of days later my inbox showed an email from their father. He was trying to set up another visit with the kids.

"John can you ask Tom if he's available to supervise a visit two Saturdays out?"

He nodded.

"Tom's saying he doesn't see the need for it," hours later John shared as he turned from the phone to face me.

I glared John's way.

"Well, the courts see it differently!" I was emphatic.

John reached up and pushed the speaker button.

"Hi Kathleen. I saw nothing to make me worried that their father is going to do anything to the kids. He was kind to them. Looked like he truly enjoyed seeing them. He was even cordial to me."

I frowned. Lines shown on my forehead and my molars fit together so

CHAPTER 57

snug that air could not pass between them.

"I think he's okay," Tom continued. "I mean, I didn't sit with them at the same table, I stayed a few tables back, but it seemed to all be okay."

Great! He's convinced an experienced cop he's okay. I shook my head. Doubt crept in. *Maybe he's changed. Maybe I'm wrong. Maybe he's decided what's important – the kids.*

"Let me know what you decide. I'll have to change a few things around if you decide I'm needed," Tom requested.

"Okay. Thank you Tom. Give us a couple of days and we'll let you know," John said before hanging up.

"You really think you need to have Tom there? He says it's okay. The kids are okay. Mike's not hurting them," John reiterated. "The kids seemed to have a good time with their father...."

I shook my head, rubbed my closed eyes, and pinched the base of my nose. Moving the palm of my hand to my forehead – I rubbed as a headache built and won out.

"I'm getting some aspirin." I turned and headed for our bedroom.

We let the subject lay for a day. But my gut was making me think twice about this unsupervised visit thing.

~~~****~~~

"Hi doctor," I greeted the blonde lady in the white coat.

"Hi... Kathleen is it? What can we help you with today?"

"I'm new to the area. I've got a couple of kids, and we need to establish a new doctor for the family."

"Okay. How are things for you?"

"I've got some reoccurring acid reflux – it's been around for a couple of years and that's about it."

She continued with her questions and me the answers.

"Let's do some tests to see if I can help you with the acid reflux. I would like to start you off with a mammogram with the history of cancer in your family... even if you are only," she flipped through my new chart, "...thirty-eight years old. I think it would be a good idea."

I didn't disagree.

"The gal out front will give you the patient packets for the kids and I'll see you in a couple of weeks. But let me get my assistant to draw some blood before you go."

We shook hands and I waited for the trained vampire.

I made the short drive back to the ranch where I thought John and the kids were out working.

"Hi you three," I said as I couldn't help but notice the kids sitting separated in the living room with disgruntled expressions. "What's up?"

"Okay girls, why don't you go play," John instructed.

The girls got up and headed off to their room. John motioned for me to follow him out onto the balcony. He shut the glass door behind us.

"What's up?" I repeated it as dread spread throughout my body. John's stern face gave me little hope all was well.

"Ethan was chasing after and hitting the girls with a stick today."

I watched John's face for *it-was-all-in-fun*, but no such luck. Panic surged through me. I shook my head, my mouth downturned.

"He's been increasing with his expression of anger and taking it out *on* his sisters in the last few weeks," concern dripped from my words. Confusion covered my face.

"Maybe he should go stay with his father. Didn't you say he's staying up here, over in Pinehurst? I mean if it will keep the girls safe," John chose his words carefully.

My eyes widened as acid bubbled in my stomach. I reached up and rubbed below my sternum.

"Tom said he didn't think Mike was a threat to the kids…" John reminded me.

I turned toward the railing, gripped it to steady myself as my head felt like it was spinning.

The safety of the girls over the safety of the three of them. Will my boy be safe? Will he learn more abusive ways that are not acceptable? God I hate having to choose. This is ridiculous. But the boy can't keep doing this to the girls!

CHAPTER 57

"It's not going to stop, it seems," defeat laced my words. "Ethan's gotten worse," my voice dropped to a whisper. "I just talked to him about this a couple of days ago!"

We stood in silence for a few minutes.

"Let me go email Mike."

My despair-filled eyes were met with John's compassionate ones. He placed his hand on mine.

Chapter 58

**Me:
Mike,
Ethan is hitting the girls and I will not have it. You are not dead so I think it might be a good thing for the boy to come stay with you for a little while. He continues to get worse and worse with the girls. This is not good for him to be around the girls at this time. When can you meet me to take him with you?**

My fingers hovered over the keyboard as my labored breaths and racing heart made for unsteady hands.

Moments stretched as my worries built. Was I making a good decision or a bad one? Was I overreacting? Was I being too protective of the kids from their father? He's shown to be less likely to hurt the children... except for those couple of times....

My mind filled with the *enlightening* conversation with the kids a month or so after their dad went "South of Colorado" ... to Montana.

"Mom, while you were gone, in California, Dad was taking us over to his Jewish girlfriend's house. She was in Pueblo," my 8-year-old, Emma, had shared.

Anger flourished in me.

"Emma told Dad he was wrong. He wasn't supposed to be dating. Because he's married to you Momma," Ethan added, sadness laced his words.

My emotions flip flopped. My anger changed to happiness at the mention

CHAPTER 58

that my daughter stuck up for her Momma. But the anger, with notes of sadness, quickly returned. I mean, after all, my husband should not be dating! We're still married. He's the one who sent me away! *And* my kids should not have to stick up for me. This is so effing wrong!

My son was not willing to make eye contact with me.

Who's shame is my son carrying?

"He pulled the truck over on the way," Ethan continued to tell me what had happened. "Dad told Emma to get out. He put her out on the side of the road! On the highway! And started to drive away!" sadness and apprehension laced the boy's words.

Rage flashed throughout my body.

Ethan glanced up at me. My son's concern about his oldest sister still lingered today, a month or so after the event. Sorrow filled the blue eyes of my baby boy.

"I told him he couldn't leave her on the side of the road. He was going to leave her there, Momma!" Ethan said as confusion still filled his eyes, even in the retelling of the event.

I scowled. Since the misery expressed by my son, a couple of months out from the incident, was conveyed so fully. Damn!

"On the side of the effing highway! He really put your sister out of the truck on Hwy 50 because she objected to him having a girlfriend?"

Disgust vied with rage as it flooded my senses.

Because his young daughter knows he's married, and she didn't approve of him 'dating' while married. What an ass! What an effing ass!

"What else happened while I was out at Grandma and Grandpa's?" *Where your father pushed me to. Where your father's calculated sleep deprivation, mind games, etc. wore me down…. What else the eff happened?*

"That's when Bella got that scrape on her nose," Emma filled in some of the blanks. "We were on the swings. Bella fell off of it. She fell forward and scraped her nose…."

Yes, that scrape on my baby girl's nose I came back to. Just before she started kindergarten a few months ago! He had just poo-pooed it when I asked. Asshole!

"Oh, she just scraped her nose," he had said.

I looked over at my youngest who now sported a scar on her nose. "Where was your dad at this time?"

My eyes narrowed. I squinted. My jaw tightened as my anger grew.

"He was drinking a beer with that lady," Emma reported nonchalantly.

"He *what*?"

He hasn't drank since our first anniversary... over eleven years ago! I go out of town, at my husband's insistence, because he called my daddy to 'send a ticket for me' and now he's effing dating? DATING! And taking our kids WITH HIM on his effing dates! And putting our beauty out on the side of the effing highway because she doesn't approve of his behaviors, and she calls him on his shit!

That was a year and a half ago. But am I doing the right thing... trusting him now... with our boy... with our kids on visits? If he couldn't do right by our kids before... a year or so ago... will he be able to do well by them now? Is the retired cop right? Is Mike *not* a threat to the kids? Is John right? Am I just overprotective? Overreacting?

No.... Yes.... No.

I can't have Ethan beating on his sisters. I hope John and Tom are right. My stomach tightened. Maybe – **I am** – overreacting. Being overprotective. The bastard isn't dead. I don't seem to know how to take care of and control my boy's anger.... Their father effing followed us up here. Maybe he wants to see his kids. Maybe he wants to do something different this time. Maybe. I sure hope so. Because... I'm really not sure right now!

I let my finger depress the mouse which sent the email to Mike.

~~~~****~~~~

"Pack your stuff son. You're going to stay with your dad for a while," I tempered my words to camouflage my anger and worry.

The boy's eyes were wide with disbelief and maybe some fear at being told he was being put out of the house. Ethan's surprise was expected.

I put two empty boxes on his bed and walked out of his room – relieved my welled tears waited to fall.

An hour later I helped him carry the boxes out to the car.

CHAPTER 58

"We're gonna put them in the trunk," I informed him. With the boxes in place I added, "Get in."

He stood still. I motioned for him to get moving as I shut the trunk lid.

"Go ahead and get in the back," I instructed as he reached for the front passenger door. "We're, I mean I'm picking up Miss Andee to go with me."

I was grateful that Andee, a five-foot-ten plus, solid-built new-to-me girlfriend had agreed to come with me. I was hopeful that bringing another substantial female with me would keep Mike at bay. John's buddy Ben and his wife, Andee, had been a welcome blessing in my new circle of limited friends. It was a long shot asking her to go with me, but I was relieved and grateful she had said yes.

A few minutes later I pulled up in front of Andee's log cabin. With the car in park, I got out to knock on the door, but as I did Andee pushed the screen door open.

"Hi," she greeted with glee.

"Hey there Andee and Ben!"

Her husband emerged from the lean-to attached to the cabin. He smiled. Compassion filled his eyes. He tilted his head, holding me with his eyes. I drank in the comfort.

"We shouldn't be too long. If he's on time," I said as Andee got in the car.

"No worries. Take your time." Ben wiped his hands on a shop rag. "I'm heading over to John's. We'll be making sure the girls have something to do."

My eyebrows arched. I nodded at the new information as I didn't know he was going out to the ranch until now.

"Yeah, so you can just drive back on out to the ranch. Maybe we'll all go have lunch after a while," he kept his tone and volume low, but his jovial smile conveyed a hug.

I buckled up as I drove out their "U" shaped drive. An uncomfortable silence filled the car. I glanced in the rear-view mirror. No bright blue eyes to greet me as usual, just the top of my son's head as he studied his lap.

"Is that his truck?" Andee asked pointing at the brown truck as we neared the prearranged Pinehurst location.

"Yes."

The closer we got the faster my heart raced. I searched the interior of the truck. I did not see him. Adrenaline surged through my bloodstream. I fought the queasiness.

Thinking it not best to park directly behind his truck – in case he got pissy and pulled out while I was still parked there – I pulled up past it. With the car in park and the engine turned off, time slowed as moments stretched. I decided to get this over with.

As I reached the back of the car I saw him. I saw my ex-husband. I saw my abuser whom I hadn't been this close to in nearly a year. He was brooding, crouched near the front of his truck. Staying nearly out of view. Nearly.

After hefting the boxes onto the tailgate, I wrapped my arms around my boy. While I focused on my son, I kept an eye out for any unauthorized movement from his father. Our son's light trembling telegraphed his uncertainty.

"Don't worry son. We'll get to see each other. I start being the parent T.A., like you asked me to, in your classroom... on Monday."

My body absorbed his tremors, his body calmed. I kissed the top of his head, lifted his chin, my green eyes locked with his blue eyes. Blue by pigment. Blue by sadness. I forced a smile, hoping to encourage my first born.

"I just can't have you taking your anger out on your sisters," my soft voice kept our conversation just between us. "I'll see you on Monday Lovie."

He released his arms from around my waist.

"Okay," I raised my voice loud enough for Mike to hear me at the front of the truck. "I'll still need the address where you are staying in Pinehurst."

"Okay. I'll email it to you. What about the visitation next week with the girls?"

"Well," I frowned. "I guess you can pick them up at the end of the driveway Saturday next," I conceded. "Eight a.m."

"See you on Monday son. Love you," my maternal softness returned.

Ethan turned toward his dad. Andee and I got back in the car, and headed away. Wanting to decrease the unease I felt within me I didn't look back,

CHAPTER 58

although I wanted to. I swallowed my fear, my frustration, and my feelings of failure.

"Thanks for coming with me today," my unsteady voice telegraphed more than I liked.

"Kind of creepy the way he was lurking," Andee more than adequately surmised.

"Yeah," I forced my tight throat muscles to swallow even as my dry tongue stuck to the roof of my mouth. "It wasn't the 100 yards that's required by the restraining order …but… at least he stayed back."

We got to the highway. I headed West.

"I hate that I had to do this." I shook my head. "I don't trust Mike. He's abandoned so many people – kids. Including," disgust washed over me. *This family included.* I chose not to belabor the point. I knew Andee had listened to the saga before. "But … he's not dead … the doc putting that stent in a few years back saw to that."

I released a half-hearted snicker.

Andee patted my thigh.

"It's going to be okay. He's not going anywhere. Ethan's gotta go to school. Did you say you were assisting his teacher, in class?"

"Yes."

I forced a smile as I saw Andee's positivity shining through my fog.

"Yes, three times a week."

"Hold on to that. You'll be able to tell if he's all right."

"You're right."

"And you said this was temporary at best and you can get him back, even if you have to go to the cops to do it. I think the cops in Pinehurst will be glad to help a mom out like that."

I exited on Coeur d'Alene River Road. Within minutes we found the guys and the girls down at the barn.

Chapter 59

I kept my focus on the girls over the next few days. I forced a positive demeanor. But it was hard seeing Ethan's undisturbed bed sheets and quiet bedroom each time I walked up or down the hall. By Monday morning I was ready to see my boy.

"Okay girls let's go! Mom's drivin' us in today," my voice was upbeat.

"Really? We don't get to take the bus?" Emma said half enthusiastic-half disappointed.

"Well, you can still ride the bus… if you want but…." I rinsed my coffee cup out and put it in the dishwasher. "I'm assisting in Ethan's class starting today, a couple of days a week," I added with a cheerful tone.

I kissed John on the cheek.

"See you later," he said. "Enjoy your day girls!" he added as the three of us headed down the stairs.

"So, are you going to wait for the bus or?" I asked my older daughter as the end of the driveway was in reach.

"No. I'd like to ride in the car with you Momma."

"Okay … thanks … Lovie," I teased.

"I just think it's real pretty out here," Emma expressed with a recognized awe in her voice for the beauty of the lands we currently lived in.

"I want to stay with you Momma!" Bella chimed in with glee.

Our eyes met in the mirror. Her crystal blue eyes, and her big smile greeted me.

CHAPTER 59

"Okay Lovie."

I reached over and squeezed Emma's leg just above the knee. She broke out in giggles and love filled the car. I kept to the speed limit to soak up as much as possible. After the car was parked we all walked into the school.

"Whatcha doin' Momma?" Bella asked.

"Walkin' to your class with you!"

"Really!"

A bounce in her step showed her excitement.

Emma grabbed my arm, lifted her chin, and strutted us to her sister's class. A hug and kiss was shared before the older sibling continued back down the hall, arm-in-arm with her prize – me – so it seemed.

She proudly introduced me to her teacher before releasing me to go to her brother's class. But not before getting her own hug and kisses in.

"Bye Lovie. See you later. Take the bus home... okay?'

"Okay Momma. Love you!"

I walked down the hall to my son's classroom holding my breath with anticipation. How could I miss him so? He'd only been gone for a couple of days! Relief washed over me at the sight of my handsome boy. Elation came when he smiled.

"Hi baby," I mouthed.

His smile remained.

"Son, do you want to introduce me to your teacher?"

Just then his teacher walked up.

"Oh, Ethan... is this your mom?"

He got up out of his combo desk-chair and walked up to the teacher's desk. His introduction was short and to the point. I resisted my urge to wrap my arms around him – and not let go.

"Thank you Ethan. You go ahead and take your seat again," Miss Simmons graciously instructed, "while your mom and I talk."

"So, how can I help you today?" I asked.

"Would you mind grading some math papers?"

"If that's what you need help with then by all means, yes."

"Okay! Here's assignments from last week. And if they don't have a name on them please set them aside." She led me to the table on the far side of her desk and placed a stack of papers down. "Let me get you a red pen." She reached back over to her desk, grabbed one, and handed it to me.

"Great."

Every now and again I'd sneak a glance at my boy. Sometimes I'd find him looking at me, other times he seemed to sense his Momma watching him and he'd look up.

"Okay, so these three assignments don't have a name on them, but this stack is done," I said a couple of hours in.

"Attention kids," their teacher said. The murmuring stopped. "Ethan's mom is helping me grade your papers and she found three of you forgot to put your names on your assignments!" She held up the pages. "How is his mom or I to know who's these are?"

Silence remained.

"Remember ... we talked about this?"

Still nothing but widened eyes communicated their worries.

"You guys need to do better... okay? After all, you did the work, and you deserve the credit for it," she encouraged. "Why don't you get ready for recess."

Students lined up at the door.

"I'll be right back Miss Kathleen."

Miss Simmons went to the head of the line and led her students out and to the left. Moments later she returned.

"You've been a big help. Do you have to leave?"

"No. I've got an hour or so more."

Before the hour was up I presented Miss Simmons with a small stack of fill-in the blank English papers. And shared a smile with my son.

Chapter 60

"I saw dad today," Emma announced as she plopped in the front seat of the car.

My hands tightened around the steering wheel, my teeth clenched tight, and I reminded myself to keep calm.

"Where?"

"At school."

Oh. Maybe he was just dropping the boy off. Darn Mike still hasn't given me the address they are staying at.

"What do you mean? In his truck droppin' your brother off?"

"No. He was standing at the back of the bus waiting."

I looked in the mirror to see Bella's reaction to her sister's declaration. Her eyes were downcast.

"Did you see him too, Bella?" I forced cheer into the end of my question.

"Yes," her tone telegraphed trepidation.

"Well, he just waved. I guess you're okay, so…"

"No. He came up an gave me a hug," Emma shared. "Both of us." There was a lack of excitement or glee at seeing their father.

I put the car in reverse as anger flourished. The girls did not seem comfortable with their father's breach of the court order.

"Okay girls," I said as I pulled up to the house. "Let's have you go upstairs and change out of your school clothes. We'll get to your snack and homework after that."

I let the girls run ahead of me.

I'm not going to stress the girls with their father not having permission to see them at school.... I'll just go to the school tomorrow and report it. Get them keeping their promise. But this is not acceptable. The damn judge saw the need for the restrictions of his parental access.... He can't continue to just do whatever he wants. And where's he keeping our son! If I'd been in front of a mirror I bet I would have seen the smoke coming out of my ears.

~~~****~~~

"Have a good day Lovies." Hugs and kisses were shared with the girls before I walked into the main office.

"I need to speak with the principal."

"Okay," the secretary said. "Let me see if he's able to do it now."

"Thank you."

Minutes passed.

"Hey Kathleen. What's up?" the principal asked as he approached.

"Well... my kids are saying that their dad's breaching the custody order."

The head of the school paused as his eyes widened.

"Come on in," he raised an arm and motioned me to come farther into the office.

"I need you to watch my kids better," I sternly informed him as we stepped into his office.

"What's up?" his tone showed his confusion.

I shared with him the girls report of Mike parking near the bus and all.

"Okay, I'm glad the girls told you. I'm sorry we missed it. I'll have a teacher out there specifically to make sure your girls are safe."

I let the principal know that their brother was staying with their father on a trial basis, before I headed off to help out in the boy's class.

"Hi son," I mouthed as I walked into the classroom.

Seeing him changed my mood, brightened my day. I went to grading the stack of papers.

"Mom..." a beautiful voice said. "... Dad asked me to give this to you."

CHAPTER 60

Ethan handed me a scrap piece of paper. Once unfolded I saw an address.

"Thanks, son."

I stuffed the paper in my pocket as I glanced back up at my son's hands. Blood red lines ran across the back of his fingers.

"Lovie... what's this from?" I said as I gently took his hand in mine.

He shrugged his shoulders and pulled his hand back.

"Don't worry son. Go, go out to recess. I'll be here when you get back."

When he got back, as promised, I was still there. I spent the next hour or so watching him out of the corner of my eye. He was nervously running his top teeth over his knuckles. I motioned him over to me.

"Lovie... how about I bring you some gum so you can chew that instead of your knuckles?"

He put his hand behind his back.

"Don't worry son. I'll get you some. You try it... okay?" I smiled warmly at him. "Okay. I'll see you tomorrow, son. Love you."

~~~****~~~

The next morning, I walked up to Ethan outside his classroom at his locker.

"Mornin' Lovie. Here's that gum I said I'd bring you."

He smiled but couldn't hide the surprise in his eyes.

"The only thing is, you can't blow bubbles or chew it with your mouth open. The other kids really can't have gum, but your teacher approved it for you. Do you think you can do that? I mean ... it would be better for you then you continuing to cut your hands like that."

He nodded.

"Thanks Mom."

"You're welcome."

Chapter 61

"It would be best if you went to the Pinehurst P.D. and reported these incidents that the principal told me about," the Kellogg Superintendent and fellow church member recommended after calling me into his office, the following day.

I nodded as my jaw muscles clenched.

"As a matter of fact, I'd feel better if you headed over there now," his insistence was not lost on me.

"Okay. Let me grab my purse."

The drive from the Kellogg Middle School, where I was tutoring, to the Pinehurst Police Department seemed to take too long. It was only five and a half miles, but the miles seemed to stretch.

What if he breaches the court order again? Keeps doing this at the kids' school where they can't seem to stop him? Ethan's not doing well staying with him. My boy is so sullen. He looks unhappy as hell. Miserable to tell you the truth, God. They need to protect my girls better. These states make us send our kids to school... they need to protect them in our stead! I need to get Ethan back in my house, God. I know. You're right.

Acid bubbled in my stomach.

Moments after stepping into the lobby an officer had me follow him back to his desk.

"So, what can I help you with today ma'am?"

I handed him a copy of the divorce papers and explained the custody

CHAPTER 61

order, the stalking, the reason my son was with his father, the multitude of wrong addresses Mike had given me, his mental destructiveness, and his lies. Including the lie that our middle child wasn't his. A lie Mike decided to spew at the second visitation which caused the girls to cut it short.

The officer's eyes widened.

"He told your daughter he had two children in the marriage, and you had three kids in the marriage?" the officer repeated back to me. "Did he tell that to your daughter? His daughter?" The officer's face contorted with compassion, making me think he was a parent. "I can only imagine what else he's saying to the kids. WHY would he say that?"

"Because he doesn't like the happiness the kids and I have found without him in our lives... is all I can figure out." I shook my head. "I guess."

"What page is the custody order on?"

"Page nine."

"Did he request paternity tests on any of the kids?"

I rolled my eyes and frowned.

"No sir."

Why would he? She looks like a female version of him.

The cop took a few moments to confirm full custody being ordered to me as well as the visitation restrictions and the permanent restraining order to protect me.

"And you say he's showing up... here... at the elementary school?"

"Yes. My girls are reporting him parking over by where they get out of the school and get right onto the school bus. It'd be one thing if he just waved but he's coming over and stopping the girls from getting on the bus, demanding a hug.... It's makin' my girls feel uncomfortable."

"Do you know what he's driving?"

I gave a description. The officer's fingers began hitting the letters on the keyboard.

"What did you say his name was?"

I gave Brown both the birth name and the alias my ex-husband had been going under. The officer typed.

"What's his birth date?"

I gave him both.

"And his social security number?"

I gave him both.

We waited in silence as the officer studied the computer screen intently. His eyes moved back and forth as he read the information that popped up.

"Well.... It seems there's already an NCIC file on him," the officer informed me.

"A what?"

"Oh, sorry. A National Crime Information Center report..." he looked at me making sure I was now on the same page as him. "There's a cop out of ... Florence... who started it," the officer said refocusing on the monitor. A few clicks here and there and the questions started again. "He has a fake birth certificate?"

"Yes sir. It seems he bought one."

"Do you have a copy of that?"

"I do sir."

"Can you bring this to me..." a scowl now accented his expression, "... so I can add this to the file? Because I will need that. Oh yeah! I'm gonna need that."

"Sure. I can go get it and bring it back. I've got time before school's out."

"Okay." He nodded more to himself and the monitor than me. "And I'll go by the school. I'll keep an eye out for him. But he should only be coming by to drop off your son and pick him up, so I don't expect it to be much. I'll call you in a couple of days."

I headed back to the ranch, retrieved my envelope with Mike's fake birth certificate, and dropped it and other papers off with the receptionist. She made copies. I returned to the ranch determined to distract myself with my sewing project, but my heart was heavy. Measuring three times, or was it four, before cutting the fabric became necessary. Agitation won out. By the time the bus pulled up that afternoon, I had been parked at the end of the driveway for ten minutes.

The Superintendent... this new cop... they think there's something not right. It's not just me this time! Maybe I'm not crazy. Maybe I AM right! God, I swore to

CHAPTER 61

you... I'd never again *not listen to those gut feelings you've given me. Never! This just doesn't feel right, God. Thank you for those you've put in my life who believe me. I wish everyone believed me.*

I shook my head as I waited for the girls.

"Hey girls!"

My heart pounded with excitement (and relief) at the sight of my beauties coming down the bus steps. The pain of longing to see my son disembark the bus hit me on my out-breaths... sucking life out of me.

A day later, I made dinner, and the girls did their homework as they sat nearby.

We continued running through Emma's list finding more than one definition for some of the words. Dinner was cooked in between words. My youngest colored and did her first grade counting images of fruit math. That's when the phone rang.

"It's for you," John said as he handed the receiver to me.

"Hello Miss Kathleen, it's Officer Brown. Could you meet me at the Pinehurst office in... about ... thirty minutes?"

Something hit the pit of my stomach and I became light-headed.

"Yes. Yes sir... thirty minutes."

"Okay ma'am. Thirty minutes."

We hung up with no further information. I sucked air into my lungs.

Why does he need me? Now?

"What's up?" John's voice broke through my internal dialog.

I turned toward him.

"Um... Officer Brown has asked me to meet him in thirty." We nodded in agreement as John knew I had already been to the station. "Let me get supper served up for yah'll."

"Don't worry 'bout that. I'll get the girls fed. You go deal with what you've got to deal with."

"Okay, thanks." I kissed the girls on the top of their heads. "I'll be back in a bit."

The girls were focused on their homework and seemed not to be alarmed by the phone call and me heading out. This provided me with a moment of relief. One less, no two less things to worry about.

Not stopping to change into long pants, brush my hair, or anything like that – I grabbed my purse and keys before heading to the car. I tried not to run down the stairs as I headed to this mysterious meeting.

Officer Brown did not leave me waiting in the lobby for long. He jumped right into the facts of the day.

"You were right. We watched him do more than just come to the school and wait for the boy. He drove by the school more than once," Brown explained in his matter-of-fact tone.

I breathed a sigh of relief at someone else seeing proof of what I'd been warning others about.

"I'm glad I reported it to you."

"I'm glad you did too," his stern expression emphasized his words. "I've got your boy for you. That's why I called you down."

My jaw dropped and my heart skipped a beat before my body filled with excitement. The hall door opened. A dark-haired beefy officer escorted my son into the lobby. My very angry son reluctantly walked in – arms crossed over his chest, holding himself tight. I couldn't help but notice the skin around his eyes was red. The blood vessels in his eyes read like a road map to hatred.

Oh damn ... he's been crying! What happened?

I wanted to wrap my arms around him, but he had a 'go to hell, it's all your fault' look in his stare. My forward movement was arrested.

"Mom," he nearly spat out my name, "why'd you do this?"

"Your mom didn't do anything wrong," Brown spoke clearly as he stood up even straighter, puffing his chest out a little, causing the young boy before him to change his focus.

"They didn't even let us ride in the same car!"

He glared at the officer and then me.

"No young man we didn't. We couldn't. Because ..." Brown waited for Ethan to look at him again, "...because you are *not* in trouble. Your dad is."

Ethan clenched his jaw, narrowed his focus, fought back more tears.

Oh Lovie... that must have been scary, not knowing what was going on... the

CHAPTER 61

cops.... My heart was breaking.

"Your dad was ordered by the courts to go by certain rules," the officer's voice, while stern, softened as he intently watched the 10-year-old before him. "Your dad moved from Colorado to here... only seven miles away from you guys. Which was okay until he began following and watching you guys again..."

The boy did not break eye contact with the officer.

"That's called stalking," the officer accented his words by leaning his forearm on the butt of his gun held in his holster, supported by the belt around his waist. He kept the boy's attention with a simple upper-body movement. "Stalking is against the law."

Ethan's eyes widened as he realized what the cop said was true.

The Sargent let the silence linger. The boy was not giving in as he processed the information. Or was he? Was the boy blinded by love for his father and anger toward anyone he could pin it on? Angry at me, the best target in the room.

"Your mom should *not* need to keep moving you guys around because your dad keeps following you guys." The master of silent punctuation waited before sharing more. "You need to stop giving your momma such a hard time. She loves you. She's tried to give you a chance to be around your dad. He refuses to do things right. He wouldn't even give your mom the right address – four times! Your dad gave her four *wrong* addresses, on purpose."

Ethan seemed unwilling to accept the information. His focus changed to the floor. He wouldn't even look at me. My heart sank.

"So you're going back home to live with your mother and sisters.... Just as the judge ordered. And you're going to listen to your mom. Do what she says... Okay?" he punctuated his orders with his firm voice.

The boy nodded.

Not accustomed to being a witness to this level of anger in my son, I could only stand there in silence and wait. The pregnant pause became uncomfortable for me. I looked over at Officer Brown. He raised his brow and chin.

"Okay ma'am, you can take him back home with you."

My son turned his back on us and stepped closer to the door.

"Thank you," I said, with compassion filled eyes as I glanced from one officer to the other.

Both officers smiled with parental empathy.

"I'll be in touch," Sargent Brown said with his hand extended.

We shook hands before I placed my palm between my son's shoulder blades. I pushed forward ever so slightly.

"Okay son, let's get going."

Both Ethan and I glanced to the right as we walked down the steps. We saw the two police cars in the drive. Without moving closer, we searched the back seat of each cruiser, but Mike was nowhere in sight. We were both disappointed, but for different reasons.

Chapter 62

The drive back to the ranch was painfully silent as my son processed being a witness to his father being arrested, which I only knew the interim results about. I really didn't know how scared Ethan might have been. It must have been so upsetting for him. I was flooded with dread.

"Are you hungry, son?"

He said nothing, just sat buckled in the passenger seat with his arms tightly wrapped around his belly. His silence lasted the entire ride and longer. Once we pulled up to the house, we sat in the car for a few moments. The hush stretched into the uncomfortable.

"Let's get out … go upstairs. I'm hungry. If you're not, you can just go to bed," my soft tone welcoming but not pushy.

Ethan chose to go to bed.

The girls smiled at the sight of their brother rounding the stair rail.

"He's tired," I explained to John and the girls.

"Is he okay?" his youngest sister asked.

"It's been a long day for him." I sighed. "Let's let him rest."

I let my hand slide down her blonde hair.

The next morning a cloud of anger emanated off of my son as he sat with us for breakfast. The anger was accented by a dullness in his eyes. I walked over and put my hand on his forehead.

"Eu…. Lovie, you don't feel too good… do you?"

He moved his head side to side.

"Let me get the thermometer."

I walked to the nearest bathroom and retrieved the mercury filled stick of glass. With it under his tongue for only a couple of minutes it helped me to know his body was burning up — 102 degrees. My lips pressed against his forehead and nearly burned at the touch.

"Oh Lovie, you're not going to school today." His shoulders dropped. "Sorry Lovie. But you need to get in bed. There's a chance you should have been at the doctors already. Let me get you some aspirin and you go rest, Lovie, until I get an answer about us going to get your stuff."

His heavy eye lids showed he was not going to object to more rest.

"Son. I'll put a call in and see if we can go get your stuff today… while your sisters are at school, if you're up to it."

He did not respond.

God, I hate this. He's so angry! Will he ever get over this?

After the girls left for school and Ethan was off in his room, aspirin already taken, I made a call to the police department.

"Hello Officer Brown. Thank you, again, for helping me get my son back where he belongs."

"Glad to help."

"I was a bit surprised it happened so fast."

"You were right. Your ex-husband was going by the school at all hours. He tried to say he was just going somewhere and going by the school was the direct route to the freeway. I let him know that I knew where his house was and that was *not* the direct route. And with his history we figured he wasn't going to take the advice about driving straight up his street, Main Street, to the freeway. Then he came by after school again, and I got the complete NCIC report. So… I thought it'd be best to get your son back in your home sooner than later.

"He's going to be deported," the officer jumped right into the facts. "He won't be allowed back in the United States for thirty days."

"Oh …." I didn't know what to say. Guess I'd never thought about the deportation issue. Knowing he was an illegal in the U.S. was one thing, but deportation? I mean, he's been skirting around that fact for so long.

CHAPTER 62

"Um... okay. I'd like to pick up my boy's stuff from his dad's place. Is it okay if I drive out there and get it?"

"No," the Sargent was definitive. "You better go up to Wallace and get permission from him. Get it in writing, 'cuz he'd be the first to say you took something, even if you didn't."

"Oh... okay. How do I...?"

"Let me call up there so the deputy on duty will be expecting you. How about that?" he offered. "Would that help?"

"Um, yes. Yes it would. Can I just head up there?"

"Yeah, I'll make the call now."

"Thanks."

"Let me know if you have any trouble."

"Sure will, Sargent Brown."

I drove up to Wallace where a deputy waited for me in the lobby inside the jail. I explained what I needed.

"Okay. Sargent Brown said something about that. Why don't you wait here," he ordered. "I'll get Walton to write it," the deputy informed.

Twenty minutes later the deputy came out from where I assumed the cells were, beyond the designer-influenced lobby.

"Okay. I was finally able to get him to agree to let you go over there. Once." The deputy smiled and rolled his eyes. "He doesn't want *you* to go inside. He really doesn't want you to go over there at all, but... I told him you needed to get your son his stuff." The deputy sighed. "You can only be on the outside of the mobile. So take your son with you. He'll have to go with you. And remember, Walton's only giving you permission to go there once," the deputy stressed. "Once."

"Okay. I'll go there in about ..." I scrunched my nose and checked my watch, "...an hour. I have to go back and get my son."

"Right." He nodded. "Good." He handed me the scrap of paper with the permission written in Mike's own hand, even though he signed it with his alias. "Remember, *only once*. He *doesn't* want you inside."

I rolled my eyes.

Not like he's got anything I want.

"Oh and keep that piece of paper with his permission with you! Okay?"

"Yes sir," I lifted the paper and headed for the car.

Within the hour Ethan and I pulled in the driveway of where they had been staying. This time I pulled in past the line of pine trees that buffered the dwelling from the road noises and from view. Coojoe got up from his vantage point on the porch. I hoped he recognized the truck from a couple of weeks ago when I finally found where Mike was keeping our boy. But, just in case I called out the dog's name. He started wiggling his docked tail and backside at the sound of my voice.

"Let's get out son."

Coojoe met me as I got out of the truck. I dropped to one knee, and wrapped my arms around his thick neck. He put his head on my shoulder. We snuggled for a bit.

"Okay, Coojoe, we've got to get the boy's stuff."

I stood and the dog walked with me.

"Mom... can we feed the horses for dad?" Ethan said noticing his dad was not home.

"Um..." keeping the impending deportation of his father to myself, I agreed to it. "Sure. Just this once." I glanced around and didn't see the mares. "Where are they?"

"Behind the house."

"Okay. Before we leave, sure." We walked up the ramp to the porch, all three of us. "Do you have the keys?" I asked.

"Nah. It's not locked."

His answer made me wonder if Mike was squatting here or.... Ethan opened the door exposing a living room with a couple of saddles on the floor.

Oh... nice.... He's still got my saddle! Bile rose up in my throat.

Making sure my toes stayed on the porch I stretched my neck to see past the living room. I couldn't help but notice this mobile was like our first one. It had a similar pony wall that defined that kitchen space. I saw the edge of a table and the metal legs of a chair. But nothing else.

"Did you have a bed to sleep on?"

CHAPTER 62

"No. We slept out here," he motioned toward the saddles.

"Oh…" I was able to hold my smile. *I sure am glad this was temporary. Sorry son. Why did I think he would step up to the plate?* My jaw tightened. *He didn't even think enough of you, or himself, to pull the queen-sized mattress out of the big rig for you to sleep on!* "Go pack up Lovie. It shouldn't be more than those couple of boxes you brought over here."

"Can't you help me?" he requested.

My body started to move forward. I halted.

"No. I know you aren't feelin' great but…" I pulled the paper out of my back pocket. Held it up. "Your dad said I could bring you here, but he was specific … he didn't want me in 'his house'. He didn't give me permission to go inside at all. Sorry Lovie. You'll have to pull your boxes out here to the porch, then I can put them in the truck for you."

Ethan looked back at me, disappointed that I was still true to my word.

"I'll go visit the mares while you do this, okay?'

He disappeared around the door.

"Okay Coojoe, let's go find the girls."

Down the ramp and around the nose of the mobile home we went. That's when I noticed the rope tied amongst the trees. And the mares. Rosie, the bay filly nickered.

Where are the corral panels he took with him?

"Hello Rosie. Guess Mike made use of these trees?" I asked my "old mare" as my eyes followed the picket line snaked between the the sapling lodge pole pines.

I stretched out my hand caressing the brownish-red hair of the youngest mare. She turned her head, licked her lips – showing her submissiveness to one of *her* humans. A human she showed she missed, as she moved her muzzle to my waist. My desire to wrap my arms around her barrel and show her I missed her too was hard to resist, but I did. Ducking under her neck, I noticed she was securely tied to the field line that Mike had strung between the trees. I let my hand trail along her chest, knowing this was my last chance to love on her. After all, Mike would be pissed if he thought our mares still showed – their human momma – compassion after this long. I snickered.

The Pinto mare turned her head toward me. Our greeting was mutual, low keyed and cautious. Yet, it was like we'd never been apart. The year and a half melted away without effort.

I noticed the mares had been bedding down right where they stood. The pine needles were mixed with some hay and were depressed as if they had laid there recently. Greetings completed with It's The One I moved down the line to Cee Cee.

I stretched out my shaking hand. She swung her head over to smell my upturned palm. As the familiar aroma of *me* bounced back into her nostrils she thrust her muzzle back into my hand. Tears welled in my eyes.

"Yep. It's me Cee Cee," I whispered as I stroked her face.

She made eye contact with me. Disbelief mixed with soul-bound sorrow was reflected in her dark orange-brown eyes.

"I miss you too Cee Cee," I admitted in a library whisper – just loud enough for her to hear me.

I wrapped my arms around her neck, at her withers, and leaned into her. She breathed in a long breath, tucked her chin, and reciprocated the embrace. I don't know how long we enjoyed our chance visit, but I did not move until my son announced he was done packing.

"Where's the hay son?"

"Right here."

We both grabbed generous flakes of alfalfa from the bale.

"Good, let's feed them a little heavy. It wouldn't hurt," I encouraged.

Ethan took a moment, saying goodbye to the mares. I stayed with Cee Cee a smidgen longer but let my hand trail down her side and off her bum as I walked back toward the truck. None of the mares flinched at my hand lazily making contact with their hindquarters as I passed them. Maybe we all knew it would be our last stolen moment.

"Did you have food and water?" I asked Coojoe.

"The bag of dog food is open on the porch Momma. And they all have water," Ethan shared.

I grabbed Ethan's boxes off the porch and we walked to the truck. Coojoe

CHAPTER 62

went to the back of the truck, his backside wigglin' as he looked from me to the tailgate, to me and back to the tailgate.

"I'm sorry." I sniffled and wiped my nose as salty tears slid into the corner of my mouth. "I can't," my stomach knotted. "I can't take you with me. I didn't get you in the divorce. If I took you... it'd be stealing. And Mike would love to have something to hold against me... charge me with.... Plus, I can't have another dog at the ranch," sorrow saturated my words. "I'm more sorry than you know. He'll get someone out here to feed you," I promised my dog.

My heart cramped as I closed the truck door. *This saying goodbye over and over needs to stop! It's killing me.*

Chapter 63

With boxes back in his room, my son came down into my sewing studio. He was not as happy to see me as I was to see him. His questions started.

"So, what's going to happen with dad?"

I took a sip of coffee, stalling. Not being accustomed to lying to him, to any of my children, to anyone – willingly – I did not think today would be my day to start.

"Well, Officer Brown said, because Mike is illegally here in the United States, it looks like he'll be deported."

"What?" His beautiful face was awash with confusion.

"Yes son," I worked to keep my voice devoid of the smart-ass tone that fought to accent my words. "Americans don't like people who refuse to go by the country's rules. And your father's broken enough laws and shown a disregard for the requirements for residency – and more … so he will be deported to Canada."

"You know he was going to take me there… to meet my sister Tina!" Ethan spit the words out placing blame on me with his disgruntled tone.

"To meet Tina, your half-sister?" I tried to keep the shock and fear out of my voice.

"Yep."

"When was he going to do that?"

"In a week or two. And now I can't go! He was going to leave me with her too," Ethan sniped. "Now I can't even meet her!" Ethan spewed his words and stomped off.

My heart raced. I searched for my stepdaughter's phone number, and immediately took my phonebook upstairs – the urgency had me taking two steps at a time.

"Hello Tina."

"Hello Momma K," the cheer in my new-to-me, now 28-year-old, stepdaughter's voice was welcoming.

"So is it true?" I jumped right in with my questions. "Did your dad make arrangements with you to meet your brother Ethan?" my words rushed out of my mouth.

"Ye... yes. We were going to meet at the border. He's going to give me a chestnut mare too."

"Really?" I drew the word out as sarcasm separated each letter I spoke. "Tell me more?" *My mare! He's now giving away the mare he took... just so I wouldn't have her?*

"Why? What's up?"

"Where did you say you were set to meet?" my interrogation began.

"At some state line rest stop."

I huffed the air out of my lungs. My mind whirled around the probabilities of what Mike's plans could have been. Anticipatory panic surged within me.

"Well, according to your little brother, Mike was planning on leaving him with you.... Did you know that?"

I listened intently fearing my stepdaughter might try to skirt around this, all while hoping she didn't know of her estranged father's plans.

"What?"

"Yeah." My mind was working overtime. It ran fast trying to figure out what Mike's plan was as my stomach knotted. "I bet he was planning on making *you* a kidnapper."

"A what?"

"You know... when he was plannin' on havin' yah'll meet up... if you took your brother over the border... then he wouldn't have been the one who kidnapped him. You'd've been."

"What was he going to do?" An angry surprise filled Tina's questions. "Go to the bathroom... and never come back? Leavin' Ethan with me?"

Her disbelief at the possibilities was undeniable.

"Well, your brother is back here, living with me, and Mike is getting deported."

"Oh great!" It sounded like she was not ready to have her father living in the same country again yet.

"Yeah, sorry."

We shared a half-hearted chuckle before I caught her up on the recent happenings, including her father's break-her-heart lie about her little sister.

"So, Mike and Ethan will not be meeting you. Thank you for being so honest with me today. I'm sorry it's going to be a bit longer before you get to meet your younger siblings."

With the handset back up on the wall, I filled my coffee cup and walked toward the TV room to bring John up to date.

"John..." I said as I walked into the TV room. The tone in my voice told him something wasn't right. "Tina just confirmed that Mike *was* planning on taking Ethan up to meet his sister!" disbelief at what I was hearing come out of my own mouth caused my mouse-like voice to quiver.

"What do you think he was going to do?" John said with an inquisitive irritation.

"I'm not sure," I shook my head, "but he was bribing her to come meet him, after over twenty years of not even talking to her, with a horse – a chestnut mare." *My chestnut mare!*

"Well, it might have been nice for the siblings to meet."

"Oh... sure... no, I know the kids would like to meet their older siblings and visa-versa, well, at least the girls. I still haven't met their half-brothers..."

My mind raced.

"I don't get why he's being such an ass. You'd think he'd be happy that someone was helping take care of his kids for him. That they are living so nicely...." John interjected.

CHAPTER 63

My eyebrows arched and my frown grew. As the conversation lagged my curiosity of where they had planned to meet was getting the best of me. It was time to get some information.

Once back downstairs, I fired up the computer, pulled up Internet Explorer, and typed in 'State Line Rest Stop.' A map came up showing a couple of border crossings. I zoomed in.

Oh ... that's too close!

My stomach knotted up.

I clicked on "Directions" and typed in 'Creston, BC' and 'Pinehurst, Idaho.'

Oh my God! It's only 144 miles away. That's only like… about… a three-hour drive. The knots doubled in my belly.

I didn't see a rest stop showing on the map.

Was he gonna use one of those back roads he said he knew about and had used many times before and skirt around the cops?

Swallowing was a challenge. I forced the tightness to recede in my throat. The phone rang. Like a well-oiled friendship, Claudia instinctively called for an update. I filled her in on Ethan being back home and the Canadian trip that was thwarted and unraveled.

"That's scary," she confirmed I wasn't overreacting.

"Yeah. I'm sure happy he's being deported."

"I'm glad you got Ethan back."

"Me too. I hope he doesn't stay mad at me for too long."

My vision diverted to my feet. I traced the course of my laces in my view.

"You dodged a bullet there," she added.

"Yeah," dread fought with relief within me.

"Mom?"

"Yes Lovie?"

"Can we go feed the horses for Dad?" my son asked.

"I gotta go, Claudia. Gotta explain to Ethan why we can't go feed the horses."

"Oh ... I don't envy you. Talk to you later."

A sigh escaped my lips as I hung up the phone.

"No son." I shook my head lightly as he walked up to me. "No we can't.

Your dad only gave me permission to go there *once*. And I've already been there when we went to get your stuff."

"But who's gonna feed them?"

My heart sank at the realities of that loaded question.

"I just don't know son." I motioned for him to come closer. "It's up to your dad to figure that out. You know those animals are no longer mine."

Oh God I hope he gets someone to feed those mares and my dog....

We both lost all cheer. Our shoulders dropped. Tears welled in both of our eyes.

"Come here Lovie."

I opened my arms wide.

He hesitated but finally came to the comfort of my arms.

"I'm sorry Lovie," I said softly as I wrapped my arms around him. "But I'm glad we fed them heavy when we were there."

I might have held on a little longer than I should have but he wasn't objecting. It seemed he missed me too. My heart swelled.

~~~~****~~~~

A couple of days later, John got a call from Joe, the owner of the Snake Pit.

"Are you sure?" I overheard John say into the receiver. "Okay. I'll tell her. Thanks Joe."

"What's up?"

"It seems Cody's back," John shared.

"Wait... what?" My jaw fell open wide. "But he was deported!" Energy drained from me replaced by defeat.

John shook his head.

Resting butterflies took flight in my stomach. I took a few steps toward the kitchen counter, reaching out my hand to steady myself.

"Yes. I guess he was at the Pit last night. Joe was saying Cody was being really loud, making sure Joe noticed he was there."

Why do people still call him by that name? It's not even his real name!

I rolled my eyes at Mike's reported overt actions. Of course, he was loud

CHAPTER 63

and celebrating. He had to make sure Joe would call us. He succeeded.

Minutes later I was on the phone.

"All I can tell you is he was picked up by I.N.S. and taken to be processed out at Bonners Ferry... by Agent Archer," Officer Brown shared what he knew.

I located the number for the Immigration and Naturalization Services via the Internet, dialed the office, and waited impatiently with each ring ratcheting up my agitation.

"Agent Archer please?"

After the introductions, I started with my questions.

"How long was Mike's deportation supposed to be for?"

"Thirty days."

"Do you know it didn't even last a week?"

"What do you mean? I deported him myself, three days after he was arrested," the agent's voice was not devoid of surprise.

"Last night, he showed up at the restaurant a mile and a quarter from the ranch the kids and I live on. He was havin' supper and being loud and all... making sure he was loud enough for many people to notice and hence have the owner call our house to tell me he's back in the states."

"Um. I wonder how he got over the border," the agent contemplated aloud.

"Can I ask you a question?"

"Yes ma'am."

"Did you take his fake I.D.s away from him?" my voice lightened and teetered on sarcasm.

"What do you mean?"

"Did you take his Colorado Driver's License or his green military base access I.D. from him?"

"No," he said in an authoritative matter-of-fact tone. "It's not illegal to possess them, it's only illegal to use them," Agent Archer added as if reading out of a textbook.

"Oh... okay... do you think he stepped up at the border crossing and said, 'I'm Michael Patrick Walton and I've been deported this week, but I want back in the United States?'" I did not try to restrain my sarcasm. "No. I bet he used his United States issued I.D.s and said he was just comin' home." There was silence on the other end of the phone. "Does it take an ex-wife to tell you that he'd use them?"

"Um. I'll have to look into this."

I brought the agent up to date with my son's report of his father's unauthorized travel plans.

"So you see sir, I am a bit concerned about the safety of my children."

"Yes ma'am. If I were you, I wouldn't go anywhere without your sidearm. I don't trust him one bit either," the agent cautioned. "I'm sorry this has caused your children and you so much worry," he sounded somewhat genuine and irritated all at the same time.

"The Sheriff down here gave me permission to carry, so I do. Thank you."

"Thank you for the call."

"Yes, sir."

Chapter 64

A black and white pulled up the drive. Because I sat facing the windows at my sewing table, I was quick to answer the door after the officer knocked.

He uttered my first and last name to confirm he had the right person.

"Yes sir. How can I help you?"

"I've got these papers for you."

I opened the screen door and accepted my summons to court.

"A Restraining Order?" I asked, seeking clarification, and making sure my eyes were not playing a game on me.

"Yes ma'am, so it seems," a frown accented his words. "You know I don't know the situation, I just got ordered to serve you."

"Oh yes, sir. I do." I put my hand up, showing the officer my palm, letting him know I didn't blame him. "Thank you. I'll be there. Thank you, sir."

The door was closed. The officer drove away. I headed upstairs. I sat at the counter, fresh coffee in my cup, to read the court papers.

"I didn't threaten to kill him! What a lying ass," I said to no one.

"Kill who? What are you talking about?" John asked as he reached the top of the stairs.

I held up the stapled packet of white papers as he came closer.

"Mike's filed a restraining order against me." I shook my head. "Now I gotta go to court."

"Why don't you go on up there, now, and see if you even have to show up for the hearing, with him being deported and all."

Feeling a need to get out of the house, I took a drive to the Wallace Sheriff's office. The nice brown-haired officer was there.

"He filed a what?" the officer said.

"Yeah, it seems he's filed this restraining order."

"Is that what he was doing last week when I saw him?"

My eyebrows knitted. I squinted showing my confusion.

"I saw him pull up in front of the courthouse the other day. And I came in here to call the I.N.S. and check to see if he's even supposed to be here. After all, when they picked him up, they said he wasn't supposed to be here for thirty days."

"Really?"

"By the time I got an answer and back out there, his car was gone. I've been instructed to arrest him and take him into custody if he shows back up again. They want to put him in federal lockup for coming back in the states."

"Okay, well that explains a lot." I scratched my head. "Doesn't my restraining order, the one the judge already acknowledged, still take precedence?"

"Yes ma'am it sure does. It's still on file here and we are still here to enforce it, even out at the ranch you live on."

"Okay. Thanks for lettin' me check on this." I turned to leave. "I guess I'll see you," I confirmed on the court papers, "in two weeks."

Not long after I got back to the ranch, the phone rang.

"Kathleen, it's for you. Some lady named Karen," John said.

"Karen?"

We both shrugged our shoulders at the unknown caller.

"Hello. This is Kathleen."

"Hi. My name is Karen."

"Yes?"

"I'm Cody's girlfriend." A silence hung in the air. "Can I ask you a question?"

I took a deep breath as I heard the *please* in her voice.

"Yes. Go ahead."

CHAPTER 64

"Do you have my handgun?"

"Your what?" the disbelief in my voice was not lost on her.

"My handgun. Cody borrowed it and now it's missing. Cody said you stole it when you came over to his place last week."

A chuckle escaped my voice box.

"No, why would I need your gun when I've got one in every room here?" My bravado grew with each word. "No, I did not take your gun," I added dismissively.

"I didn't think you did."

"Miss Karen, Karen is it?"

"Yes."

"Cody, as you call him ... but know his real name is Mike, first of all ... he gave me written permission to take our son over to his place, in Pinehurst. He did not give me permission to go inside his dwelling. So, I didn't," my flat matter-of-fact tone was not friendly but not aggressive either. "Only our son was allowed in that house."

"I really didn't think you did," she repeated with a kind, yet irritated tone in her voice. "He just said you did."

"Sorry. He's probably sold it, like he did mine years ago."

"Yeah." She sighed. "I've already put a call into a couple of pawn shops around here."

"That's a good call on your part."

"Do you know where he is?" she asked in a friendly tone.

"No ma'am. But I know he will, most likely, be at the courthouse in Wallace, as we have this hearing."

"How do you know that?"

"Because he filed a restraining order against me and we have a court date on Wednesday of next week."

"He ... is he staying over there in Pinehurst?"

"I'm not sure."

"He asked me to move over there to take care of his son," she shared like I would welcome commiserating with her.

Bile rose up in my throat.

"I'm just not up to that," she continued .... "My kids are all grown and out of the house. And I don't want to start raising kids again. I'm sorry. You really do have a nice son. He seems like a good young boy."

"You don't have to be sorry, Karen. It's a lot to consider. And you don't have to be worried, the boy is back here living with me. It didn't work out. It wasn't a healthy situation for my boy. Plus, it was just a trial stay anyway."

She was on an information-gathering mission. But I don't think I helped much.

"You said your court hearing is next Wednesday?" she asked.

"Yes. It's a 10 a.m. court call, at the Wallace Courthouse."

"Do you mind if I show up? To confront him?" She hesitated.... "I haven't seen or heard from him for a while."

I guffawed.

I don't think she knows he's been deported.

"I don't mind. It's a public place."

"Thank you for answering my questions," although she didn't seem satisfied, I think she genuinely meant it.

After filling John in on the conversation with Karen, he changed the focus to my son.

"I think that your son is not safe here, especially with Cody..." I scowled at John's use of the false name, "...back so quick," John said. "Add to it, his attitude and behavior hasn't gotten any better with the way he is treating his sisters."

"Right. And I worry Mike's gonna be stopping by the school again and ...." nausea hit my stomach. "Can I even keep my kids safe?" I uttered rhetorically. *I'm failing my kids.*

"Do you think your folks would be able to take Ethan?"

I shook my head as my mind remembered all of the ways someone could get into and out of my folks' ranch, without being seen.

"No, because Mike knows that ranch. We used to live there. It's too open."

"What about Claudia and Gary?"

My stomach soured and acid bubbled up into my throat.

CHAPTER 64

I'm too close to the border for this shit! I gotta keep that beauty safe and the girls... but what is the right, let alone, the best thing to do? What is the best way to protect them?

Vacillating between choices, minutes passed before I dialed Claudia's number.

"Hey... with Mike being back here and the cops not able to get a hold of him... would you mind Ethan coming to stay with you until his dad is successfully deported?" My throat tightened. "I hate to ask. I mean I just got him back... but... I don't trust me being able to keep him safe with Mike acting fishy. Let alone Ethan's still pretty angry and acting like he doesn't even want to be here, being mean and all."

I filled Claudia in on the call from Mike's girlfriend and another missing firearm associated with my ex, which only added to our safety concerns.

"Did he sell it or hide this handgun? And if he hid it... is he planning on using it?" the cop's daughter in Claudia queried.

"I don't really know. He blamed my gun, the one my grandpa Joe left for me, to have been 'stolen by the ranch hand.' But I believe he sold it to pay for his girlfriend to get home to see her grandparents as one took ill ... and I was coming to the horse show with my folks and all. Back when I was dumb enough to be trying to put our marriage back together."

"Let me talk with Gary and make sure it's okay with him. After all, you know my sister did this for me with Kurby," she finally addressed my original question. "Give me a couple of hours."

Within hours the plans were made.

"Okay, John... Gary and Claudia said that they'd let Ethan come down and stay with them. But... now I gotta figure out how to get him down there before the court hearing."

My mind was racing.

I need to get my kids safe. Ethan's not safe here. But is this the right thing to do? Why can't I just live a quiet life ... with my kids? Why can't Mike just leave us alone? Why can't he get happy with a balance of visitation and shared parenting? I was trying to work this shared parenting time out! Dam it!

A reoccurring dread started to fill me.

"What if Mike's only back to take the boy with him?" my audible words stopped my mind from running on its hamster wheel.

"Yes. Yes it would be. It's not like that hasn't been in his plans before with his visit with Tina and all. And if Mike gets Ethan over the border it will make it very difficult to get the boy back. It could take a long time to get him back, years maybe," John contributed to my worries.

My potential realities. My potential failures. I shook my head as my stomach cramped.

"This is going to be the best for your son. They are good people," John added as he watched my worries surface.

"Oh... no. It's not that I don't think that Gary is a good man and a nice strong male influence for the boy.... And Claudia is a good woman.... It's just a lot to think about. I just hate this. I hate needing to do this. I'm tired of movin' us around already, John."

As the afternoon wore on, I used the pretext of going up to get the kids from the bus as an excuse to have some time to myself.

It seems Gary had called while I was down at the end of the drive.

"Gary's gonna meet me halfway... at Winnemucca tomorrow afternoon," John whispered while the kids were changing out of their school clothes.

Damn it! My tightening jaw muscles flickered under my skin. *They made plans... for my kid... without me in the planning? What the...!*

My feelings must have been telegraphed on my face.

"Well, you have so much to do, and this is not going to be a fun trip. Gary being willing to meet us halfway will save lots of time. Plus, it will make it so you can still make it to court on Wednesday. And if I take the boy down there... and there is car trouble or something goes wrong, at least you won't miss your court date."

I shook my head. Not happy with the arrangements. Not happy with the effing logic of it all. Not happy that our life was a cluster-fuck. I seethed with frustration and anger.

Things are happening too fast! I don't want this anymore. I'm tired of all of this bullshit. But I need to keep the boy safe. I need to keep my girls safe. Mike's plans... what if they haven't changed? What if....

CHAPTER 64

John reached over and put his hand on mine, arresting my mental descent down the *what-if* rabbit hole.

"This will be for the best. Ethan will be in safe hands, and he'll get to see his grandparents, I'm sure, as they are so close down there. You need to be here, taking care of the girls. You can't be in two places at once," he directed me with his 'I-know-better' tone of voice.

Effing logic again. I'm starting to hate effing logic. How much tearing apart of this family must we endure?

It was time to set the kids down and have a chat with them. So, as soon as they came out to have their after-school snack, John and I brought them up to date on Mike's return, the pending court hearing and John taking Ethan down to meet with Gary.

"Son, I need to make sure you are safe. I don't know what state of mind your dad is in, but ... he's really mad and ... well, we've seen him mad before and sometimes it's not pretty." I looked into my favorite blue eyes. "I don't want you to get hurt Lovie."

Ethan nodded ever so slightly.

"You get along with Gary... and Claudia's not a bad lady. Strict, but not a bad lady," I put some cheer in my voice.

My boy smiled halfheartedly. I couldn't tell if he was glad to get away from me, away from the turmoil, or just glad to go be where he was the only kid in the house.

Ethan packed most of his stuff and I assured him he'd be gone for a short time. I think the determination in my voice helped.

"We'll speak each day... okay son?" I said as he made sure he had his belongings all packed.

The next morning, we shared a hug, after the girls got theirs in.

"I love you son."

"Love you too."

"It won't be long. Go for a visit and go see G-maw and G-paw. And your Brax. You'll get to go see your Brax-dog."

We both smiled as we searched for the positive in this turbulent time. We wrapped our arms around each other. Minutes later, after letting him go, I kissed him on the top of the head as he buckled up. The three of us girls stood at the top of the driveway, waving as John and Ethan drove out.

My heart sunk.

God, how long will I be without my son this time?

"Let's go get you ready for school," I encouraged, hoping to keep something normal.

That day, a couple of hours later, I put the girls on the bus and then headed to my hairdresser's salon. As with many stylists, half of her job was listening to the changes in her clients' lives. She was akin to my counselor for the day, and counseling she did. We chatted about my current worries as she washed my hair.

"May I make a suggestion?" she asked as she unwrapped the towel from around my wet hair.

Making eye contact with her in the mirror, I lowered my chin and gently raised it twice.

"Keep a journal."

My expression contorted awash with confusion.

"You see my two boys out there?" She tilted her head toward the door and the two tall young adults I passed as I came in today.

"Yes."

"Those are my sons. I didn't get custody of them in the divorce."

"Right," I said as I remembered that she had shared this before.

"Well, at that time someone suggested I keep a journal ... a journal for them ... to them. To write in, whenever I wanted or needed to.... So I would have proof ... that I thought of them. So I'd have proof that they mattered even when they weren't with me. So I didn't have to try to remember things ... like the answers to the questions they are asking me now! Now that they are back in my life."

She stopped trimming my layered cut and looked me square in the eyes... in the mirror as she was still standing behind me.

"I didn't do it," sorrow was present in her voice as well as her eyes. "But, now that they are nineteen and twenty... and asking all of these questions, I sure wish I had."

CHAPTER 64

I swallowed hard as if her lesson was *my* hard pill.

Oh God, please! My Ethan won't be out of my home that long... will he?

After my hair was cut, dyed, and dried, I went to the grocery store. I grabbed a faux blue jean-covered Composition Book as I picked up stuff to make a homemade seafood tomato sauce-less pizza. After all, my acid reflux couldn't take the tomato sauce tonight and, with all of this stress, the last thing I wanted was for Emma not to be able to eat as I wasn't sure she might not have a flare-up of her Geographic Tongue. We still didn't know what caused it. It was time to make a meal that was sure to bring some smiles to the girls and me.

I started the journal that night, after supper. I wrote on the inside cover:
To Ethan,
  For while you are out of my direct care, I still care.
  Kathleen, your loving mom
As I dated the first journal entry "Early Feb. 2003" I reminded my son of some of the background events that included:

  me toughest thing to do was packing your stuff so you could lay with your choices. mat is until I had to 'hand you over' to your father. It would prove to be a small disaster in the weeks that followed.

I also apologized to him, in the journal, for putting him in the middle when I asked him to give his dad an envelope on Valentine's Day –

...one that was just the torn-up card that your dad sent me this week.

I shook my head. Still disgusted that my ex-husband was sending me love notes over a a year and a half after we had stopped living together and four months after the divorce was final.

I fell asleep with the journal and pen on my lap and tears in my eyes.

Chapter 65

John made the handoff of my beautiful boy and was back on the Idaho ranch late Monday night. I heard the car pull up outside, below the second-story bedroom. I looked at the clock and saw it was 11:48. I sat up and moved the journal and pen to the bedside table. I wiped the crusted tears from my eyes and waited for John to come upstairs.

"So... how'd it go?" I barely let him get through the threshold of the bedroom.

"It was an easy drive. Ethan did not talk much with me on the way down," John said as he disrobed. "Gary and I met up at noon." He crawled in under the covers and we snuggled. "All three of us ate lunch and then headed off back to our own homes."

He yawned. The sound signaled my brain and, unintentionally, I mimicked his yawn.

"You can call and check on him in the morning," John said as we both drifted off to sleep.

"How's he doing?" I abruptly asked Claudia the next morning, after she answered the phone.

"He's okay. I'm gonna take him to school today and get him registered. Get this back on track – the store is open today and I'm expecting a shipment of fabric," there was that shared joy in her voice that we all used to get when a bunch of fabric was due to come into the shop.

My mind raced back to last summer and the handsome blonde UPS driver,

CHAPTER 65

his well-built body, and those shorts. The man wore brown uniform shorts during the summer. Yum. And added to it... he was bringing us fabric. Pretty fabric. It was a two-fold summer treat for us all. I shook off the distracting memory.

"Okay. Thanks. I hope I sent all of the right papers to you."

"Yes. It looks like you did. The permission slips... temporary guardian, medical treatment.... It all seems like I've got what he needs."

"Okay. I'll be sending you a hundred a month, right?"

"Yes, that should be enough. If not, I'll let you know."

"Thanks Claudia. Tell 'im I love 'im, please."

"Will do."

And with that, I hung up and made sure the girls were ready to head down to the bus.

~~~****~~~

A day later, with the girls off to school, I put on a skirt, blouse, and ankle-high boots before heading off to court.

"Tom is going to meet us at the courthouse," John said as he drove.

I breathed a sigh of relief that was only made better as we pulled up to the courthouse and there he was. Tom was waiting for us. After 'thank you's were said the three of us headed to the courtroom. But not before I looked for Mike.

John and Tom flanked me. They sat like unmatched bookends. We were shoulder to shoulder in the small courtroom.

"So what does he say are his grounds for this restraining order?" Tom asked.

"He says I threatened to shoot him."

"Did you?"

"No. I promised."

Tom's eyebrows rose and he narrowed his gaze.

"Last time he hit me," I explained, "was when I was nine months pregnant. He snuck up and hit me from behind. So, after he tried to deny hitting me, a couple of hours later, I told him, reminded him really... 'first-time shame on you, second-time shame on me, third time you will not survive a hit.' He was a bit ignorant, so he asked me 'what you gonna do?' So I helped the fool understand the lengths I would go to protect my children and myself." I watched Tom's expression. "I merely said, 'You know how well I shoot.'"

"Well... was that a threat?"

"No sir. It was a promise. After all, I know threatening is illegal."

"You're right. Threatening is illegal. And if you were not threatening him... then you can admit that to the judge."

We both smiled.

Just then a medium-built, strawberry-blonde lady, whom I estimated was in her early to mid-fifties, walked into the room. All three sets of our eyes focused on her. She nodded at me before sitting behind me in the only other row in this small-town courtroom.

"Who's that?" John asked.

"I don't know, but I think it's Karen... Mike's girlfriend. She said she might come, to confront him... about her gun and all. She hasn't seen him in a while," I shared.

I checked my watch.

The judge should be here any minute. In anticipation, I rubbed my hands together. *Remember. You know this is bullshit. You didn't threaten him. It was a promise. After he laid that last whoopin' on you. It's not illegal ....*

"All rise!" the bailiff ordered interrupting my silent coaching.

The same dark-haired man in a black robe, who presided last time I was here, walked in and sat at the elevated desk. The bailiff gave the four of us permission to sit. We complied as the judge reviewed the case file. He looked up. Surveyed those in attendance and then reviewed the documents. We all saw him lift his left arm, and pull back his sleeve, exposing his watch. He then glanced up at the clock on the wall opposite the bench.

I took a deep breath as I was expecting Mike to walk in any second.

The judge checked his watch again. His eyebrows came closer together as wrinkles grew on his forehead and his lips tightened his already closed mouth.

"We have before us a restraining order request, but it appears the

CHAPTER 65

requesting party is not here." He looked up again, hesitating a moment to see if Mike was going to walk in the door. When the door remained still the judge continued. "Misses Walton," he gestured for me to come to the respondent's table.

I stood and swallowed hard as I knew I needed to explain my actions from about five years ago that could, depending on the viewpoint and mood of the judge, get me in trouble. My confidence was bolstered by Tom's recent assurance that I was in the right, as I walked where directed.

"Misses Walton, thank you for showing up today. I am sorry, it looks like the court's and your time have been wasted as the requesting party is a no-show."

I nodded.

"Do you have any questions?"

"Well sir," I hoped my timid voice was loud enough, "isn't the restraining order you granted me a few weeks ago valid for both of us? I mean… it says he has to stay away from me, but it also says I have to stay away from him… doesn't it?"

A smile grew on the judge's face.

"Yes ma'am. Which makes this request for a restraining order on you unnecessary."

"Okay, thank you, sir. That is what I thought." I breathed a sigh of relief.

"Now, also, because Mr. Walton is not here, the court will dismiss his request for protection, and you are free to go and continue on your way." The sound of the gavel hitting its wooden block pad accented his words.

"Thank you, sir."

My protective bookends rose and we walked out of the courtroom, flanking me again, not stopping until we were out by the cars.

"Where I come from, we call this harassment," Tom commented. "Forcing someone to show up, just in hopes of making them look bad, make them worry, and waste time is harassment," the harsh tone in the ex-officer's voice made me think he'd changed his opinion of Mike by now.

"By the look on the judge's face … he thinks so too," John added.

"Well, it won't go well for him when they catch up to him," Tom said before we got in our cars and left.

"Breakfast?" John offered as he drove us to the riverside restaurant.

Chapter 66

Each time I walked past Ethan's empty room my heart ached, so much so that I put pen to the page after the girls went off to school. I wrote in my son's journal.

It's only been days, my love, but I already miss you more than it is, most likely, safe to admit. I feel like this missing you is going to consume me. You sound ... better, on the phone. Better than you did when you were staying with Mike. At least you will talk to me now. I'm sorry if you were uncomfortable talking to me while Mike was around. That is not how it is supposed to be.

With the house quieting down and the defunct restraining order hearing behind me, I decided to keep my doctor's appointment. I checked my date planner.

Okay, 1:30... it shouldn't take too long, and it'll leave me enough time to get back here and get the girls from the bus at 3:12.

I busied myself with cutting out individual oak leaves from some of my fabric to applique on the Log Cabin quilt. This kept me distracted before I headed over to the doctor's office. After signing in, with fifteen minutes to spare, I sat in the waiting room and read a magazine.

One thirty came and went. The nurse called me back to a patient room about a quarter 'till two. She took my vitals and left me in the room waiting for the doctor. The silence left me checking the face of my wristwatch to make sure the hands were moving.

One one thousand, two one thousand, three one thousand....

There was a knock on the door just before the doctor walked in. He got the small talk out of the way, but not quick enough for me.

"You've written down, here, that you've had this acid problem for a while?" The doctor sought clarification.

"Yes. It even put me in the hospital for a night... back two years ago. My husband gave me one of his nitro pills, 'cuz we thought I might be having a heart attack, and it seemed to help. But the docs said it wasn't my heart. The one doc said it might be due to the stress of our house burning down."

I frowned.

"Well, if it's acid reflux, then the nitro worked on the smooth muscle of the esophagus," the doctor explained. "What's brought you in now?"

"I've been forced to stop drinking coffee," I tilted my head and shared one raised eyebrow and a cocky smirk, "because it is setting off the acid in my stomach. And that's just not right!" I allowed a short chuckle to escape my lips. "It's even bubbling up into and burning my throat. I tried tea, that was bad too. And ... now," my eyes dropped as did my shoulders, "over the last few days... water is doing the same thing. Water!"

I shook my head over the stupidity of water hurting me since it is part of our life force.

"Okay," he scribbled notes in my file, "I'd like you to have a test before you go today. My nurse, Nancy will take you upstairs, to the x-ray room," he said as he opened the door to leave.

"Follow me," Nurse Nancy said, and I did. "Okay, it shouldn't be too long. Doc wants this test run and there is only one person in front of you."

"Do you know how long this is going to take?" trepidation laced my words.

"Oh, don't worry, it's only about a ten- to fifteen-minute test," the nurse said.

I fidgeted as I heard the tech grumble.

"Darn it! Why isn't this working right!" he said, not once but three times over the course of ten minutes.

I checked, checked, and rechecked my watch. The minutes ticked by. My

CHAPTER 66

agitation grew.

"Do you know how much longer?" I kept my tone kind, but there was a warble in my voice. "Maybe I should just reschedule?"

"No. Please don't. He's got it working again," a nurse said as she patted me on the shoulder.

But I really need to get home. It was 2:30. *If this test doesn't start, I'm gonna have to leave. They don't understand. I need to go! I need to be there... for the girls. Damn it!*

"Okay Kathleen, you're next. Please put on this gown," she said with a light blue garment in her outstretched hand.

With the stylish medical drape tied in the back, I waited. I kept my socks on as the linoleum tile squares were cold.

"Okay ma'am, please lay down on this x-ray table. Please lay still," he said as he walked away.

The minutes seemed to stretch only adding to the acid buildup in my stomach. I burped and my throat burned. The safety of my daughters bounced around like a ping-pong ball in my head.

I really need to get going. I shouldn't have waited so long. I should just get up and get dressed and get going. I promised the girls I would be there. Damn!

"Okay, hold still…. Hold your breath. Don't move."

The whine of the machine took my focus as I held my breath.

"Just a couple more shots," the technician said as he pulled the quarter-inch metal plate from a slot in the cold table. He walked back behind the protective wall.

"Hold your breath."

Then the mechanical noise was repeated.

"Okay, we're done. You can change back into your clothing."

I rose and placed my feet heavily with each step on the floor, not wanting to have my socks make me lose traction.

Falling won't get me to the girls any quicker.

With my jeans, shirt, and shoes back on I grabbed my purse and walked out of the office, not stopping to say anything to anyone.

If I hurry, maybe I can make it home before the bus gets there, I'm only here at

Kellogg!

The acid continued to bubble in my stomach. I reached for the antacids I had become accustomed to carrying with me everywhere. A couple of nickel-sized chalky tabs sat momentarily on my tongue before I chewed them as I tried not to exceed the speed limit. But, as I checked my watch, my foot laid heavier on the throttle.

The highway was free of 'black 'n whites' – *thank God*. But as I got off the freeway I was more mindful of the multiple changes in the posted speed limits along the river. Once I rounded the curve of the west end of the ranch I sped up. My eyes scanned the field, barn front, and driveway that last quarter mile. As I pulled in the drive, I noticed the barn's big sliding door was partially open, but there was no sign of the girls or the dog.

The antacids were not working.

I rolled down the car windows, willing my ears to hear their laughter.

But there was nothing.

I accelerated up the drive. As I crested the knoll, I glanced up at the balcony.

No sign of the girls there either.

My heart raced as I got out of the car and opened the unlocked door to the house. I breathed a sigh of relief.

Well, if the door is unlocked, they're here! Yes!

"Girls! Emma, Bella!" I hollered as I climbed the stairs.

Just then I saw the girls' red, white, and blue matching jackets in a heap on the kitchen floor.

But wait... who's jacket is this?

I lifted the blue-green jacket that was about the same size as Emma's.

Who's coat is this?

"Emma! Bella!" panic infiltrated my voice.

My head was on a swivel as I turned and went down the hall, looking for them in their bedroom. But nothing.

Oh God! Where are they? What if he's got them? I knew I shouldn't have stayed at that effing doctor's appointment! Damn it. I knew I should have left and rescheduled. It just doesn't pay for me to try to take care of myself. Stupid,

CHAPTER 66

stupid, stupid.

A queasiness hit my stomach and a dizziness made thinking difficult.

Wait! Their jackets are here. Think. Think. Maybe they are playing or hiding? God let them be hiding and not ....

I opened the back door. Lifted my fingers to my mouth and whistled as loud as I could. I was rewarded within seconds.

"You who!" Emma responded in her usual manner as she hadn't learned to whistle yet.

My heart skipped a beat, or two. And that is when the phone rang. I stepped back into the kitchen and lifted the receiver.

"I've got them. They're over here. Come over," Maggie's familiar Swedish accent served to calm the panic, but not for long.

I hung up the phone, headed out the back door, and down the steps – taking them two at a time. As I did so, my eyes searched the horizon.

Is he still driving that brown truck?

Halfway down the driveway between the main house and the rental house I noticed there were vehicles across the road, but even farther than I expected. They were on the other side of the river.

What? How can there be cars over there? Oh hell... there isn't a road over there... is there?

I swallowed the lump that had built in my throat.

Shit!

Quickening my pace, I ran up Maggie's drive and up the steps. There, waiting for me, with Maggie were my two beauties. I wrapped my arms around them. It was only then my pulse slowed.

"Oh Kat'leen, he was 'ere," Maggie said with wide eyes.

Adrenaline surged through my body once more.

"We got off the bus and we were showing Jenny," Emma gestured over her shoulder to her little friend, "the horses in the barn and dad pulled up, outside the barn."

"Outside... the barn? He was on the property?" I asked for clarification as fear and anger gave me a bitter taste in my mouth.

"Yeah. He tried to get us to come to him and get in the truck." Emma's eyes were wide with terror. "So we ran out the back of the barn, then up to the house and called Maggie!"

"Okay, Maggie can I use your phone I need to call the cops!" My urgency almost made my tongue trip over my own words.

"I already called 'em," Maggie admitted. "They should be here any moment. I've got the girls watching some TV." Maggie smiled trying to keep things calm.

"Oh… okay… why don't you girls go back in with Jenny while we wait for the officer to show up," I suggested heavily in my best and kindest motherly tone.

My girls walked back into Maggie's house.

"Maggie… is there a road on the other side of the river?"

My face contorted as I was not able to hide my anguish.

"Yeh, yeh there is." She shook her head. "You didn't know that?"

The queasiness returned. I placed one hand on the balcony railing and one on my stomach.

"No. But," it felt like my heart did a splash landing into my stomach, "that tells me how he's been watchin' this place and how he knew I was late gettin' home to the girls," I said in a low angry tone. *Effer.* "I knew I shouldn't have stayed at the doctor's." *Never making that mistake again!*

Maggie stood close. Supportive. But not knowing what to say, she remained quiet. She was a rock. I was glad to be friends with her, even if I was sorry I had to involve her in this mess.

"Emma, come here please," I requested.

A moment later my beautiful brunette was out on the balcony with Maggie and me.

"Lovie, who is that girl and why is she here?"

"I told you. It's Jenny. From school. You said she could come over."

"I said, she could come over, but not without me talking to the kid's parents and … me making sure I was home. You just can't make plans without clearing them with me. Because…" I looked into her big brown eyes, "because … things like today happen. All because I was held up at a doctor's appointment."

CHAPTER 66

Emma's eyes widened with understanding.

"Let's call her folks."

"I'm sorry Momma," sorrow and frustration filled her voice.

"I know Lovie." I gently stroked my oldest daughter's hair, grateful for every last hair on her head. "And so am I. I'm sorry we have to live this way."

I don't know whom the soft tone of my voice calmed more, but I knew being close to my beauties was what was really calming me.

Chapter 67

"Hi Jenny," I said as if we'd met before. "Can I get you to call your folks and let me talk to one of them?" I asked just as I walked through Maggie's front door.

"Sure. My dad said he'd be home this afternoon and he should be home by now."

"Great."

It didn't take long for her dad to get here after I gave him the address and lightly explained why I couldn't bring her home today. Once her dad pulled in behind Maggie's car, the girls and I went down to meet him.

"Hey, Emma... would you get Jenny's jacket? It's up in the kitchen." I asked knowing it was going to be cold in the morning.

"Oh, sure."

"This side door is unlocked. Why don't you go on up and get it for her?"

"Okay Mom."

I turned to Jenny's dad. Made eye contact and kept my volume low.

"Thank you sir. Sorry for this inconvenience. My daughter didn't know I had a doctor's appointment today and I didn't expect it to run late. Normally I'm here when the kids get home from school," I said in hopes of not having him feel as much unease as I know I would if I had been called with the *'sorry, your daughter can't stay here and I can't bring her home, 'cuz the cops are on the way'* from a parent who I assumed my child would be safe with.

Our daughters were saying their goodbyes.

CHAPTER 67

And going forward I certainly will be here. I won't EVER be late again! Never! I won't ever take that chance and put my beauties in that much danger again. Oh how scared they must have been.

"Well, maybe," Jenny's dad's words pulled me out of the spiral my mind and soul were falling down, "it would be easier for your daughter to come over on a weekend and spend the night at our house… like on a Friday? We're just a few miles up toward Cataldo…."

Yeah, and I bet it will be safer too for your daughter … and mine.

I was surprised he was even offering… maybe he was just being kind. Either way, his kindness was appreciated.

"Let me check on some things before I say yes. But…" I smiled and nodded, "it might just work out in the next week or so."

And with that, there was one less child's safety to concern myself with.

The minutes lagged before the Sheriff's cruiser pulled in the driveway. Both Maggie and I smiled, as relief washed over us.

"Hello Officer," I greeted as I walked down the stairs with Bella following close behind.

"So what's up today?"

"He was here!" my little, now 6-year-old exclaimed stepping in between the officer and me. "He came all the way up to the barn!" She stomped her foot. "And he's not supposed to do that!" she accented her emphatic words as she crossed her arms over her chest.

The Officer and I shared a look as we both worked to keep our – *how cute is she* – to our adult selves.

"You might be right, young lady," the officer said. "Why don't you let your momma and me chat a few minutes and see if we can't stop him from doin' that?"

Bella leaned her head back, looked up at me, made sure I was okay being left to talk to this guy. I put my hands on her shoulders, but not without caressing her blonde hair first, in an effort to reduce her worries.

"Mum's gonna be just fine. Why don't you go on up and finish watchin' that show with Maggie? And I'll send Emma up in just a few minutes."

Bella pursed her lips and walked off in a huff.

"Guess she's not too happy her ... dad is it... came on the property?"

"No sir. I don't think she is either."

We both let out a lighthearted chuckle.

"So..." he pulled out his notepad from his breast shirt pocket, "can you tell me what happened today?"

"Well, my ex-husband breached the restraining order. ..." I brought him up to speed on it all.

Emma, now standing beside me, repeated her account of the incident.

"Thank you young lady," the officer said.

Emma walked back to the stairs and stopped halfway up them. Turned and sat.

"How do you think he knew you weren't here?" the officer inquired now that we were alone.

"Well," I pointed out down the driveway, "it seems there's a road over there, on the other side of the ponds and North Fork!" I frowned, still pissed at myself for not knowing this before.

The officer's eyes followed my arm's movement.

"Yes ma'am, there is. I know it's hard to see from here, especially if there's no vehicle on it. So what makes you think he's been watchin' this place?"

I quickly covered my ex's previous behaviors.

"Okay," he said after closing his notebook. "I know the high bushes and grasses make it a great vantage point..." he bobbed his head toward the river.

Was that a tinge of frustration I heard in his voice?

"Your girls did really good today. They were so brave," his admiration for the girls was undeniable.

One side of my mouth lifted into a smile.

"You tell 'em for me? They did real good today." His focus moved over to Emma sitting on the steps up to Maggie's. "She still looks pretty worried."

I glanced over my shoulder.

"Yeah. She does."

"Well, I've got enough right here — between what both girls told me and your extra information — to arrest him. Plus, it seems there's an arrest

CHAPTER 67

warrant out for him by the I.N.S."

I allowed my chin to bounce, a smidgen.

"So I've heard."

"We'll do our best to see he stays out for thirty days this time."

"Good luck with that," cheerful sarcasm fed my words.

"I guess I don't have to say, be careful. Stay close to them. And if you need us, just like you guys did today, don't hesitate to call us. We'll get out here as soon as possible. He's gettin' pretty brazen though. Makes me worried he's getting desperate." The officer made eye contact with me. "Be careful. It's not just you ladies here … is it?"

Trying not to be insulted by the *'just you ladies'* part … I shook my head.

"No sir. Maggie's husband and my boyfriend are both due back before nightfall."

"Okay." He opened his car door and slid behind the wheel. "One of us will let you know if we're able to get him into custody. I'm heading over to his residence now. You just sit tight… okay ma'am?"

I nodded as I thanked him for coming out.

"Hey Lovie," I greeted Emma as I got closer to the steps. She stood. "Did you hear? That officer thinks you were really brave and did the right things today. We're both really proud of you! Let's go finish watchin' that movie now."

We climbed the rest of the steps and went into the brown house to sit with Bella and Maggie for a bit.

Chapter 68

Later, after we all settled down and finished watching whatever was on the TV, I excused the girls and myself – homework and chores needed to get done. Let alone some sense of normalcy.

An hour or so later, a truck pulled up the drive. Although I recognized the sound, I was glad to see, as I looked out the kitchen window, it was John. He was filled in, by the girls as much as by me what happened this afternoon. John didn't hide that his hackles were up.

"The cops were here! At the ranch today? At my ranch, today?" John's angry tone was just shy of yelling.

"Yes. The girls were so brave. They called 9-1-1 and waited over at Maggie's until the cops got here. I got here first. Then we all waited," I reiterated.

"I've never had the cops out here. What are they going to think?"

"I don't know. I'm sorry. Calling the cops was necessary. Mike's been on the ranch, against orders. And most likely watching from across the river! The kids did the right thing. He tried to get the girls to go with him!" my voice cracked. I scowled. "I'm sorry if we've embarrassed you," sarcasm and disappointment accented my words. "Girls, you can go wash up. So you can help me make the salad," I suggested in a loud enough voice the girls could hear me in the TV room.

"Why can't he just be happy someone is taking care of his kids? You'd think he'd be glad he's not been asked for a lot of child support for these

CHAPTER 68

kids! They're living in a nice house, have nice clothing, shoes, beds…." John did not hold back his growing irritation. "He's being an ass!"

"So, the cop said someone will call when they have him in custody," I changed the subject… a little.

"Then he's to be out of Idaho for thirty days?"

"Well, out of all of the U.S. for thirty days, really," I clarified.

The sound of that potential break from this mess gave me hope.

Minutes later the girls made the salad, I put the dressing on after making up the spaghetti. I dished myself up a salad and buttered noodles.

"You only eating that?" John inquired.

"Yeah," I said with downcast eyes. "My stomach is really bothering me. I may have to go back to just bread if this doesn't sit right."

As I rinsed the dishes and Bella put them in the dishwasher, the phone rang. I gripped the sink's edge tightly.

"Kathleen, it's for you," John announced.

"Oh, hello officer…. Yes." A smile graced my face. "In custody…. Out for thirty days this time. … Sure, sure. I'll still keep my eyes peeled, just in case. Great. Thanks Sargent. Have a good night yourself."

Chapter 69

I opened the journal, again, and put pen to paper, as I'd been doing every day.

March 15th, 2003
Well, it's family time. My birthday worries you. Don't. Within hours of you coming back to my home, [weeks ago] you said, 'Mom, I have a birthday card for you!' It was me who told you not to give it to me right away. After all my B-day wasn't for another week or so. I should have let you give it to me. Sorry, Lovie. You sent a wonderful, thoughtful card. And you made sure we spoke on the phone. Thank you, Lovie. I wish you were here with me so I could wrap my arms around.

As I closed the journal, my hand lingered on it, as if it was on my son's shoulder. Even if he was over 900 miles away, it was my way of staying close.

In the ground floor sewing room, the CD player turned the disc. The lead singer from the Dixie Chicks sang about pursuing dreams, getting away from home, landslides, life changes, and then the lullaby *Godspeed* came through the speakers. The simple strumming of the guitar strings started tears to well, which became a gut-wrenching torrent. Glad for the sanctity of the downstairs space, I sat back on the futon as I closed my eyes and saw my son the only way I could – in my mind's eye.

CHAPTER 69

Since Ethan had been gone, the words of this song had taken on new meaning. Bringing me to tears every time I heard it. They triggered memories like never before. Dragons....

Dragons are Ethan's favorite critters.

Superman....

Oh how he'd loved the impromptu Superman costume I pulled off with the blue sweatshirt and the red lace I hand-stitched on the front, in the shape of an S! That seems so long ago. Was it... five, or was it four years ago? Wish I had a picture of that. Did I ever? Did that photo burn up in the house, too?

I shook my head as tears fell. And now, not just because my son was only going to hear my wishes and prayers for him on the wings of angels, but for how he got a couple of burns on his head the night the house burned down.

The rabbit hole was slippery and the only traction I could get was... to change one of the words repeated by the singer to something that rhymed with it – E-*man*.

You are my E-man.

It took minutes for me to stop the mourning. The anguish. But, when I did, I changed the CD to Shania Twain's upbeat *Come On Over* album. I needed something upbeat.

~~~****~~~

"With Emma spending the night at Jenny's ... what movie would you like to get and watch Bella?"

We headed to the grocery store as it had a movie rental department – gotta love small towns. With a couple of movies chosen, popcorn, and tasty homemade pizza makings in the bag we drove back home. I attempted to keep my sadness away from everyone else.

"Why don't I go down to the Colorado house with the handyman, Dan? We can put that sewage system in and make it legal and sellable," John suggested.

"I don't have the money to pay for any of that..." concern filled my voice.

"I didn't ask you for the money to do this. I'll do it. It needs to get done," he said patting me on the leg as we idly watched the movie with Bella. "Dan's already said he could go. He's a good worker. We could fly down on Monday and be back by the next weekend."

I grimaced, not used to having things done right. Still not comfortable with letting others do things for me. Let alone how much this would cost me financially and ….

At what cost is this going to be accomplished? Nobody does things like this without it costing…. What's this going to cost me? My trust wavered.

"Okay. It would be helpful. Yes."

"Okay. I'll book the flights tomorrow," he said draping his arm around my shoulders.

At 4 p.m. the next afternoon I pulled up to the wood-sided single-wide. Emma and her friend were playing out back, their giggles were a welcomed sound.

It's nice that she's able to have a good time. She needs it.

"We'd love to make plans to do this again," Jenny's mother said.

"I'll check to see if we can even do this over at the ranch," I fibbed, I knew asking John for the girls to have a sleepover was out of the question.

The friends made promises to see each other at school on Monday. Then my two girls and I headed for home. John was packing when we got there.

"So … you're flying into Colorado Springs?" I asked. He nodded. "Here are some directions to get you to the ranch from the airport. They may be hand-drawn, but I've made that trek so many times… I could almost do it in my sleep." I gave a cheeky smile. "There aren't a lot of motels or hotels real close to the ranch…"

"Don't worry about that. I'll find us one."

"Try Cañon City. It's only about a fifteen-minute drive from the ranch. There's a nice enough Mexican-style restaurant to the West of the ranch, about five miles up. And some other places to eat in Florence itself, too."

"You said the renter's name was… Mary, right?"

"Yep."

"We'll get this done. Don't worry," John attempted to reassure me as Bella shared the movies with her older sister.

CHAPTER 69

I smiled as the possibilities started to form in my maternal head.

"Things are finally comin' back around," I said as we shut down the TV room a couple of hours later and all headed off to bed. "Maybe now, with the semester coming to an end, Mike out of the country... maybe Ethan can come back here," I tried to share with John, even if I was saying this as much to myself as him.

"You want your son to come back and live with you, you'll have to find your own place to live," he said over his shoulder as he headed down to the shower.

My jaw fell open.

What the eff? What did he just say? He must have been joking. It's just the stress of what's been going on here. He doesn't mean it... does he?

I got ready for bed. Pulled tight to my side of the king-sized mattress. Still not liking what had come out of John's mouth, I acted like I was asleep as I heard him enter the room and drape his towel over the footboard post on his side of the bed before he slid in under the covers. The gurgling in my stomach was my acidy lullaby.

Two mornings later, John was ready to go to the airport by the time the girls left for school.

"You sure you don't want me to drive you and Dan to and from the airport?"

"No, it's all right. We'll just leave the car in long-term parking. That way, you don't have to have the girls out late when the return flight gets in," John said.

I assumed he sounded pleased to not cause us any additional worries while doing things for me to make it so I could sell my Colorado ranch.

After hugs and kisses were shared it was time to ... do what? No kids. No John. Horses, dogs, and the barn cat were all fed.

Wow... this place is quiet.

I got a cup of hot water, turned on the CD player, and the computer.

Maybe I can write something. Write before I go out and work that pretty bay mare.

I couldn't concentrate on my writing prompt.

"Hey there Dad," although my dad sounded glad to get a call from me, my tone was somber. "Yes, John and Dan are headed down to the Colorado ranch. Yes. The sewer needs to get done. Glad I had the leach line test completed before we left."

"Why aren't you happy about this?" my dad asked.

"Oh, it's just something John said the other night." My dad let the dead air lie between us as he patiently waited for me to continue. "We were talkin' about the semester coming to an end, Claudia and Gary coming up to pick up this bay mare and bringing Ethan home, now that it's safer."

"Well, when is Ethan coming back to live with you?"

"That's just it... John said, 'You want him to come back and live with you, you'll have to find your own place.' He's not saying my son's not welcome here anymore... is he?" my voice was down to a whisper in disbelief.

"I don't know why he would, the boy was welcome there before. It's not Ethan's fault his father was trying to kidnap him?"

"Maybe I heard him wrong. Maybe he heard me wrong." My jaw tightened. My teeth fit together like LEGOs. "But daddy, I'm gonna tell you what... if he says it again, then I'll know he wasn't kidding ... and... I'm outta here," the defiance telegraphed through my hostile tone.

"Yeah, it will be the best thing for your family. Where you thinkin' of going?"

"Well as much as I love it up here and could afford something up here...I've been lookin'... it's still so close to the border with Mike around."

"You *would* be challenged to protect the kids well enough, once he found out you were out there on your own."

My tears flowed freely accompanied by sniffles.

"So... I'd have to come back home. I need to be able to keep them safe. Us safe," the timidness returned to my voice. "Would that be okay, Daddy?"

"Yeah. We've got the bunk bed set up in the spare room. You'd all have to share that room. All four of you, but you can come here."

"Are... you ... sure? I mean... if I heard him correctly?"

"Yes. I'm sure," my dad's words sounded reassuring. "Just let me know."

"Thanks, Dad," I managed between sniffles.

CHAPTER 69

"Why don't you go ride that mare of Claudia's? You've said you enjoy working with her," his voice encouraged his youngest who had been blessed with both of her parents' affinity and connection with horses.

I wiped the tears from my cheeks.

"Okay ... Dad ... thanks."

And with that, I pushed the off button, hung up the phone, and walked down to the barn. My heart and soul calmed as my palm made contact with the mare's neck. I drew my hand down from her ears to her withers, again, again and again. Slowing my breathing with each stroke.

Chapter 70

While John was gone in Colorado I met with the doctor.

"Thanks for changing my appointment to mid-morning, doc. I..."

"No worries Kathleen," she said flipping through the chart. "The tests you've done have shown that you have H-Pylori."

"Wha...what is that?"

"It's bacteria that is in your stomach. And it is causing your acid reflux." She looked up from my chart. Hesitated. "I've got this ... successful procedure ... medicines...."

Why is she hesitating so much?

"I've already sent your prescriptions over to the pharmacy in case they had to order them in."

Them?

"It's six prescriptions. You'll have to take them more than once a day. But it comes with a reminder pad..."

"In the prescription?"

"Yes," she frowned, "I guess people tend to get a little discouraged."

My eyebrows dropped. but I mimicked her smile.

"Please take all of your prescriptions. It's really important," she pleaded, just a little, as she spoke.

"Thanks, doc. I'll go get these now."

A couple of hours later I had the six amber-hued plastic bottles with their

CHAPTER 70

white tops sitting on the kitchen counter along with the encouragement post-it notes. I thumbed through them. They instructed me to take one of each of these pills four times each day for the next ten days.

I can do this. I won't need this set of notes. Notes that instruct me to read, then rip off and discard the one each time I take a set of the pills. Silly. But in reality... by day nine I was glad there were only two days of notes left.

After John returned from Colorado and got a full night's sleep he filled me in on the successes in Colorado.

"...I met the renter," John shared. "She said, months ago, Mike told her the sewer was going to be done. Said she'd even paid the rent a week early to help get it done. But he never showed back up. Just loaded up the horses, even though he said he was just going roping, she said he never came back." John and I shook our heads. "She hasn't seen him since."

"Guess 'cuz he's been up here."

"I can't believe he left that lady and her kids with that open sewage trench too." The sick-to-stomach look on John's face only added to the disgusted tone in his voice.

"Unbelievable," escaped my voice box. My eyelids dropped to slits as I scrunched my nose and scowled. "That's just not right. So, it's not just his wives and kids he doesn't care how he lets them live." I snipped and shook my head.

"I'm glad we got it done, she could have sued and since you were awarded that property in the divorce... she would have won, and you would have had to pay!" John emphasized with protective concern.

"Well, thanks. Thanks again. Maybe I can list this now and get it sold. I'll call Randy, the Realtor tomorrow." Moments passed as I began to cheer inside. "So, Ethan gets out of school next week and Claudia and Gary are planning on bringing him back up here... since it's been safer now with Mike not showing up since the second deportation. And it's time for my son to be back under my roof."

John sat up straight, stiffening his back.

"And she'll pick up that bay mare I've been training for her and take her back with 'em."

"If you want that boy to live with you, you'd better find somewhere else to live," he said before walking out of the TV room.

I pursed my lips. Nodded although I was filled with confusion. My body heated up. I walked over, grabbed the cordless phone.

He said it again! I gripped the oak railing letting my hand haltingly slide down with each step. *Oh my God! I **did** hear him correctly, before. Damn it! Just what I need.*

He walked past the sewing room without a word to me. Once in the truck, he drove down to the shop. I dialed Claudia's cell phone. Shared with her what John had just said.

"Hey, how about the kids and I follow you guys back to Tehachapi?"

"What?"

I filled her in.

"No man, no man *ever* will separate me from my children!" hostility filled my words. "Can you imagine if he was able to get me to be *okay* with **not** having Ethan live with the girls and me...? Bet he'd work on separating me away from the girls too!"

"Sounds like you'd be right," Claudia said with a hint of irritation in her voice. "Well, let me get back to you. We were heading out tomorrow and heading straight up there. But I don't want to stay there at the ranch anymore. I'm gonna find a hotel. And ... this changes our plans for the vacation. I'll call you later today or tomorrow."

"Sorry to drop this on you."

"No, no. Don't worry about this. It's not you who's changing things."

Later that afternoon, after John got back from where ever he chose to eat and sat down to watch TV, I addressed him.

"I'll be out in four days," I spat out, satisfied I could just follow my friends back to Tehachapi on their way home. "Hope that's fast enough for you," I said defiantly with my chin up as I looked John – square in the eyes.

"Four days?" John parroted in disbelief.

I turned on my heels leaving John by himself.

CHAPTER 70

~~~~****~~~~

"What are your plans?" John's gruff voice interrupted my packing.

"Since I will be following Claudia and Gary back to Tehachapi they have changed up their plans and will be going by way of Yellowstone National Park before they get up here instead of on the way home."

"How are you going to get all of your stuff back there?" John demanded to know.

"I'll be going to get a U-Haul and finish packing up."

He turned and walked back out of the house. I took the next half hour to re-run the conversation in my head before I picked up the phone, again.

"Hey Dad," I began leaving a message on Mom and Dad's machine, "he said it again. I hadn't misheard him. I'll call you later tonight. I'm off to pack boxes."

And boxes I packed, but not until after I found the local rental truck place's listing, reserved a smaller box truck, and made arrangements to come by in the morning to pay for the rental. Hours later, with much of my sewing room boxed up I made lunch with the girls.

"Let's go into the sewing room," I suggested after our meal. Once inside the girls couldn't help but notice the packed boxes. "Well, when Claudia, Gary, and E-man get here we will go ahead and follow them with their horse back to Tehachapi."

"Why Momma?" Emma asked.

"Because our family needs to be back together and that is where we can do it. Plus, this way... I can save up enough money to get a house for all of us. Just us."

The girls seemed to accept the impending move.

"I've put some boxes in your room. Please start packing. We'll be leaving in about four days."

"Okay Momma," the girls said in unison.

Chapter 71

The next morning, just before the rental place was scheduled to open, I got the address from the yellow pages, wrote it down on a scrap piece of paper. John loomed behind me at the kitchen counter.

Don't cower. Don't let him see he's too close. Don't get into an argument. You already know there's no way anything he can say will change your mind.

"What are you doing this morning?" he demanded to know.

"I'm going to book the rental truck and then pack our stuff," I didn't look back.

"You need to give me the credit card back that I gave you!"

"Um…" my eyebrows knitted, I turned to face him, "…no. I will be using it to rent the truck and I won't be giving it back to you until I get my kids back home safe and sound," I added standing tall, awaiting a battle.

John's shoulders slumped momentarily.

"How do I know you'll send it back? That you'll pay for what you spend?"

"Because," I glared at him before walking past him, "I've always been a person of my word," I finished saying as I hit the top of the stairs. "Oh … I'm using the car today," I informed Mr. Control over my shoulder.

Only after I got the car pulled out onto the road did I stop looking in the rearview mirror with anticipation that he'd come after me.

I'm glad he didn't try to stop me. What does he think? I've got money hiding in my pockets, like he does? He knows I haven't been working. That job at the school dried up.

CHAPTER 71

A couple of hours later, back at the house, the packing continued, and I consolidated the boxes in the sewing room.

"When are you picking up the truck?" John inquired from just inside the sewing studio doorway.

Two days left. You can do this... it's just two days.

"Tomorrow. It's gonna take me hours to load it," I admitted.

"Do you want me to take you over to get the truck?" he offered.

Oh now, now you're gonna be nice. Or are you just making sure I got the right one?

"Um, sure."

"Why don't you ask the guy if you can pick the truck up late this afternoon so you can get an early start on packing," a kindness in his voice had returned.

"Yeah, I will do that. Would you be willing to drive me over later?"

He affirmed with a nod.

"Great. Thanks. I guess I could use the extra day to pack." *It's only twenty dollars more, what the heck.*

The next morning the phone rang.

"Hey there Claudia!" was that cheer or relief I heard in my own voice?

"We'll be there in about a hour. What do you have planned for breakfast?"

"Well, I don't know. All I know is I was going to pack the rental up this morning."

"You aren't packed yet?" she scolded.

"No. You weren't supposed to be here until tomorrow...."

"Well, why don't we meet for breakfast and then pick up the truck? Can we do that?"

"Oh, I already have the truck, I picked it up last night."

"Who's that?" John asked as he walked into the room.

I put my hand over the bottom of the handset.

"It's Claudia. They'll be here in an hour or so and were wondering about breakfast. But I need to get that truck loaded and...."

"Is all of your stuff ready to put in the truck?"

"Yes. Yes it is."

"Then go on. Go have breakfast with them. Let me pack the truck for you. I want to make sure you get it packed right," he said with his I-know-more-than-you tone of voice.

"Okay Claudia. The girls and I can meet you," I rolled my eyes as I spoke with a mixture of cheer and frustration.

We agreed to meet in Kellogg for breakfast.

The girls and I waited outside the eatery with much anticipation! They were antsy. Fidgeting and adjusting their weight from one foot to the other. As the brown truck and trailer pulled in the parking lot the three of us squealed – a little.

Just the mere sight of the top of my son's head, as he opened the back door of the club cab, made my heart skip a beat. Although I wanted to race across the parking lot and hug him, I restrained myself.

Don't smother him. Don't make him want to pull away. Be patient.

His smile told me he was glad to see me too. See us. He walked over to the three females in his life who missed him.

"Hi son!" I said as we embraced.

"Hi Ethan," was echoed by both of his sisters.

Mere moments later there were two more sets of arms wrapped around us. His back stiffened a little. Oops, the girls and I held on maybe longer than he wanted, but he didn't fight it too much. I kissed the top of his head as Claudia and Gary walked up.

"Hey you guys!" I said as we released our boy.

After a few minutes of stretching their legs we all went in for breakfast.

"So you've got to pack when we get back?" Gary asked.

I rolled my eyes and grinned, which drew inquisitive looks from both Gary and Claudia.

"John's packing the truck," I accented my announcement with a smirk.

"What? He is? Is he trying to get you out as quick as possible?" Claudia asked.

I guffawed.

"He said, he 'wanted to make sure the truck was packed right.'" I added

CHAPTER 71

air quotes around – *packed right*.

"What a control freak," she added.

"Yeah, he treats me like I haven't packed and loaded a truck or two ... what twelve times in my first five years of marriage with Mike and at least that many times since the stalking began. Only broke one dish in all of those years!" I didn't hide my pride.

"Let him do it. When we get back, you can check to make sure he got everything and we can be on our way," Gary encouraged.

"Yeah, 'cuz I don't want to stay here at the ranch tonight," Claudia shared her decision. "Do you think there's so much that we would need to wait until tomorrow to leave?"

"No. I could pack the truck myself and still have us leaving today." I shook my head. "The truck won't even be full."

"Bet he's just making sure you aren't taking anything that's not yours," she sniped.

"Nah, this is just his way of having some sense of control," I responded. "We can go have you meet up with your mare... if he's not done packing the truck. You can stay down there, groom her.... I know the girls would love to help you with that, wouldn't you?"

The girls nodded as glee sparkled in their eyes.

"Do you think the mare has had enough time on her," Claudia asked.

"Well, as I've told you... this sweet mare you chose is broke enough that both of the girls were riding her out in pasture with me, more than once."

The girls bobbed their heads as they ate. Ethan sat quietly and the adults continued to speak of things to come.

After I paid the bill, we all headed for the ranch.

"You wanna hop in with mum?" I welcomed my son.

He did.

We pulled into the drive and as planned, stopped in front of the barn.

"Why don't you kids stay down here and help Claudia with her mare. I'll go up and pack the truck."

The girls got out together and worked to slide the large barn door to the side. Ethan got out only to be greeted by Psycho, the dog.

"Can I just tell you I don't even want to go up there!" Claudia was not hiding her complete irritation with John.

"Kathleen and I will go up. I'll see if I can help with the packing of the truck. And then… we'll load the horse and start out as soon as possible," Gary offered.

"Okay. Thanks. 'Cuz he's pissed me off!" Claudia fought to maintain her Christianity.

"Jump in Gary. Let's go up," I invited, then drove up to the blue house.

The box truck was backed up to the first garage. Both roll-up doors – on the back of the truck and the garage – were open. John was inside the truck securing a box.

Gary and John said their hellos.

"Can I be of any assistance?" Gary asked.

"No, thanks." John shook his head. "I've got most all of their stuff packed."

Upon visual inspection of the container, he was correct… it looked like he did, in fact, have *all* of the boxes packed.

"Why don't you go inside, make sure I haven't missed any of the boxes," John ordered more than suggested.

Walking through the garage, I entered the house through the side door, and started in the sewing room. Satisfied nothing was being left behind I headed upstairs to Ethan's room, but I stopped off at the phone first.

"Hey Dad and Mom. It's Saturday afternoon. We're heading out today. I should be home no later than late Monday night… early Tuesday. Love you."

After I left the message on my folks' machine I headed through the house, to make sure there was nothing left behind. Ethan's room held the fully made queen sized bed and no other signs of us. Next was the room I used to share with John. I checked the walk-in closet, the standing jewelry box.

No clothes or trinkets left here.

The bedside table and bathroom held no remnants of me either. I stopped and gazed at the antique settee. My hand caressed the plush green velvet. I smiled at the woman's face carved in the wood frame.

"Good-bye mystery lady."

CHAPTER 71

I grabbed the small box from the kids' bathroom with the toothbrushes, etc. as it was all that was left of us. At a glance, I confirmed only the quilt I made for John was in the TV room, all of our stuff was packed. And I didn't need anything in the kitchen. Nothing. We have it all. The stairway called to me. I halted, looked up at the six-point buck's trophy head above the fireplace. I sighed.

Never got to bring my own deer or elk down. Disappointment flowed through me. My eyes glanced around the room. *We probably pissed off the furniture store when we sent the leather couch back twice. But the delivery guys loved seeing our 10-year-old driving the truck up by himself up from the barn. They were so shocked to see such a young boy driving a truck... alone.* I smiled almost as big today as I did last fall. Guess city folk don't teach or maybe it's trust their kids to learn to drive that young. *It was fun picking out the furniture and helping decorate this place.* I shook my head. *But it wasn't worth it. No way. All of this is not worth it.*

I glanced out the open drapes. The tree trunk where the mineral block was ... stood as a sentry.

I'm gonna miss this place. Thank you God. It's been good for us, kinda. Thank you for giving us a chance here. I frowned. *We tried. But ... he crossed the line. And God, I promised to take care of these gifts, these beauties you've entrusted me with... to the best of my ability.... I'm tryin'.*

The carpet muffled John's heavy ascending steps.

"You're all loaded. Gary's walked down to load the horse."

"I'll drive the box truck down after grabbing my purse out of the car."

He walked to the kitchen. I walked down the stairs. As I did, Ben came through the foyer. Mid-climb of the staircase, Ben gently placed his hand on my forearm. I halted. He waited for me to make eye contact.

"I'm sorry," his soft voice was filled with compassion. "I told him to be more considerate and told him to think twice before he ever brought you up here. That this wasn't all about him."

Ben shook his head as tears welled in my eyes. I diverted my focus to the flagstone floor in the entryway, blinked time and time again to clear my view. He lovingly squeezed my arm. A deep breath in through my nose helped me regain my composure.

"Thank you my friend," I finally managed to utter, before looking back at Ben.

We shared a light smile.

"Tell Andee..." the tears showed back up again, he bobbed his head, I walked on.

With the small box in the back of the truck I pulled down the door, checked the car one last time, grabbed my purse, got behind the wheel of the truck, and drove down to the barn. The bay mare was loaded, and the kids were giving hugs to the dog.

I stroked his coarse black hair, kneeled near his shoulder, and wrapped my arms around him. He laid his head on my shoulder.

"Bye bud. Thanks for still being mine when I got here." I smiled but couldn't stop my throat from tightening as tears stung the back of it. "Thanks for still loving me and the boy, and taking to the girls so..."

Just then I heard Maggie.

"Kat'leen, Kat'leen..." She was walking fast toward me. "I jus' saw the truck... John's jus' told me." The tears were not just in my eyes, now.

"Yeah, sorry. I didn't have time...."

"Noh, noh, I understand." She held out a red apron. "Here's a little som'thin'. I'm gonna miss you."

"Me too Maggie. I love this."

"Did you take yer stool?"

"Oh yes I did. It was one of the first things packed."

"It wasn't much, but..."

"No Maggie, I love my Maggie stool."

She looked up at me and we shared tears as well as smiles.

"I will never forget you and our friendship. He can't stop that... now can he?" I tried to reassure her.

We shared a loving embrace.

"But I just need to..." I added.

"You take care of these beauties and y'urself."

She broke away, retreated to the brown house. Good-byes seemed

CHAPTER 71

difficult for her too. The tears continued to sting my throat. I sniffled, wiped the moisture from my eyes, and refocused.

"Okay. Shall I just follow you Gary?"

"I think that would be best. We'll just drive as far as we can and decide where to stop along the way."

"Okay, who's gonna ride with Mum?" I asked.

"Girls, you wanted to ride with us, come on," Gary welcomed them.

"Okay. That means you and me son," I smiled. "Let's go!"

The cheerleader in me was in motion as I looked at my watch. It was only 10 a.m.!

As we pulled out of the drive and made it around the bottom curve of the property, I couldn't help but smile at the clutch of well-aged Cedar trees we had picnicked under, once. All four of us. That was the day I got stung by a bee. I laughed to myself at the memory.

"Well, we do have a few good memories from here don't we?" I looked over at Ethan, patted his hand and drove on to our next chapter of life.

Chapter 72

We couldn't get out of there fast enough, so the ever-changing speed limits along the river was daunting as the adrenaline pumped through me. By the time we headed West on the freeway, I relaxed my grip on the steering wheel. Shared a smile with my son.

The hours slipped away as did the miles. Not caring what roads Gary had chosen to drive back on I merely followed him and stopped for gas when he did.

"The drive's going very smoothly. I'm thinking about stopping about dinnertime. But I'm not sure what's up the road," Gary said on our second fuel and pee stop.

"Well, this looks to be the same road Mike and I traveled down when we moved from Washington. There's a town a couple of hours away and there are places to eat. It's before we head up a good-sized hill into California... if memory serves me, but I could be wrong."

"Okay... we'll drive for a couple more hours, stop to eat, and evaluate how long you and I want to drive."

A couple of hours later we pulled into the parking lot of a Mexican food restaurant.

*I hope I'm not smiling too big! My son chose to slide in this half-round booth... beside **me**! Don't smile too big.*

"Do you want to share a dish with me Lovie?" He nodded. "Girls, what

CHAPTER 72

would you like?"

"A burger and fries," Emma admitted.

"Well, okay Love, they don't have them on the menu. What about a taco, some rice, and beans? Those will be soft on your tongue," I added just loud enough she could hear me as she sat on my other side.

"How are you feelin'?" Gary inquired near the end of the meal.

"Good."

"You want to try to make it all the way tonight?" He watched my face for a change in expression.

"Sure. I'm up to it."

"We might not get in until early tomorrow morning... but we can stop at any time."

"Let's go for it. I think Mike and I made it back to Tehachapi after this stop."

We all headed out to the truck, the kids swapped ride-along spots and off we were.

Thanks to the sun being up almost fifteen hours on this mid-July day we drove well into the night. At about 10:30 Gary pulled in a gas station.

"I think it'd be best if we topped off our tanks. Because," he smiled widely, "we can be home in a couple of hours and there's few, if any spots, on the 395 for fuel between here and there."

My smile grew at the thought of being home... tonight and laying my head in a safe place.

"You don't look too tired. You wanna keep going?"

"Sure. Be home an entire day early! Yes. That would be great," I said.

"A day early?"

"I told my dad we'd be home Monday night or Tuesday."

"Well, at this rate," Gary put the gas cap back on. "It will be Monday when we get there. It will be damn early, but it will be Monday."

We shared a healthy laugh.

"Yes... let's make it home Monday," I agreed. "Plus, it will give Claudia time to rest. I know she still has to do a bit of that even if she is cancer-free... right now."

333

"Okay, why don't you plan to pull off at Tehachapi Blvd. and I'll just keep going the extra miles to our offramp. You can come get the boy and his stuff later. Let's just get us all home and rested."

"Sounds good to me Gary." I wrapped my arms around his beefy frame. "Thanks. I'd still liked to have had you as my brother." I kissed him on the cheek, peeked in on my son – asleep on the back seat – and got back behind the wheel.

A couple of hours later I lifted a finger, and my turn signal was on. It was time to get off this freeway! Instead of honking I flashed my high beams twice as Gary continued driving down Hwy 58. I didn't want to wake the girls who were sound asleep on the bench seat beside me, Bella with her head on my lap and Emma with her head on her little sister's lap, like tipped-over Dominos.

Only eleven more miles of freeway for them! Good night. Love you. I thought as if Ethan could hear me. I hoped he could.

Only fifteen miles to a bed for you girls and me. I looked down, again, at the girls, asleep on the bench seat.

I yawned as I came to the signal at Tucker and Hwy 202.

"Just of few more miles. You've got this," I whispered to myself.

Once onto Banducci I knew I needed to keep my wits about me. The mountain curves didn't need to win another life tonight. I dropped the tranny into a lower gear and managed the turns and the lower speed. The all-too-familiar rumble of the tires going over the cattle guard made me smile wide.

Almost there!

The second cattle guard came under the tires and woke my oldest daughter.

Even Emma's senses know she's back.

A surge of positive energy made its way through my body. Emma sat up, rubbed her eyes. She peered out the window and then over at me, her eyes widened.

"Yes Lovie, we're almost back home to grandma's and grandpa's," I kept my volume low to not wake the youngest.

CHAPTER 72

I placed my foot on the brake pedal and slowed the truck before taking it off the pavement onto the dirt drive, moved the transmission into first gear, and made sure I avoided the holes.

"Do you want me to get the gate Momma?" Emma's sweet voice was welcoming.

"Oh, Lovie... are you sure?"

"Yeah," she said, sitting up straight.

"Okay then Lovie. Make sure you re-latch it, okay? Because I don't know where the horses are," I said scanning the dark horizon.

"Okay Momma."

I brought the truck to a full stop before she got out of the truck. She unwrapped the green chain, freeing it from the "V" catch, and walked back opening the gate wide enough for me to drive through. Once I pulled in far enough for Emma to swing the stock panel clear of hitting the bumper, I stopped the truck. It wasn't a long wait for her to close it, latch it, and get back in the truck.

"Almost there baby!" I said as she climbed back in.

Two turns later I parked the truck just above the house, turned the lights off, and gently woke the youngest.

"Okay girls, let's go in and go to bed."

"Do we need to take anything in?" Emma asked.

"No Lovie. We're just goin' in and hittin' the hay. Just make sure to shut the door softly."

We made sure we didn't slam the truck doors, didn't need to wake the dog or my folks at this hour. Glad for the near full moon, the three of us navigated the uneven dirt as we walked over to the sliding door.

"Woof, woof."

"Shh Brax," I said as I reached for the door handle. He stopped barking. "Hey there boy, it's just us." He did not feel the need to continue to bark at his humans. "Good boy." His stumpy tale was wagging. "We don't need to wake Mom and Dad." His nose was on sniffing overload. "Back up boy. Let us in."

The dog who used to protect us backed up.

"Off to our bedroom girls."

Emma led the way. Bella, Brax, and I followed, but not until I slid the glass door shut.

The girls sat on the bottom bunk. Their heavy eyelids and yawning didn't stop Brax from loving on them.

"Do either of you need to go potty?"

They shook their heads. I pulled their shoes.

"Okay, up top. One of you needs to go on the top bunk."

"I'll go," Emma offered with a yawn.

She finished petting the dog and climbed the ladder at the end of the bed.

"Okay, scoot in Bella." She patted the Rotty's head. "Okay boy." I yawned. "I need some sleep."

I joined my youngest on the bottom, queen-sized bunk. We laid our heads on the pillows and the dog assumed his regular protection spot. He lay down on the ground beside the bed, just like he'd last done a year earlier.

Hours later, after the sun rose, I heard my father's voice.

"Where's my dog?" he said as he walked across the house. "Brax? Where are you Brax?"

I lifted my head off of the pillow, opened my eyes to daylight, and saw the dog still beside the bed, sound asleep.

"Shhh Dad. He's in here with his kids," my voice was groggy.

"Wait! You're here? Already?" My father now stood in our doorway. "When did you get here!"

"This morning about midnight or so."

"I didn't hear you come in? What a good guard dog," loving sarcasm could be detected in his voice.

"Well heck no. He didn't bark much once I spoke to him." I reached out and stroked his big head.

The dog looked up at me and then moved his eyes from me to my dad.

"Are you puttin' coffee on Dad?"

"Yes." And with that he turned to brew a pot.

Chapter 73

Within weeks I got a job – waiting tables both in the dining hall and the bar, six to eight shifts a week is what it took to stay ahead of bills and purchase a vehicle. Thank goodness, my folks liked having the kids around. I couldn't do this without them.

The Colorado Ranch was put under contract and sold within sixty days. I was able to pay off the six surprise liens businesses had put on the ranch.

"I am really glad to get those businesses paid off," I shared with my parents one evening. "Their bills shouldn't have been left unpaid," I frowned and shook my head.

"But you did right by them, bills are paid," my dad encouraged.

The phone rang. It was John.

"I'm coming down next week to California," John said. "Wanna spend the weekend together?"

Oh sure, that's what I want to do… be your booty call when you don't respect the biggest part of me… me being a mum. Yah… right. That's what I'm NOT attracted to.

"No. Nope," disapproval was evident in my tone. "I'm dating someone else," I stretched the truth since I'd only served the prospective date a few meals – at the restaurant.

"Yeah, what does he do?" Mister Nosy asked as if he had a right to know.

"He's a test car research mechanic," I retorted.

"You're dating a mechanic?" disapproving sarcasm dripped off from John's words.

"I've told you before… it's never been about the money John." I tired of this banter and ended the conversation - stating the guidelines. "If we're gonna focus on keeping this decade-plus-long friendship you gotta know, there's not going to be another time for us as a couple. It's just not open for discussion. And if you can't stick to the friendship, I won't be takin' your calls anymore."

"No. You're right. This friendship is what's important. We can't let the fact that we can't live together ruin an eleven-year friendship," he conceded.

~~~****~~~

Six months later, as Christmas Eve came around, my new boyfriend and I spent time wrapping presents for the kids in my parents' living room well into the early morning. We tried to not wake the kids or my folks.

"Well, it seems you two love each other," my mom said Christmas morning.

"Yes, and he's talked about marriage."

"Well, that's not a big surprise," she added as she made a cup of tea. "And he lives all the way across the U.S. ….." Mom let her attention to detail hang in the air. "I know it's been quiet for the last six months, but it wouldn't hurt if Mike didn't find out you and the kids were here. So moving wouldn't be a bad thing," she added as she sat on the couch across from me.

"It has been quiet. It's been nice, this settling back into a less stressful routine," I concurred, lifting my coffee cup up to my lips.

"Maybe this will be your last move," Mom encouraged.

But if I leave … is this still running? I swallowed my mouthful of caffeine comfort. *Or will this be the traditional home I've been told I could have? A traditional family I want to provide for my kids?*

~~~****~~~

At the end of January 2004, I packed another U-Haul and loaded my vehicle on the rented car trailer before the kids joined me four-wide in the cab of the moving truck. Three evenings later we pulled into Ohio. Good timing – it was my to-be husband's birthday. Unpacking took a day. The wedding was two weeks later.

CHAPTER 73

Wow... a house, a husband with a job, a job with the temp. agency, kids in school only blocks away, and a church we can go to at the end of the block. Thank you Lord. I prayed as I laid my head down. *I don't have the white pickets, but the neighbor does....* I chuckled out loud. *I am following your lead, Lord.*

~~~~****~~~~

Our Ohio life grew its rhythm. A calmer rhythm. With no emails from Mike, which I waited to see each time I looked in my inbox, there was no one stirring the pot of our existence. We worked through the bumps of melding a new family. The kids seemed to like my second husband's playfulness as it balanced my sternness. And he didn't contradict me like John did.

A year and five months later my cell phone rang. I recognized our landline number.

"Hello Lovie? What's up?" I asked.

"Mom! Mom! Mom! It was him! It was him!" the low volume did not hide the panic in Ethan's voice.

"Who son?"

"It was him," Ethan's voice trembled. "It was Dad! I'm unplugging the phone. I'm unplugging the phone," his words came fast.

"Oka..." The line went dead. Panic surged through me.

Shit. Here we go again. Please God, protect my beauties.

I went to my manager and sped home.

Breathe, breathe, get home. The boy only said Mike was on the phone. Lord, please let Mike only be on the phone! I repeated as I cut fifteen minutes off my drive home from Dayton.

The beauty of the spring day did little to quell my fears. But as I turned the corner I could see no additional cars near our home. I pulled into the driveway and breathed a sigh of relief.

He should have emailed me. It's not like I've changed that, it's in the court order. I would have been able to prepare the kids. I calmed my breathing. *God, calm the kids and let's get this figured out. Maybe it's going to be okay. Maybe Mike's just in a position to see the kids again, or at least start the bi-weekly calls.*

Thoughts on Abuse

Abuse is evil and more of a sin than abandonment. Some abusers use the sanctity of marriage for satanic ends. A spouse who is abusive has already abandoned the marriage. God condemns abuse of a spouse or a child throughout the Bible as well as a spouse who takes advantage of being able to hurt those who are weaker. The spouse or child is not at fault if the home is made unsafe by the abusive spouse. The abused should flee without condemnation, even in divorce.
(Ps. 9:18; Isa. 3:14–15; Ezek. 18:12; Amos 2:7; Mark 9:42; etc.)

Domestic Violence Help

~~~~****~~~~

If you know someone who could use some encouragement to get safe
Please give them this book and/or
the number for the
National Domestic Violence Hotline
in the United States of America
Call: 800-799-7233
And if you're not in the USA please just look up the
Domestic Violence Support in your area!

~~~~****~~~~

~~~****~~~

If you enjoyed this read, this book ~
Please go to the online source
you purchased it from
or on social media
and
LEAVE A REVIEW.

Thank you very much ~
Kathleen
Survivor and Author

~~~****~~~

~~~****~~~

Kathleen can be reached at:
Kathleen@DragonflyEditingAndPublishing.com
Instagram: TheKathleenKline
TikTok: @KathleenMKline
Author Page: KathleensDragonflyDesk.WordPress.com

About the Author

Kathleen M. Kline is an author who has chosen to use her wordplay to share, encourage, and let others know they are not alone while braving any judgment as she shares the path she traveled — with her nonfiction works. She has enjoyed writing and editing since 1991, is an author who writes fiction as well as nonfiction. She lets you see the hope in possibilities, hints at love, and the presentation of strong women. This is an author who has worked in the newspaper and magazine industries, while writing and editing for others world-wide as a writing coach. She helps others bring to the page what is in their hearts and minds. Her published credits are many including her books: *When You Only Have Time For A Quickie- Volume I: A Collection of Short Stories* and the *Weekly Writing Planner*. While others stories of Kathleen's have been included in *Stories That Lift*(.com), *Tales of Our Lives*, and *What's Your Story? A Memoir* and other places.

You can connect with me on:
- http://kathleensdragonflydesk.wordpress.com
- https://www.facebook.com/kathleen.klinelivingston

Also by Kathleen M. Kline

Weekly Writing Planner
Kathleen wrote, designed, and paginated a Weekly Writing Planner that provides writers and aspiring writers an undated 52-week planner (so it can be started any week of the years), a page per week to write on, and the bonus of 10 vocabulary-building words per week.
https://amzn.to/3UT8SaV

When You Only Have Time For A Quickie
Inside these pages, you will be treated to 22 tantalizing short stories for the times, in your busy life, that you only have time for a *short read*.

Let your lunch breaks, train rides, or soaks in the bathtub be a time for a little reading break – a gift for you, for your favorite reader in your life, or for someone you want to build the desire to read in.

amzn.to/42awYBu